GEORGE FRANCIS

Trainer of Champions

GEORGE FRANCIS

TRAINER OF CHAMPIONS

GEORGE FRANCIS

AND GRAEME FIFE

MAINSTREAM
PUBLISHING

EDINBURGH AND LONDON

First published in Great Britain in 1998 by
MAINSTREAM PUBLISHING COMPANY (EDINBURGH) LTD
7 Albany Street
Edinburgh EH1 3UG

ISBN 1 84018 059 5

A catalogue record for this book is available from the British Library

Typeset in Benson Old Style Opti-Medium and Plantin
Printed and bound in Great Britain by Butler and Tanner Ltd, Frome

Contents

Foreword

I first met George Francis 13 years ago. His son, William, had been, and remains to this day, a close friend of our family since he began working for The Police about 20 years ago. Billy had told us stories about his father many times so, even before I met him, I knew him to be a real character.

George looks exactly like you'd imagine a boxing trainer to look. He is compact, solid, fit and strong, and certainly doesn't look whatever age he currently admits to being. Hard as nails, he has a twinkle in his eye that lets you know his heart is in the right place.

I enlisted George's help shortly after giving birth to my son, Jake, now 13. I had always been quite fit, doing aerobics and the like, but I felt that I needed some serious work to get back in shape. I didn't really know what I was letting myself in for.

I don't think George had ever trained a woman before. John Conteh, Frank Bruno — and me! I found it a daunting prospect, and at the time it felt like George made few allowances for my sex. It certainly seemed like he trained me like he would train a fighter. After a warm-up run down to Highgate Ponds (and back up the hill again), there would follow unforgiving, demanding, gruelling training sessions. He worked me very hard, but made me very strong, particularly my stomach muscles. When someone is throwing ten-pound medicine balls at your abdomen, you make sure you can take it!

Despite the extremely hard work he put me through, training with George was always fun. He kept me laughing through the agony with many interesting and often hilarious stories about his life.

This biography is a wonderfully warm and true reflection of George Francis, against the backdrop of some fascinating eye-witness history of London. He is unique, the original rough diamond. George will always have his own special corner in my heart.

Trudie Styler, 1998

Introduction

I met George at the Highgate Men's Pond where I swim every morning. This is the place where he'd taken all his boxers for early morning training. We got to know each other and, as he'd put it, we clicked. In the course of desultory conversations he told me many stories of his early life — very little about the boxing — about his childhood in the Camden Town slums, scrapes with the law, bunking off school to run errands and earn extra cash for the family and so on. It seemed to me that here was a story which ought to be recorded, a remarkable life encompassing setbacks which would have finished off most men three times over.

One day, we were sitting in the sun over at the Pond before our swim and George told me that Joan, his wife, was away on holiday, so he'd set about decorating the bedroom, had come across all his old scrapbooks and decided they were cluttering the place up, and dumped the lot — 'just a trip down Memory Lane' he called it — in the dustbin: the entire George Francis archive gone. I didn't say anything but when I got home, I wrote to him suggesting that maybe this needn't be just a trip down Memory Lane and if ever he thought he might put the story down on paper I'd be glad to help. He phoned me up, said I wrote a good letter but, no, he didn't want to stir up the past as there were too many people around who might be hurt.

A while later, he said he'd been thinking things over and decided that we might do the story after all, but not till after the Bruno v Lewis fight that October.

I turned up at his house the first day, laden with tape recorder, notebooks, pens, loose paper. We sat down in the living-room and at once I realised that a tape recorder would be a hindrance: with that confessional machine rolling I wouldn't *listen* as hard as I should. So, George talked flat out, I scribbled flat out then cycled home and typed it up flat out; that was the pattern of our work. He scoured his memory with the same energy and whole-hearted enthusiasm he brings to everything he does. He shirked no enquiry, gave up on no detail, held nothing back. He faced the pain of much that he had to dredge up with the same vibrant courage that is the hallmark of his spirit. We continued the work in the course of long walks over Hampstead Heath, filling in the gaps in the story. We never fell out; our friendship only deepened and if the essential generosity of the man does not emerge in this account of his extraordinary experiences the fault is mine alone.

When we were finished he told me: 'Graeme, I'd like to just say this. I know it's out of context but just sitting here thinking about something, I recall, when I was in South Africa last year, staying at my daughter's wonderful home, I'd had a great day. I'd taken the children out in the morning, running. We came back and swum in the pool. In the afternoon we went up and they got their ponies out, I hired one and we trooped up to the top of the mountains there, looked across and could see Table Mountain — wonderful views. Then we came back, and we sat by the swimming-pool. The kids were all having fun. My daughter's maid had just brought us a cold drink, and sitting there, with everybody, I pinched myself. My granddaughter looked at me and said: "Grandad, why are you pinching yourself?" That made me chuckle. It was one of the moments of my life, thinking what had happened down the years. I said: "Well, it's a long story and maybe one day I'll tell you."

'I don't judge people by what they've achieved. It's their self that counts and the kindness that they can spread. There's a saying that I keep on the wall at home: *People who take kindness for weakness are the weakest kind of people.*

'I've been lucky and I've worked hard for what I've achieved myself. But I don't think I could have achieved what I have, in later life, without the help of the Good Man, out there looking after me. And, of course, Joan, my wife. She's been my backbone all these years and it's been tough for her, probably more than for me. She had the job of looking after the children through all those long, lean years; and also looking after me, particularly twice when I was very, very ill. I owe everything to her.'

I would like to record my own thanks to Joan, for jokes and kindness, cups of tea and coffee, sandwiches, cakes and biscuits; to George's family for their cheery support throughout; and to Maggie Laville for invaluable help in legal matters and for securing the loan of Bill Hemmings's notebooks from which I reconstructed the Old Bailey trial.

Graeme Fife, 1998

Chapter One

No One Said it Would be Easy

Wembley Arena, 2 September 1995, Frank Bruno makes his fourth attempt to win the world title, this time against Oliver McCall; Bruno's been written off before and he's been written off this time. Nine years ago in this very stadium he took Witherspoon 11 rounds then lost when he was knocked out. Two years ago, in Cardiff, he was leading Lennox Lewis all the way until the seventh-round punch which ended the fight and — in the view of both pundits and supporters — put paid to the career of Frank Bruno, the nicest guy never to win a world title. He kept saying: 'This is my time.' Who listened? Frank Warren listened. Without Warren's belief and faith there might well have been no contest tonight. Frank Bruno's wife Laura, his manager, listened. I listened.

Fourth time lucky? Luck didn't come into it. Jersey Joe Walcott took five attempts to win the title. We were already one ahead.

It's rehearsal time. Bruno's loosening up in the dressing-room by stretching, exercising and skipping. He is very calm and quiet. The time for the bandages to go on; and as this is a title fight, the officials have to be in attendance. They watch exactly how the bandages are bound and the tape is put on: you can't tape over the front of the knuckles, only the bandages protect them, and the British Boxing Board of Control stewards sign all the tapes to make sure that not only are they on correctly but that you can't put on any more.

The stewards leave. The time left is for relaxing, drawing on the concentration. When it is time to glove up the referee comes in. Tony Perez, a veteran referee, officiated at the second Ali v Frazier fight. He says to Frank: 'Look, I want a good clean fight. When I tell you, step back and break. I don't want any rabbit-punching behind the neck. I don't want no low blows. In the case that one man goes down, the other boxer who's standing must go to a neutral corner for me to take the count up. I won't start till you're in that neutral corner and you stay there until I tell you to box on or it's finished, you know? When I say "break", you punch your way out, don't drop your hands. You've got to guard yourself at all times.'

That's the most important thing the referee can stress — protect yourself at all times — because if he starts to talk to you while you're boxing and you turn your head to look at him, you get punched on the chin.

Finally, he repeats: 'I want a good clean fight, and may the best man win.' He hands over the gloves and we're on our own again. I tie on the gloves and we do three rounds warming-up, with me on the pads. He's ticking over now, nice and ready to go. I grease him up with Vaseline all over his face and body and check my bag to see that everything we need is on hand. There's a knock at the door. Frank's brother — a great guy, very supportive — and the keep-fit man, Keith Morton, as well as John Bloomfield, my own man who helps me in the corner. At 6ft 6ins, John is very handy at passing me up the boxing paraphernalia as I call for it. I've known John for years and years and he's placed what I need in my hand almost before I've asked for it.

Suddenly the door opens and it's the officials with the television people: 'You've got five minutes . . . four minutes . . . three . . . two . . . one . . . go.' Then we're out in the corridor heading for the arena, the cameras trained on Bruno the whole way. I take him to where he's going to walk up the slope to make the spectacular entrance. The rest of us go around the side and wait down at the bottom of the overhead ramp. It's a long walk down, way above the heads of the crowd, over twenty thousand of them. The lights go up; music and cheering, thunderous applause, shouts of 'Come on, Frank!' and 'Bru-no! Bru-no!' That much was the same as any fight he's been in.

Being the challenger, Bruno has to get to ringside first. Soon after, McCall's famous entourage arrives to wait in their corner: the whole gang, American flags waving, and the abuse began. I'd warned Frank about it; they'd play that ploy, to keep us waiting, to soften him up. They're grinning across and shouting: 'You're going down. It's our fight. You've no chance. Take a look at the belt now it's the closest you'll ever get to it.'

They were gesturing, thumbs down, holding the belt up, taunting Bruno, grimacing, yelling, sneering, trying to catch Frank's eye. He couldn't help but hear them, but he ignored it all, kept himself completely to himself.

The psychological war had begun at the press conference when McCall had called Frank an Uncle Tom, which was plain crude and disgusting, but then he said: 'I'm going to do to you what Benn did to McClaren.'

That was sick: McClaren had fought Nigel Benn and got a blood clot in his brain; he's now incapacitated. That kind of intimidation is ugly, unsportsmanlike. The British Boxing Board of Control made McCall apologise.

'You've got no chance, Bruno. You're out of here.'

Frank is jiving to the music, paying no attention. Across in the far corner, joining the pro-McCall abuse is Lloyd Honeyghan. Thanks for nothing, Lloyd. Taking the heat off Frank is Nigel Benn. Giving the other side as good as they're giving us. Waving the Union Jack. Supporting Frank to the hilt as Frank had supported him at the ringside in the ill-fated fight with McClaren.

No sign yet of McCall. We wait. Minutes go by. Part of the war of nerves. Grind Bruno down, rattle him. He knows he shouldn't be here. He's an Uncle Tom. He's a no-hoper.

'You're going to be in a fight tonight, Bruno, you haven't been in a fight since Lewis.' Bruno hasn't been in a fight because he stopped everyone he's fought in the first round.

Fifteen minutes go by. I've never seen Frank look so calm, so collected, so much in charge of himself. He's in amazing shape and so detached, so self-contained and in command that none of the verbal stuff gets to him. He ignores the antics, the whole charade. 'This is my time.'

At last, Oliver McCall deigns to appear. As before the fight against Lewis, when he became world champion, he's so emotional he can hardly force back the tears, his face is screwed up, he's tight to the brim with passion. He's the hard man, the man who knocked out Lennox Lewis, the man no one has ever put down, best chin in the business and a puncher — a big puncher. He doesn't believe Bruno has the stamina to put up any show past seven or so rounds. He'll wait. He'll still be coming when he thinks Bruno will tire. On the way to the ring, Don King has his arm round the champion; he's saying to him: 'Ain't nobody going to stop you tonight.'

As soon as he gets to the ringside, McCall starts prowling, his face scrunched up with both emotion and ferocity. He's acting like a dangerous animal aching to be let off the leash. The hostile tension is spilling out of him. And Frank? Nothing of this has touched him. He's ready. We've got a plan, worked out to the detail, rehearsed and rehearsed. This is our time.

In the ring the referee brings the two fighters together. McCall is scowling. I've seen it: it's nerves. He's also shooting Frank the mean look. Frank's expression is impassive, cool and detached. This feels good to me. I'm not in the least bit nervous. I've only ever felt nerves once: first time in the amateurs when my kids went into the ring. It felt as if it was me going in there. Never since, especially as a pro. It's my job to get my man ready, to be confident, to give him the benefit of that confidence. He's the one who's got to get in there and do the business.

Round One

Bruno starts needling McCall with a series of right jabs which penetrate McCall's guard, one after the other. He's taking the fight to the champion from the off. McCall seems to be asleep. His corner shouts something; he looks across and smiles. The crowd are already shouting 'Bru-no! Bru-no!' He's giving McCall no space, no opening. And suddenly, he unleashes his Sunday shot, a big left which catches McCall full on the jaw. Any other fighter would have been down; it's the hardest punch in heavyweight boxing; but McCall just staggers, leans groggily against the ropes, then he's steady on his feet again. Still, it's shaken him. He's already beginning to hold, to ward off the relentless jabbing of Bruno's left. It's what we'd worked on so hard, so long. I knew that if you throw a right at McCall he blocks and comes straight back with his own right. It's how he finished Lewis. Keep the left going, Frank, and remember his right.

Bell

My minute. I'm straight out into the ring the second the bell goes. I look Frank in the face, let him know I'm there on the instant, with him as closely as I can possibly be. Wipe his face down, little to say yet. The game plan is working fine; exactly as we trained to do.

I say: 'That's as perfect as you can be. Stick to the game plan. Centre of the ring. Don't let him back you up. Pick him off with the left hand as he comes, you know. Left hand, left hook. You can start bringing up one or two uppercuts and crosses in there. Well done, Frank, keep at it.'

Round Two

Bruno moves in, steady and in command. Once again McCall is ducking the punches, weaving and holding. He's holding: he doesn't want to know, he's giving in, yet he thinks he's cruising, that's what he's told himself: Bruno hasn't the staying power; he can't survive past seven rounds any more. McCall's trying to throw punches but none of them get through. His corner are chafing him: 'Wake up. What you doing? Come on, man.' He nods at them. Bruno is varying the jabs, to the head then to the body. He's smothering any attempt McCall makes to come out of defence and into attack. McCall is relying on his chin and his stamina, but he's giving points away the whole time. Bruno is tying him up: all he can do is duck and hold.

Bell

'Frank, you're doing a great job. Keep at him, take it steady, he's getting nowhere. Move him forward, just like you're doing. Well done, well done, well done.'

Round Three

No one has ever put McCall on the floor. He's already taken and forgotten Frank's big punch. He's acting as if he can take another any time, if necessary. He's doing nothing to shake off the relentless hammering Frank is handing him. The fact is Frank is boxing at a level no one has ever witnessed before, except me in the gym, where I've seen him mature into the rounded pro now in the ring with McCall. Everybody wrote Bruno off; they said you can't teach an old dog new tricks. But Bruno is like a good wine: he's improving with age. He's showing nous, he's displaying a variety of punches, devastating accuracy and consistency; he's doing what is the mark of any champion — happy to go for small percentage gains as well as looking for the big flattener. He's never given up learning. And here he is, showing a stature of world class. McCall doesn't know what to do as Bruno probes, teases and feints. McCall reads a fight well, there's no doubt of that, but he's foxed. It's as if he can't be bothered to go for points; he's accumulating none. I knew that McCall had a good left hand, so, for this fight, I set out to make sure Frank's was even better, and it worked a charm: those opening three rounds I have never seen Frank box better using his left hand. Three months solid work, the plan unfolding exactly as we'd wanted.

Bell

Into the corner. I don't waste a second. Sixty precious seconds, the only time I have with my man. In that time I have to see to any cuts or swollen tissue — the ice-swell is in the bucket to hand. Frank's looking relaxed, breathing easily, strong. 'Now you're working nice. You've won the first three rounds. Now we start bringing the other moves into play.'

Round Four

So much is weighing on us tonight — not least the certain knowledge that some time McCall is going to come back. We know he can endure punishment, probably better than any other heavyweight, but he's being boxed out of the ring at the moment. I'm thinking: 'Keep it up, Frank. Stick to the game plan.' Bruno uncoils a second massive left hook; McCall reels, steps back, but the man is made of cast-iron, he doesn't even look like going down. His corner yells at him. He nods back; they're rattled. At this rate he's not going to win a single round. Now Bruno is taking his time. In the past, he did all the work. I didn't want him to do that, get tired and a bit lackadaisical towards the end. So, from round four, I told him: 'Steady up a bit. Don't do all the work.'

Bell

The noise is deafening. You shut it out. It's just you and your man. I know that minute to a millisecond, just like I know three minutes. I could count it anywhere, any time; I don't need a clock. And as the time comes up, I lean right down to Frank, eye to eye. It's him and me. I won't have anyone else whispering in his ear. Look across at McCall; he's staring at the canvas, across the ring, out through the ropes. His trainer is leaning over his shoulder from behind, the cut man is attending to the bruising on his face where Frank's punch drove in.

Round Five

At the ringside Frank's wife Laura watches without a flicker of emotion showing on her face. No one who hasn't been this close can possibly know how hard the punching is; how punishing the fight always is; the sound catches you in the stomach. It takes some nerve for Laura to sit there; she hasn't seen Frank for over seven weeks, as he's been away at a training camp. The tension on her must be enormous. She gives not a hint of it away.

McCall has gone into a clinch. Frank is happy to stay with it, to conserve energy. The referee shouts 'Break', but they lean into each other. They have to be prised apart. Suddenly, McCall seems to wake up — until now he hasn't just left this fight in the gym, he's left it in the bedroom — he lands two stiff jabs. You can sense a shiver of expectation go round the arena. McCall has just been biding his time, waiting for Bruno to wear himself down on the first onslaught. Except, that is, if you ever get a chance to take someone out, you do it. McCall hasn't landed any punches before because Frank hasn't let him.

The tapes round Frank's left wrist come loose — poor quality English tape; the American type is much stronger. The referee signals to me to tidy it up. I could have simply cut it, but I bind it round more neatly to take up more time. The referee gets impatient: 'Come on, come on, that'll do.' I pay no attention, concentrate on the job, make sure it's all tucked up nicely. Fifteen seconds or more. When I'm finished — there are no halos in this game — I whisper: 'Okay, Frank, you've had your rest, now get going.'

The final seconds of a round can make all the difference: what you do then can stick in the judges' minds more than any fancy stuff at the outset. Frank comes out hard, but McCall has had a rest too: he whacks Bruno a solid left. Frank goes back on to the ropes.

Bell

Frank had caught a pile-driver but there was no weakening. He marched back to the corner. I told him to breathe deeply, wiped him down, talked to him, encouraged him. He was very calm, totally focused, contained. We were well aware that McCall was going to be launching more; this was a guy who wouldn't give up until the final bell. Knowing that, and preparing for it, had formed a large part of our physical and technical work in the build-up to the fight. And it had brought Frank to a new level of purpose. This was Frank Bruno as no one had seen him before. He had developed a fantastic mental toughness which only those achieve who are denied the peak of success and who have to go right back to the bottom to start all over again. I said: 'Good, Frank, it's going well, but don't fire away all the time. Hold him occasionally, turn him occasionally. Don't do all the fighting. Don't start having a war, trading punches. Keep at it.'

Round Six
When's McCall going to wake up? He seems completely unbothered. He's done nothing so far — bar land a couple of solid punches — he's so far behind on points he must be relying on Frank buckling and laying himself wide to the knockout. And, waiting for the fabled Bruno collapse, he's prepared to weather any punishment that's dished out his way, knowing he's got the strongest chin in the business. He won't fall over, that's his stock-in-trade. He gets stronger as the fight wears on. His confidence looks to me all hot air and fantasy at the moment, but he's still champion and he's still coming forward whenever Bruno gives him the chance. He's getting through with a few jabs now, stringing some combinations together. Halfway through the contest and McCall realises that he needs to come up with some positive action. He puts together a flurry of jabs. Whatever he tries, though, Bruno blocks; he's not allowing himself to be pushed. Bruno lands a brilliant uppercut, McCall steps back and Frank grabs a breather. McCall comes on again and delivers some heavy punches; Bruno absorbs them. No sign of any distress. Never show him you're hurt. He's tying McCall up once more; he is dominating this fight by technical skill and smart boxing, and he won't give McCall any way through. In fact, the champion seems to think all he needed to do was turn up, stand up and put up; he's hardly even looking at Bruno, doing virtually nothing to match him.

Bell
It's when things are going well, when you're ahead, when you're nearly there, that you've got to be most alert. When you feel like coasting a bit, knowing you've got plenty in hand, then you have to put the pressure on.
    Frank comes back to the corner. I leap out ready for him and as soon as he sits down, I look him square in the eyes, slap his face and wake him with a start as if he's been wandering around in a trance out there. 'What the bloody hell do you think you're playing at, Frank? This is a fucking title fight, your title fight, and you're boxing like a dope. Get going. You're letting him back in. Don't give him a fucking inch.' Well, that was what I was thinking. In fact, what I said was: 'Good, Frank, it's good what you're doing, keep at it. Don't wander off. Don't give him an inch,' and I said it as coolly and as fiercely as a sergeant-major would, knowing that any fatigue,

any lapses, any complacency, anything less than total commitment and purpose, could be disastrous. Which is exactly what McCall is banking on. When you feel as if you're giving everything you've got, that's precisely the time you've got to find more. Your mind will fool you that you don't need to go through any more pain, and that's when you have to get your mind sorted out. That's my job, to remind my man of that. He knows it, deep down, but in the thick of the fight he has to be reminded to crank up the effort harder and harder. It's not his job either to tell me he can; if he really can't, he doesn't deserve to be champion. And however tired he looks, I have to get more out of him. It may seem absurd to anyone who has never tested him or herself to the absolute limit: and the absolute limit is when you pass out or fall over.

Ken Jones tells a story about when he was a junior reporter trying to see Terry Spinks after he'd won the flyweight gold medal in the 1956 Olympics. Spinks took the fight on points but was so far gone by the bell — after taking a desperate pasting from Johnny Kidd in the later rounds — that, standing in the shower aware that someone is outside the cubicle and thinking it's his manager, Sammy McCarthy, he mumbled, 'What round is it, Sammy?' Fighting through tiredness that extreme is what forges champions.

Frank looks back at me and he knows. This is the seventh round coming up; the round that Lewis caught him in Cardiff two years ago. We're halfway through, nearly half an hour to go to the final bell, with everything still to do. However far he is ahead, it can all be lost in a trice.

My last words are: 'Use your left hook off the jab. Bring your right hand in whenever you can.' As I say it, I'm leaning over him, emphasising the words with my fists; pumping the energy into him. The bell goes.

Round Seven
If Frank knows round seven has a jinx then so does McCall. He marches out ready to do the business. The noise in the arena is unbelievable; huge roars of 'Bru-no! Bru-no!' At the ringside, where I crouch just by the canvas, the clamour is deafening. McCall leads, Bruno steps back, McCall presses forward. The signs are ominous. McCall's beginning to realise this fight is slipping away from him; he's got very little insurance, only the knockout. Nigel Benn is on his feet at the ringside shouting: 'Don't let him back you up, Frank. Left, right. Don't let him back you up, Frank.' But McCall is pushing Bruno on to the defensive. Bruno's punching gets a bit sloppy and the referee warns him for hitting McCall on the back of the head. In the pause during the warning, Frank gets back on song and then both men are lamming into each other with shuddering power; a huge combined weight

of punch and full body strength, This is some of the most ferocious punching I've experienced, a full-out, toe-to-toe heavyweight encounter.

Bell
I'm relieved that round is over. McCall is showing some urgency, even if Bruno is closing him down. A hard round over, worse to come. You're equal to it, Frank. Dig deep. I know he will. He already has.

Round Eight
McCall hasn't really come in from the fringes of the fight. He'd have landed more shots on Bruno if Bruno had allowed him to. All that stuff about Bruno being a one-round hitter — if this isn't proof to the contrary I don't know what will convince anyone. His body shots are getting through and stopping the champion short. Suddenly, Frank switches guard, he goes southpaw. It's a risk going for what may be a very dodgy advantage. Southpaw means he rests his overworked left arm, plus the possibility that he takes his opponent off guard for a while. However, he has to go on boxing as well as he has, or else open himself to the knockout punch. It's a sign of great self-confidence and Frank works it to perfection. McCall — obviously thinking he can catch Frank on the hop — springs an attack, but Frank dances out of trouble, very balanced, very agile. The southpaw ploy wasn't my idea, it was Frank's. When he proposed the southpaw plan in training, I wasn't keen, because of the risk involved, but Frank insisted he felt happy about it, and that he could make it work, so it was my job to ensure it did. We exercised hard, leaving nothing to chance. Isn't that what makes champions — hard work? You can have all the talent on offer, but if you don't work it hard, you'll get nowhere at the highest level. Perfecting the basics is the key to being the best.

Bell
If you look at a tape of the fight, you'll constantly see McCall in his corner staring across the empty ring. His trainer is standing behind him on the other side of the ropes, leaning over his shoulder, talking into his ear. The cut man is peering at his other cheek, working on the abrasions. In our corner, Frank and I are locked face to face, as if there were messages on the whites of our eyes. I'm saying: 'Well done, Frank. This is your fight. Good, Frank. Keep at it.'

Round Nine
Time is running out fast for McCall. He's stepping up his effort, throwing loads of bombs. He's seen the recordings of the Witherspoon fight, the Tyson fight, the Lewis fight; he's depending on doing the same. He's boasted about all the trouble he's given Tyson in sparring, but not about

any problems he caused Bruno. Still, he knows this title is being torn away from him, and Frank knows he's in this fight to the finish. Bruno's driving in some lovely jabs, bringing the fight under his control, matching any manoeuvre McCall attempts. It's a display of immense boxing savvy; it made me very proud of him, the way he's never given up learning, never given up his dream. Nonetheless, he's got no room for slacking off.

Bell

Another round to Bruno. That morning, John Morrison, the chairman of the British Boxing Board of Control, had said: 'Bruno deserves to win the title for everything he's done for British boxing.' Nice words, and undeniably true, but this isn't going to be any honorary victory. What is also undeniably true is that Bruno is outboxing the champion.

The tension is enormous. I'm quite het up. I'm feinting punches as I hunch over Frank. 'Keep those jabs going, Frank. You've got to start increasing it a little bit more. You've got to go on controlling the fight. You've worked all these years: don't do nothing stupid. You're well in front. Don't try to knock him out. Just box nicely; box, box all the time. Ice-cold aggression (my catchword), Frank. Ice-cold aggression. Let him have it.'

Frank nods. The bell goes. I duck away.

Round Ten

Frank goes straight out into the stormiest onslaught yet. Heavy punches to his body; probing jabs. Any slackness and your wind gets squashed out, your knees sag, hands go down, you're open. The willpower to stay on your front foot, guard up, has to be heroic, there's no other word for it. Bruno is fighting his own past tonight, the history of three losses to a single punch. He's also battling through tremendous fatigue, the exertions of every round on the attack. To lose now would be unthinkable but it's still possible. This man McCall has got the punch — if only he can land it.

Frank is boxing beautifully; jabs and combinations. A tribute to how far he's come, to step up another gear so late in the fight. The tempo may seem slower; the energy and force of the punching hardly diminished. McCall catches Bruno with a terrific uppercut; Bruno's head goes back, but not for long. He rolls with it, rides it, unlike in the past. This time he's prepared.

Frank has said often enough that anyone who steps into the ring — especially at this level — has his respect. This attitude makes him a gentleman; it also, sadly, encourages idiots to think he's a patsy. What they don't realise is that true respect, such as Frank accords his opponents, is rooted in self-respect. Bruno is a fighter; he just doesn't happen to be a loudmouth.

Bell

I readily admit I was happy to hear that bell. The fight was beginning to get to me. I don't mind telling you that that was the most emotional evening of my life. I didn't lose my head — my old headstrong street-fighting instincts are all dead and buried. I've been a pro too long to let emotion creep into my work, but I knew for sure that with two scorching rounds left to go, I had to gee Frank up so he was not only boxing out of his skin, his nerves and brain lit up like Christmas, but that every instinct for survival out there was pinging like an alarm clock. Having been a Covent Garden porter, my language can be a bit rough diamond. I'd taken off the throat microphone the television people put on me, but the Sky TV microphone picked up the saltier samples of my encouragement, as my family in America who watched the fight told me. 'Frank, you've worked so fucking hard to get this far, don't fucking-well give it away now. You've got hold of it so bloody tight don't let it out of your hands. Hold on. Keep at it. Bite on your gumshield. Go for broke, all the fucking way. The only way you can lose now is if you get careless. They must be telling him you're a fucking mile ahead and he's going to throw the works at you.'

Which he did.

Round Eleven

McCall is going for broke. There's no doubt this was his best round, with some almighty punches, some left hooks, some crosses, and it was a very rough passage. Bruno catches him head and body, but the stupendous effort he's put in earlier is taking its toll. He goes in to hold, something he's never done in his life, to his cost. Before, he was always too proud to hold. In fact, there was a loud chorus all round the ring: 'Hold him, Frank. Hold him.' Some people watching on television, not because they're boxing fans but because they sensed this was Frank's night, were saying: 'But he's not allowed to do that.' Frank is holding like a good 'un; McCall is rolling his eyes, making signals to the referee — distress signals, I'd call them — as if to say 'Get him off me'. The referee breaks the clinch. Frank's guard goes up instantly and the champion stares wildly at this so-called non-boxer, non-fighter, as if to say 'What can I do?', just as Frank catches him with a left uppercut — he's gone back to conventional guard — and skips back in to hold again. And this is the man they accused of boxing like a tin soldier, without guile, incapable of using his feet. McCall's survival instincts are pumping adrenalin through him; he's taken almighty stick from the start; he's storming in, punches flying, the Atomic Bull on the rampage, his last charge maybe. Bruno stands up to it and moves forward; he refuses to be forced into error or haste. That's the worst temptation at this stage: to let go, panic, rush at it, out of control, anything to finish the business, get out of the torture chamber. Bruno has won most of his fights early and it could easily become the pressure of pride to try and end this one with a bang. I've warned him off it, over and over again. This time he's not prepared to give anything away, he's showing fantastic nerve and patience and raw courage. You can't give anyone heart: they have to be born with it.

Bell

I lean over Frank, my mouth close to his left ear, I'm almost embracing him. The bond between us at this moment is as intense as I have ever known. The clock is ticking the time out; we're nearly home. I say: 'You've got to remember everything you've ever learned in your life for the next three minutes because your life is going to depend on it. Three minutes for your dreams, Frank; three minutes, that's all. You're so far in front: don't let him put you down. Everything you've got. He'll be going for you because he thinks he's on top. You're going to go out there and one way or another you're going to survive.'

Frank nodded and said: 'No problem.' That's all. Enough to show I'm getting through. I give him a crack round the head, just to get him together and say: 'Come on, come on.'

Final Round

Bruno and McCall touch gloves. What happens next is totally predictable – Custer's last stand for McCall. He's probably thinking he's softened Bruno enough so that he's ready for the taking. All he's got to do is whack Frank with the sort of 'Goodnight Vienna' punch that Frank has got and that's that. If he can find him. Frank didn't stand and box, stand and box; he'd do a little bit then grab McCall, lock him up, waltz him across the ring, give him a couple of cracks and then hold him again. All the planning worked out. A few nettling jabs, then hold.

Forty seconds to go. My heart is beating out those seconds down to zero. Frank is breathing heavily, blood oozing from his nose. Both men are tottering with fatigue. There's still time. One ramrod from McCall ... but then the bell goes, it's all over. Pandemonium. I can hardly believe it. All the sparring, all the hundreds of rounds, the terrible disappointments forgotten, because we knew he'd won it. And all through the training for this fight in the gym we used to shout: 'And the new champion ...' and that was the word we wanted to hear. The waiting seemed to go on and on, just like at the beginning of the fight. Then the announcer's voice comes over and at last the words we'd been wanting to hear all those months rings out: 'Introducing the new heavyweight champion of the world ... Frrrank Brrruno!'

Bedlam. I hugged Frank, the *noo* champion of the world. 'At last. You've done it, Frank. No trainer could ask for more.' And suddenly the ring is full: officials, friends, his lovely wife. He'd got probably the best wife I've met

22

in boxing; she's wonderful. She takes the pressure off us because she arranges so many things that would normally land on our doorstep. She does a million and one things for us. She's great. She leaves us to do the fighting side, and she looks after all the trimmings: the press, dates of different commitments. It's lovely that moment, to see her with her husband in the ring. I just step back and wonder when it will sink in, that it's another world champion I've got. Not *just* a world champion, either, a *special* world champion. The Americans had always written off our guys, called them the horizontal champions. One commentator was even nastier about it when he said: 'The difference between American boxers and British boxers is that our champion is in jail and yours is appearing in pantomime.' Frank changed that.

Harry Carpenter came over and said: 'George, you've taught him well.' And someone else told me: 'That was a very educated display.' It was music to my ears, because going the full 12 rounds to win a world title by skilful boxing is special. One of McCall's ex-sparring partners, Lyndon Jones, came over. We'd hired him to help us prepare and he was very useful. I don't know why he and McCall had fallen out, but when he nudged me in the ribs and gave me the widest smile I'd ever seen, I knew what pleasure he'd had seeing Frank win. Me too. I've worked with a lot of boxers, some good men, some bad, some downright diabolical as blokes, but Frank is a diamond guy.

The jibes that had been thrown at Bruno before the fight had obviously hurt him very deeply and in the interviews at the ringside he was crying with the emotion of victory and the sense that he had overturned those insults. There's something very innocent about him; as if he could hardly believe that from all the pain and toil of climbing back up after defeat, of the long waiting, that his time had — as he'd said it would — finally come, insisting that it would be against all the smart money, all the so-called expert opinion. That innocence reveals how genuine and open, how very 'frank' he is. It comes through the way he is with kids. He'll visit hospitals and sit on kids' beds for hours, laughing and joking with them, cheering them up. At one press conference after the fight in Wembley, he kept seven camera crews waiting because there was a little girl some folk had asked him to see because they were raising money for an operation for her. He's like the Pied Piper, kids just follow him. A room can be full of celebrities and he walks in and everyone homes in on him. It's his directness, his simplicity and honesty and his total lack of vanity that shines through — he always gives his true self, no fancy façade, no falseness. He has never forgotten his origins as a wild, unruly kid, making life difficult for everybody else because he couldn't cope with life himself. A lot of people who make it to the big-time forget where they started out — not Frank. He came through a tough schooling in the way of discipline, not only the discipline others imposed on him but the discipline he took on his own shoulders to achieve what he always believed to be his destiny.

I'm proud that what I believed to be my destiny came to be linked to such a man. And if I never do anything else in boxing, I can regard this as the pinnacle I wanted to reach and have reached. Success can waft up as swiftly as it wanes, but this . . . no one can ever take this away or diminish it or belittle it.

There was a party to celebrate and I was asked to go, but I'm not a party man. Frank didn't go either, because he'd been away from home that long he wanted to get back. I'd been away an age too, so I came home to Highgate. My wife, Joan, had watched the fight on TV with the rest of the family. Apparently she ran out of the room during the tenth round — she couldn't bear the tension.

When I got in, it was around 3 a.m. Joan went to bed. I couldn't sleep so I played some music and then I thought: 'I know what I can do.' I put on some warm clothes and went for a walk across the Heath, over the fields where I did much of my training — right from the earliest days — stood up on to Kite Hill where I gazed out at all the lights across London, one of the best views around. I stayed a while, drinking it all in. We'd been down there and we'd done it. Frank Bruno had just become the first British heavyweight to win the title in the ring for 98 years. The first time since Bob Fitzsimmons knocked out the champion, James Corbett, in the fourteenth round in Carson City in 1897. And this was the belt, the cream of the cream. And somewhere among all those lights was Camden Town, where I started off as a kid in a dingy backstreet in 1928.

Chapter Two

Childhood and Early Life

Just opposite the end of the turning where we lived, on the other side of Great College Street where the trams ran both ways, was a snobs — a cobbler's. As a kid I used to go and watch the cobbler working, tapping pins into the leather on the metal last.

One day, I stood outside the shop, looking through the plate-glass window watching the old boy repair a shoe. He had his mouth full of sole tacks and as he needed one he'd spit one out into his hand and tap it into the leather. All in a fast, smooth rhythm — lips, fingers, shoe, hammer, tap, lips, fingers, shoe, hammer, tap. I was hypnotised, I didn't know where those pins were coming from. It was as if he was making them in his mouth. Then I heard my mother call me from the end of our turning: 'George!' I didn't look where I was going, I just flew across the road, smack into the tram coming from Kentish Town, straight under the metal cowcatcher at the front and was dragged 20 yards before it stopped. All I remember was waking up for a few seconds, seeing legs all around me and a fireman with his arms around me, pulling me out from under the tram and saying: 'He's alive.' I was four years old.

I was in hospital for about six months and in a coma for quite a long time, which affected my brain. They were going to put a metal plate in my head, the crack was so bad. In the end they didn't, but for ages I couldn't speak properly. I knew what I wanted to say but I couldn't control myself. My knees shook. I used to shit my pants. So I got sent home from school all the time. I'd be in the classroom, go into a faint and fill my trousers. The teacher had to call my sister Dorothy to take me home. It made me different from all the other kids. They picked on me; 'You're just a dummy, can't talk, mess your trousers.' I used to lose my temper, all the frustration boiled up and I struck out. And that's when things went badly wrong with my father. Up until then I felt loved like any other kid, but after I came home from the hospital, getting sent back from school, not able to sort out anything in my head, it seemed as if he was always saying: 'You shit yourself again? When are you going to stop that?' Battering away, nagging, the whole time nagging.

The result was that I hated being at school, and I didn't feel wanted at home. I was a liability, running wild in the street, getting into scrapes the whole time — first thing in the morning I left the house out of dad's way and didn't come back until night, sneaked in and hoped nobody would notice. Mother tried to force me to school; now and then she hauled me off round into Camden Way, even took her shoe off to spank me when I kicked and fought. But as soon as she'd left me inside the school gate, I flew off round the opposite way and out, free for the day. While other kids got a school dinner, I was feeding myself, doing odd jobs, anything to earn some money for something to eat. I was hungry most of the time, but that was the start of working. I'd do anything to earn a few pence: errands, help, anything.

The insurance money from the accident was put in a special trust for me to use when I was 21. I was married by then, and we went, mother, Joan and I, to Duncan Terrace to collect the money. I handed over the papers which proved my entitlement and they went off to search through the files. When they came back, they said that my father had drawn it out, must have been just after I came out of hospital. He'd told them he needed it so he could pay for me to have holidays to recuperate.

He was a cruel man, my father. I was terrified of him. I'd go up to him, he'd half smile then grab hold of me and hit me because I'd been in trouble, or just because he felt like hitting me. I never knew whether he was going to hit me or give me a cuddle. One Friday night he'd seen me playing over by the canal. He got me as I came out of the bath, so I couldn't run away under the table to escape, and started belting me. I grabbed hold of my mother's stays, draped over the back of a chair, to protect myself, but he kept walloping me. My mother rushed in. 'Bake! Bake! (Charles 'Bake' Francis, I don't know why) leave him alone, you'll kill him.' He stopped long enough for me to get away and I ran up into the bedroom, trying to stifle the sobs, heaving for breath, and I heard him shouting up the stairs: 'If I catch you . . .' I was so petrified I couldn't speak. I listened as he came up into the bedroom and started beating me all over again. And, whenever my mother tried to protect me, he'd start hitting her too . . . bruises, black eyes. He was always full of apologies afterwards when he'd sobered up; crying, saying he was sorry, he'd never do it again.

We lived in Prebend Street (renamed Baynes Street because there was another Prebend Street in Islington), at number five, then 12, then 14 in the basement and ground floor of a four-storey house. Granny and grandad Francis lived at number 11, and two of my uncles lived along the street, so there were a lot of Francises in the turning. My other grandma lived across the street, too. I had four sisters: Lily, Rose, Dorothy and Mary — the baby — and two brothers, Charlie and Billy.

There always seemed to be a lot of women coming and going to number three. I asked why but nobody would say. Later I found out that the woman who lived there was a back-street abortionist. The rumour got around that she used a crochet hook and some of the young women had haemorrhages and bled to death.

There was a lot of disease: tuberculosis was rife as it was highly infectious and there was no cure in those days — unless you could afford to go to a Swiss sanatorium. And those cramped, damp, filthy, overcrowded houses were a breeding ground for germs. The railway depot was a quarter of a mile away and the railway line ran over a bridge at the end of our turning. There was a power station and a coal dump just along Great — now Royal — College Street, so the air was permanently loaded with smoke, soot, grime and damp. The Regent's Canal ran along the end of the street and barges, some coal-powered, went back and forth. In winter the cold weather, rain and fog all mixed to make the thick, choking smogs London was infamous for. Bronchitic people would be doubled up, coughing, in the streets. Even if you were healthy you could feel your nose and throat jammed up with those pea-soupers. It wasn't much cleaner inside the house: a down-draught in a blocked chimney that hadn't been cleaned for months and soon there'd be a cloud of black smoke in the room and a fall of soot into the fireplace.

There was also scarlet fever, diphtheria, meningitis, whooping cough, rickets. In the hospital on Camden Road by Rochester Square, they had a special room with blacked-out windows where they gave artificial sunlight treatment to kids with rickets. We could see through chinks in the window blinds this weird blue light in the room and the kids lying on couches. I had already lost my older sister Rosie to disease. Now young Lily fell ill.

When I was about five, my mother had to go into hospital for a serious operation on her leg. So, my sister Lily and I were carted off into care — I don't know where, I never have been able to find out. While we were there, there was an outbreak of illness, either scarlet fever or diphtheria. Lily and I were taken off to an isolation ward and put in cots side by side. She was very ill and sobbing. I was ill, too, but not nearly so badly. During the night the doctor and a nurse came in and lifted her out of the cot. I was scared witless and started screaming, but the doctor said, 'She's got to go, she's very poorly.' I was yelling: 'You can't take her, you can't take her.' They did take her. A few days later, my mother came to fetch me home, her leg done up in a thick bandage, and we went to the Dartmouth Park Hospital to see

Lily. Mother left me at the porter's lodge, and he looked after me. When she came back she was crying. She said: 'Lily has passed away. She's gone to heaven.'

The children slept as many as four to a bed, packed in feet to head like sardines. There wasn't enough bedclothing so we had coats laid over us on top as blankets, and the sheets didn't get washed very often, so we used to get scabies or 'itch'. It comes from a mite that burrows under the skin and usually starts as sores in the webs between the fingers. The more you scratch the more it spreads and the cure was a sulphur bath. The Cleansing Station was tucked around the back of St Pancras Gardens. You had to strip off and go and lie in a warm sulphur bath while they took all your clothes and baked them in an oven to fumigate them. When you came out you stank like a polecat so everybody knew where you'd been. It gave us an excuse to get out of school, though. All you had to do was scratch a raw patch on the back of your hand and say you had the itch and they sent you home.

Fleas were common, too. I always had long curly hair as a kid, but if you got fleas it was round to Mann's the barber, on the corner of Little Randolph Street, for a 'tuppenny all off', hair cropped to a quarter of an inch from the scalp. 'Come in here, Tobias,' he'd say. 'I'll soon polish you off.' And the other kids ribbed you when you came out: 'Baldy! Baldy!'

And rats. There was never a time when we didn't have rats somewhere in the house, but there was a whole plague of them once. Horrible bloody things. Everyone had them. My uncle fixed tin sheets over their holes to keep them out, but one night I woke up and there was a rat chewing a rusk at the end of my younger sister's cot. She'd been eating it before she went to sleep. I jumped up and chased it off. A dog might kill them, and a cat would get the smaller ones. You could set traps; either the flat variety with a loaded sprung lever, or a cage they crept into after the bait. You'd see people in the morning, lowering a caged rat into a dustbin full of water to drown it. A lot of families kept chickens in the backyard, so that rats came after the chicken feed.

In the backyard of most houses there was the earth closet — a wooden bench over the deep toilet hole. (Toilet paper was generally a wad cut from a newspaper or a telephone directory.) Cold in winter, but a lot less smelly and unhealthy than the toilet just inside the house at the back of the ground-floor hallway. Also in the yard was the washhouse with the copper for doing the laundry (Monday was washing day), sinks, an old-fashioned hand-mangle for squeezing water out of the wet laundry — and mind you don't get your fingers trapped as the sheets went through — two iron baths hanging by hooks on the wall. Friday night was bath night.

As we got older, we went to the public baths in the Prince of Wales

Road. That made you feel grown up. You waited till they called your turn, 'Next please', and you went along a narrow walkway between the bath cubicles. Outside every cubicle was a brass disc with a square notch cut into the centre for a lever that the baths attendant turned to fill the tub. You would lie there in real luxury and, when your bath cooled off, sing out: 'More water in number five.' and wait till the attendant came, turned his lever and the hot water flowed.

I hated dirt; probably from being locked in the coal-cellar. Outside the basement was an open well below the pavement level, what we called the 'area', and at the end was the coal-cellar — under the steps and landing leading to the ground floor of the house — with an overhead chute for the delivery and a door which opened into the area. When my father got angry, he'd grab me and say 'I've had enough of you', and lock me in the coal-cellar, shoot the bolt and leave me in that dark, dirty, stinking place with the rats and cobwebs. I hated it. It wasn't so bad being locked in the area for a bit, at least that was in the open, but that cellar was horrible. And another thing about the basement: because the window was about on a level with the pavement in summer there were swarms of flies coming into the house. Horses going to and fro along the turning left a lot of manure and in the wet, the slurry ran along the gutters, the flies were thick, everywhere. A man came round selling those roll-down, sticky flypapers. 'Flies alive. Catch 'em alive!' So, there'd be flypapers dangling from the ceiling in the kitchen where we ate, flies stuck all over them, and they never took the papers down, just put new ones up. It was revolting.

Our turning adjoined College Street at one end, St Pancras Way at the other. In College Street was a tobacconist, a baker, where we went at nine or ten in the evening — when they were baking the next day's batch of bread — to ask if they had any stale bread or cakes, only what they hadn't sold that day. You'd get them for next to nothing and I always wolfed down one of the cakes on the way home. Any time I had money, I'd buy a currant loaf in there, sit on the corner of the street and eat the lot. I can still eat a whole currant loaf without thinking.

On the next corner was Webber's the butcher. He regularly had six live sheep delivered from time to time to slaughter in a small yard at the back. We had no fridges of course; the meat and butter and other perishables went into a larder. Granny Francis, a warm, jovial woman, used to cook meals for eight or nine girls working in the Carerra cigarette factory, to make a little extra money. I used to go to Webber's to get the meat for her, so they knew me, and during the war, when meat was on ration, they often gave us a bit extra. I wasn't above rubbing out a cross on the ration book if they marked it in pencil, either. I'm sure they knew, but they never said a word.

Next door was the pawnshop. We never called it that: it was always

'Uncle's'. A busy place, which was divided in two, one side for jewellery and fine stuff (wedding rings, men's watches and chains etc.), and one for clothes. The man's Sunday suit often went in on Monday morning — two shillings and sixpence in the hand, redeemed for three shillings on Friday — if the wife had the money, and if she didn't there'd be explaining to do. After a week in working clothes, the men liked to get togged up in their Sunday best, to go to the pub, walk in the park. After the redemption time was up, the pawnbroker put the clothes on sale. We were all poor together so it was no disgrace. And, from a kid's point of view, taking a parcel of second-hand clothes round to 'Uncle's' was okay — he gave you cash in your hand, which meant grub. When I was about 12, in my first official job, my mother said: 'I'll get you a decent suit now you're working.' She went in and bought a brown suit for ten shillings, a thick brown suit with beading all round the revers. I put it on and went out, pleased as Punch, to see my pals. They all burst out laughing. 'It's a park-keeper's suit, Georgie's got a parkie's suit on.' I felt humiliated in front of my mates. I went home, took that suit off, tied a brick into it and chucked it in the canal. I've hated brown ever since, and I read the other day brown is coming back in — they even make brown suits in Savile Row now.

The oil shop, as we called it, sold everything in the hardware line — logs, bags of coal, gas mantles, shoe blacking and blanco — oil for hurricane lamps (there'd be a hurricane lamp in the outside privy, if not a road-mender's lamp that had gone missing) — and bamboo canes in bundles, thick at one end with a thin, whippy tip, at tuppence apiece. Father always kept one in the house with the end bent over to make a handle. Any time you could, you got hold of that cane and burned it, chucked it, lost it. But when one of you had been naughty, father would say 'Go round and get a cane', and you didn't know who it was for. You took it in the house, handed it over and ran for your life, as he said, 'You get first taste', and you caught it, swish! on the back of your legs as you dived for cover.

Another shop was Fischer's. Mr Fischer was German. He sold food mostly, but every now and then he'd come on a bargain and snap it up — a job lot of cheap slippers, say. He was very stern and strict, but just protecting his stock from a horde of urchins and ferrets — us. He had eyes like a hawk and he needed them. Mother sent me to Fischer's for ham for my father and soup for us. Mr Fischer would say, 'Where's the cash, boy?' and I had to say, 'Mother said can you put it on the tick, please, Mr Fischer?' which made me squirm. The same feeling I had going down with my dish to the egg shop in Inverness Street where they sold cheap the eggs that had cracked in unloading.

Along the other side of College Street near the snobs was Mrs Lambourne's café and the Eagle pub on the corner. Mrs Lambourne used to love me, and was always giving me something to eat. She'd take me through into the kitchen and sit me down to a plate of stew. She'd been so shaken by that tram accident, right outside her café, she always wanted to make sure I was okay.

There were kind people about, people who saw us kids with our noses pressed up against a cake shop window looking at the stuff on the shelves, who would say, 'Would you like one of those apple dumplings? Here's the money.' Or a teacher — who saw me outside the biscuit shop at the bottom of Georgiana Street where they sold every imaginable sort of biscuit, and a few other things too, but mainly biscuits, biscuits from wall to wall, and a twist of phone directory paper filled with broken biscuits for a penny — who would say: 'Why haven't you got any biscuits, Francis?'

'No money, sir.'

'Here's a penny, get yourself some.'

Or the people sitting in the zoo café having tea (we never paid to get in, always bunked in over the fence), seeing us with our tongues hanging out: 'Would you like some tea?' And they would set us up at a table with a drink and a bun on a plate. We were always hungry.

Mr Azapardi — Governor Azapardi we called him, a nice, nice man, from Malta — kept a greengrocer's on the corner of our turning. I loved the whole family. I used to hang around on the pavement, Governor Azapardi would catch me eye, smile and say: 'You wanna work?' And I'd help him fill the bushel boxes with fruit on one side of the shop, and vegetables the other. I can still hear Governor Azapardi's voice saying: 'You wanna work?' I repaid him as best I could: I told all the other kids in our turning that no one was to steal from Governor Azapardi, his shop was out of bounds. In the summer he made ice-cream in a metal canister. That went in a larger wooden tub and we packed ice — chopped from a huge block — round it, plus freezing salt added to two inches below the rim, to stop the ice melting, and a chilled damp sack over the ice. We loaded it on a barrow for me to wheel up to Regent's Park to sell outside the zoo. When I came back at the end of the day he'd give me two shillings or so and sometimes he said; 'Go and wash your hands, come down and have a meal.' That was brilliant. They always had glorious meals and I could eat as much as I liked: soup, meat, pudding . . .

Our treat was spotted dick boiled in the copper: flour, raisins, sultanas, even prunes, mixed up with water, wrapped in a teacloth, even a baby's nappy, in the copper. We stood and watched it with our mouths hanging open till it was done. Then inside to the kitchen, cut open the pud on a plate, clouds of steam, a hot floury pudding smell, jam or custard slurped on — if you were lucky — and wolf it down, till you nearly burst with that sticky duff clinging to your ribs.

My father was a street bookie. He'd always been very clever with figures.

He could work out complicated odds and winnings in his head. On Derby day, when a lot of people who never gambled used to have a flutter, there'd be a long queue outside the house come the evening, up to 20 people, and he could work out the totals just by looking at the bets they'd laid and the odds. He started off working at the Surrey Docks. His father was the caller-off for the timber porters. Six o'clock every morning, he went out to call in a gang of men for work that day. There were always many more men than jobs.

When a load of timber arrived, it came with a spec (specification) detailing types, grades and sizes of wood and the whole load would have to be sorted and stacked in piles on the dockside. My father could look at the spec and work out how to sort the wood so that the stacks came out roughly the same height instead of some eight-foot high and others 12 foot, 16 foot, 20 foot, as high as 40 foot. He obviously had an eye for numbers, so the local big-noise bookie, Sullivan, who lived round the corner from us in a large house in St Paul's Way (now Agar Grove), said to my father: 'You can earn more with me. Why break your back down there?' So, he left the docks and went with Sullivan. Instead of working eight hours at the docks, he had only a few hours' work in the day and the rest of his time free, and that's when he started drinking. He went to pubs till closing time, then late-night drinking clubs. Plus, there was a lot of money passing through his hands.

Off-course betting was illegal in those days, so the street bookie had to watch out for his back the whole time. We had to look out for him, sit at the corner of the street keeping our eyes peeled for plainclothes policemen. We got to know most of them so, whenever we spotted one creeping up towards the turning, we'd tip dad the wink and he'd duck into the house. They'd try anything, disguise themselves as railwaymen, even as chimney-sweeps, but we always could recognise them and give the signal, and try to get away before they landed a backhander.

With the police on the prowl, father couldn't always use the house. He dodged about. Camden Road station had two exits: he stood at one and if the police nosed up he could dart off through the side entrance. And there was a house on the corner of a mews in our turning, Mrs Sibson's. He could look both ways up the street from her front window and disappear through the side door if he had to.

If the dick loitered about, father would give him a 'body'. He'd call me and say, 'Go and get so-and-so.' Anyone would do, so long as they were over 18. Father would give the 'body' a couple of betting slips to put in his pocket and the police would frogmarch the punter down to the station in Platt Street to charge him. Father could carry on with his business and the police had an arrest. Next day, up in Clerkenwell Magistrates' Court, the decoy was fined ten shillings, even five shillings, and father paid the fine plus five shillings. In those days a week's wages was about three pounds. He even had housewives volunteering to be a 'body'.

Sullivan employed four or five street bookies, of which Bake was one, each taking bets from his own house. At noon people arrived to lay bets on the afternoon races and when my dad had gathered in so many bets, he'd tell one of us kids to run round to Sullivan's with the betting slips: straight bets, accumulators, trebles, hedging against losses. We'd fold the bets up, put them in a bag and take off, nip over the wall, through the stables and on into St Paul's Way. Only ever betting slips, never money. Sullivan had phones so he rang the bets through to the racecourse (hedging bets of his own if he had a lot of money staked against him) and sent runners back with the results. That went on till about four o'clock and the last race and there would be a break, when father worked out all the winnings and losses ready for six o'clock when people came round to collect and lay bets for the evening dog races. Father used to count the money out on the square arms of his chair; heaps of coppers, tanners, bobs, florins, half dollars (old ladies always bet in coins) and sometimes he'd knock over one of the piles. Our job was to collect the coins up, but sometimes they'd roll down inside the chair. One day, before bonfire night, he told Billy and me to carry the old chair out and get rid of it — he had a new one coming. We got the chair out and scrabbled down the sides of it and rooted out two quid in lost coins. We had a good lot of fireworks out of that.

Gambling was a curse. A man might bet his wages, lose the lot and that would be that for the week. A woman might pop her husband's suit or her wedding ring and lay the money on a horse, lose, and come round to my dad and beg him for a bit of money so she could get her possessions out of hock, and promise to repay him the next week. But I heard him say to mother more than once: 'When you start doing that, there's no end to it. You make enemies for saying no, and enemies for saying yes to one and not another.' If anyone came to the house and asked for him and he knew they were after a loan, he'd tell me to tell them he was out.

You learnt to lie at an early age. So much was on tick — clothes from the Provident Clothing, for instance, which you bought with their cheques, so their collectors would be round for instalments. Every Friday you knew the rent collectors would be coming. A knock on the door and mother would tell you to go and answer.

'Mummy said she's not in.'

'Well, just you tell Mummy I know very well she is.'

And he'd stand there waiting on the front step, lean in through the open door and shout: 'Come on, I know you're in, and you didn't pay last week, so that's two weeks owing. Let it go now and it'll be three weeks next.'

She'd come out, pay one week plus a bit of the arrears and fetch me a clip round the ear for getting it wrong.

The worst thing about my father was that he was a drunkard. Mother cooked Sunday lunch and it had to be on the table when he came home from the pub at two o'clock. Either Billy or I had to stand watch and the other had to go and get him from the Eagle. He'd be at the bar, flushed red as a radish with drink, smoking, laughing with his pals. 'Come in, Georgie,' he'd say. 'Come in, son.' It was horrible, the noise and the smoke. 'Come on, Georgie, have a seat.' He'd be pointing to a chair and just as I sat on it, he pulled it away and set the lot of them laughing. Then he'd swagger out, full of booze and sway off home, then fly into a terrible rage if the food wasn't just so and ready on the table.

One night he came home, he'd had a fight apparently. We dived out of the way, but he dragged me out from under the table and wheezed his beery breath into my face and launched into how he'd beaten the daylights out of some bloke. 'I whacked him, I whacked him. I gave him one like this (and smashed his fist into the radio) and another like this (waving his fist at the light bulb and breaking it so we were plunged into darkness). What happened to the bloody lights? Georgie, where are you? Who turned the lights out?' he yelled, lurching about into the furniture waving his fists.

That image of him, his face distorted with drink, crazy with booze, stayed with me for life. I did try alcohol once, when I was working on the timber at Tottenham Hale. We used to collect our wages from the pub at Manor House. I always drank lemonade. The other blokes kept on at me to try a man's drink, so one day I did, I think it was brown ale. I had five bottles, then went for a pee in the toilet. I stood there at the urinal; there was a bloke beside me being sick into the pissing bowl. Another man in the corner leaning against the wall in a daze, his eyes glazed over, and I looked in the mirror in front of me and saw my father's face, not mine. It came back, his drunkenness and mad rages, and I suddenly felt dirty inside, didn't want any part of it and I've never touched a drop since.

The main thing was to escape. The canal was our playground; 'the cut' we called it. The Grand Union, Regent's Canal runs from the Regent's Canal dock on the Thames by Limehouse, to Paddington Basin and on west. The section we knew was from King's Cross to Camden Lock. It flows under College Street right at the end of our turning. The towpath is open now, but in those days there was a high brick wall along it. We cut grooves in it so we could climb down on to the towpath and go swimming. Our parents forbade us, but they knew we would end up in the water one way or another, so they made sure we could swim, by hitching a rope under our armpits and dragging us along in the cut till we could stay afloat on our own.

The canal copper, Long Tom, patrolled the towpath occasionally and he was supposed to stop you playing in the cut. Anyone who spotted him shouted, 'Watch out! It's Long Tom!' and if you couldn't get away up the wall in time, you'd more than likely leap into the canal fully-clothed and swim across to the far bank and stand there laughing at him and yelling, 'Can't catch me!' Fully-clothed was jumper and trousers, no underpants — never heard of them — just trousers with our bare arses hanging out the hole in the seat, like as not.

We swam in all weathers, got changed under the bridge by the Constitution pub where St Pancras Way crosses the canal. And just along from there were the hot waters — three openings which gushed out hot water in a waterfall from the power station behind. Near the hot waters the fish grew deformed; they had huge lumps over their eyes from the pollution, but we swam there anyway.

On payday, the railwaymen from the depot behind the Constitution often stood on the bridge with their wage packets and we'd line up on the balustrade ready. They said, 'Okay, son, penny a long dive', and lob a penny into the cut. You dived, and if you were lucky you caught it as it drifted down. If it got to the bottom, about eight feet deep, you had to go slow so as not to stir the mud and lose it. Those long dives from the top really taught you how to hold your breath.

The canal barges carried coal and timber, mostly pulled by horses. Or there were Gipsy boats, with an upturned V canvas-tilt over the load of corn and grain: the 'pop-pop' boats. If two boats came in opposite directions it wasn't uncommon for them to get stuck, even in the wider passing places. The horse was heaving away and if the head of the barge made a sudden swing into midstream, it yanked the horse's hindquarters into the drink. A cry would go up, 'The horse is in the water!' and we'd rush along, leap into the water, unhook the traces and get the horse out of the harness, kicking and splashing, and help pull it back along the cut to the slip where it could scramble back onto the towpath.

We had mud baths, fished with an old bicycle-wheel rim, minus spokes, with a sack tied round which made a drag-net for gudgeon, sticklebacks, tiddlers, and glided about in old tyres. After seeing *Sanders of the River* at the pictures, we tore a door off one of the empty houses to make a raft and our cut was a river in Africa. A raft came in useful for raiding Lawford's builders' yard on the canal bank for house bricks, tiles, anything in that line. We threw the bricks into one spot below the bridge by the pipe, so they built up on the bottom of the cut. When the horse came along, pulling the loaded barge which was low in the water, the barge ran into the bricks and the horse couldn't heave it past. So, the bargee would tether the horse and walk half a mile along to Camden Lock to ask the lock-keeper to let more water into the canal to float this barge clear. That gave us time to leap onto the barge, fill our sacks with whatever cargo they were carrying and away.

The canal gave off a vile smell — especially in the steam down by the hot waters — which hung over the whole area; there would often be a large wrack of dead cats and dogs, rubbish and used contraceptives swirling about on the surface, and it was dangerous, too. The banks are reinforced with metal box girders now, but there used to be telegraph poles fastened horizontally to piles driven into the canal bed. Those poles got very greasy with moss and weed, and one time a boy I knew went missing. They reckoned he must have slipped off the pole into the water, bobbed up again, whacked his head straight into the pole, knocked himself out and drowned. They dragged the cut with hooks, across and back, across and back, all afternoon then into the night with lights rigged up till they found him. I saw probably six kids dragged out who had drowned. Mother was always saying, 'Don't go down', but there was nothing that could stop us. Even in the Blitz, my pal, Darkie Frank, and I used to swim in there with lumps of red-hot shrapnel landing in the water with a terrific hiss. The people in the ARP depot, next to the button factory near the bridge, who were the gangs who went out to dig people out of the rubble of bombed houses, shouted at us to get out or we'd be killed, but we were having fun. When the bombs were raining down thick, Darkie and I used to run for it and hide under the table in Granny Francis's basement — it had huge, heavy legs and a thick tablecloth and we believed we were out of harm's way.

School had nothing to offer me, except going next door to All Saints Church (it's been a Greek Orthodox church since 1948) for morning prayers. I loved the singing, all of us together, and the stories the vicar told in the pulpit. I suppose from that earliest time I liked the security inside the church, but that was enough school for me. I either didn't go or I was thrown out and I couldn't read or write a word till I was over nine. I used to go to the gardens opposite quite a lot. The gardener there was a kind man; he taught me how to plant flowers. But mostly I was out and about trying to earn scraps of money for a bite to eat. I was a ferret; I'd do anything. There was a mansion block of flats in Camden Road where I went round knocking on doors, offering to run errands; the Veterinary College in College Street kept bin-loads of dried blood from their autopsies outside and I sold sacks of that to various allotment holders — it was perfect for tomatoes. There was a little pitch just by the railway bridge in our turning where an old guy sold firewood. I'd go across St Pancras Way to the sawmill and get a sackful of offcuts, then help him saw them up into six-inch pieces, split them and tie them in bundles to sell. He had a couple of tables for apples, too. Always got the first ones in, Beauty of Bath, bought cheap to make toffee-apples. I'd go round the streets with a pony and flat-backed cart, leading the pony by the halter, ringing a bell and shouting: 'Toffee-apples, one a penny! Toffee-apples!' Or I went to earn pennies helping the men push barrows loaded with fruit and veg up Agar Grove into York Way and across to the Caledonian Market for the auction. Every Tuesday and Friday, they sold everything from a button to a suite of furniture. The first penny that I earned meant that I could go to the bakery to buy a big square slab of Tottenham — yellow cake with jam filling and pinky-white icing — which put food inside your stomach and set you up for helping drive cattle round to the slaughterhouse by the market, blocking off side roads so they didn't veer off. That job was easier after I got a dog, Peter, from the stables, when I was about seven.

After the accident I spent a lot of time in Cooper's stables along Prebend Street, under the bridge, 30 yards from our house. Jack Cooper was a horseman, little else. A hard, unyielding man, he had no refinement. A horse to him was a creature of work, to be worked into the ground and then taken to the knacker's. He showed them no love or affection. If the harness didn't fit them, he'd say it didn't matter, get the thing on somehow, it'd have to do. But a harness is like a pair of shoes: a bad fit chafes the flesh and a horse would get sore patches on its neck and withers from where the hames rubbed. When you were on the cart and had to stop at a junction, or to give the horse a drink, the collar would ride up and expose the galling. If a policeman saw that, he could run you in for mistreating the animal. So Cooper taught me to disguise the sores — chalk if it was a grey horse, oil from the axle for a black or chestnut.

Cooper got his horses from the horse fairs at Southall, Barnet or Elephant and Castle, and he always went for the spiteful ones because they gave you the best work. They would tear at the bridle for a while, but they'd always be strong — until he flogged all the life and energy out of them, broken their spirit and their heads went down. If you backed two horses into a cart one morning and saw one of them limping and told Cooper, he'd wrinkle his nose and scoff: 'There's nothing wrong with him. Let's have a gander — give him a run down the turning.' I'd take the horse by the halter, walk him down to the end of College Street then back with the horse trailing its leg. But Cooper would stand at the entrance to the yard with his whip so as when the horse got near it knew what was going to happen and skipped into a trot. Cooper would smirk and say, 'See? I told you. Right as rain. Harness him up.' I never believed him, but he was right, sometimes. There's an old saying, 'a horse will work himself to death', and Cooper seemed bent on proving it.

I learnt most about horses from Cooper's carman, Johnny Phillips. He was a big, strapping lad, a natural horseman. He knew horses, how to handle them, look after them, get the best out of them. He loved them. He took me on the back of the van to help with loading and unloading, and to keep an eye on the stuff to see it didn't disappear off the back as we went along.

Whereas Cooper was a bully, Johnny taught me how to coax. There'd always be a stubborn nag who jibbed, stopped dead and refused to go another step, which didn't help if he took it in mind to get cussed in the middle of Camden High Street or going up the hill towards Chalk Farm. Hauling a heavy cartload up a steep gradient meant you had to get the horses going at a fair lick, and if they showed signs of dragging their feet, Johnny taught me to rattle the whip in the brass holder or flick it gently behind their ears or blinkers to encourage them, instead of out with the whip and flog them into a run, which is what Cooper did. Johnny taught me never to let animals see you're scared; you have to show them you're the boss, firmly and calmly. It's a matter of nerve. Which is where Peter comes in.

Someone had brought a dog into Cooper's yard and left him, saying he was too vicious to handle. Jack tied him by the gate and told me to stay clear of him. Needless to say, he was a brilliant guard dog — he went for everybody. I don't know what sort of dog he was; we used to say he was a cross between an Airedale and a scrubbing-brush. I started to feed him, give him water and gradually he became my dog, so to speak. I was beginning to come out of my shell after the accident and Peter helped me. He was a fighter, like me. Helping drive the cattle up York Way, Peter turned out to be a marvel. Within a month or two you'd have thought he'd been trained as a cattle dog. You could send him ahead and he'd keep them moving up the road, head them off from side turnings; he was magic.

The horses became very important to me. In the two and a half to three years it took to recover from the accident and get my speech back to normal, I can remember the terrible frustration of knowing what words I wanted to say but not being able to get them out. It was very soothing to work with horses, pat them, groom them, brush and stroke them, give them feed and water. Even when they throw their heads back, or get restless and start weaving about in the stalls, you're saying 'Whoa, boy' over and over again. 'Whoa, boy', you say it a thousand times, and that was my leader, my way back from going crazy because the words wouldn't come. Years later I was walking up Camden High Street when I recognised one of the old horses I'd worked with, Ginger. I called out his name, his head went up straightaway. I went over and said hello, made a fuss of him. He was getting on a bit. And I suddenly had the idea that I'd like to buy him. I went into Cooper's and asked how much he wanted. 'Too late,' he said, 'I sold him to the knacker's this morning.'

There were 12 stalls in the arch, six on either side. Twelve horses to muck out, feed and water; 12 sets of harness to clean and oil to keep the leather supple. Twelve sets of brassware on the hames and tack to polish. I got to the yard first in the morning and gave the horses their feed and mucked out the stables. Every evening I went over to the sawmill with chaff sacks to fill with chippings, one sack per horse to bed down on. Occasionally I had to lead a horse that needed to be reshod down to the farrier at the Veterinary College in St Pancras Way. I'd help the farrier, blowing the bellows to fire the forge up, fetch and carry while I was waiting — and that was another penny earned.

At the end of a long day in harness, between 6 a.m. and 4 p.m., hauling three maybe four loads, each of two tons apiece, the horses' legs would be near enough run off, but Johnny never just unhitched them and shoved them into their stalls and goodnight. He always had time for each one. He made sure they had fresh, dry chips to lie on, brushed them down, groomed them, patted them, talked in that gentle friendly way horse-lovers have. He tended sores they had with various oils. He spent hours with them, Sundays included. You couldn't just leave them because it was your day off. They had to be taken care of every day. That's where I learnt the professional attitude. I spent all the time I could in the stables; it's where I got attention and gave it in return. Horses weren't only your living, they were your friends. Uncertain tempers, maybe, and some of them were downright cantankerous, but they were your responsibility.

Cooper had a grey horse, it was the best worker but mean and spiteful with it. As soon as you lifted the harness off him at the end of his day's work, he'd let fly with his hooves and bite you if you didn't keep an eye on him. But I could handle him. Partly because I spent a lot of time with him and partly because Johnny taught me so well.

When Hampstead Fair came in the summer we used to take ponies up from the yard to the broad grass verge by the Heath up the hill from South End Green to hire them out for rides — threepence the small kids, sixpence the bigger kids — from eight in the morning till nine at night. Trudging back one time I said to Jack Cooper: 'I don't known who's more tired, the horse or me.'

'Well,' he said, 'the horse has got four legs.'

Hampstead Heath — the fields — was only two and a half miles away, but it was a different world: countryside. Kids from Camden Town used to take the tram up and camp on Fitzroy Farm, by Kenwood, at weekends. And there was the swimming. My uncle took me to the Pond first when I was about seven, and that was the start of something; I've been going to the Pond ever since, used the compound for training boxers for years, and the fields for our training runs. As kids, though, we went swimming in the Lido across the Heath — never paid, bunked in over the wall. You could always tell the poor kids at the Lido; they had a callus on the sole of each foot, where their pimsolls had worn through so they were walking partly barefoot on the pavement. That hard patch stood out like a stuck-on lid. You could cover the hole with cardboard but that didn't last long, especially in the wet. And we'd always be going to the hospital in Bayham Street to get a rusty nail out of a foot.

My father died aged 34, when I was eight. He'd always been a heavy smoker as well as a boozer, and as the TB consumed his lungs he was left coughing and wheezing and gasping for breath. The ground floor where we lived was a long room divided in two across the middle by glazed double doors. My father's bed was under the window on the outside wall, so he could look into the street. I was standing there once, with Granny Francis, listening to him racked with coughing. My mother came out and Granny said, 'How is he?'
    'Bad.'
    Granny said, 'He's smoking himself to death with those cigarettes. Why doesn't he stop?'
    But he wouldn't, he couldn't do without them. He called me in one day: 'Go and get me some cigarettes.' I refused. 'Go and get me some cigarettes.' He was shaking all over, screaming with fury, as if he had electricity going through him. I was scared stiff. He gave me the money and I fled. I didn't want to get him the fags but I didn't know what to do either. Then I saw a drain-grating in the gutter and that put the idea in my head. I chucked the money down it and when I went back and he said, 'Where are the cigarettes?' I told him I'd dropped the money and it had rolled down the drain. He took a swing at me, he was beside himself. I didn't love him, I didn't like him, he was so vicious and hard, but it was horrible to see him dying and still desperate for tobacco. He had TB for about two and a half years and when he knew he was dying he tried to be more friendly, tried to make things up with me, but I never trusted him.
    When he died, my mother tried to keep us kids away from the funeral. I overheard her saying that my elder sister Dorothy would take us all off to the pictures, so I hid and they had to go off without me.
    The hearse arrived, a black carriage with glass sides, drawn by two black Belgian horses in a cortège with two other horse-drawn carriages and a procession of cars and old bangers. My dad being a bookie and part of a large family, there seemed like hundreds of mourners. The whole turning was lined with wreaths from end to end, flowers everywhere. The family had gone outside to wait for the coffin to be brought out, so I stood by the front door and watched the carriage arrive and the undertaker's men get out of the hearse and open the back. When they came into the house, I ran up the stairs to the first landing to watch. They carried the coffin out of the downstairs room but, because the angle in the hallway was so narrow, they couldn't get the coffin round. They tried to jockey it out but it wouldn't go, so they turned it on end. I was very angry. I thought, 'My

father's in there.' I ran down the stairs, pushed past them and out on to the front step. One of the neighbours, Mrs Draper, saw me and said, 'He's too young to understand, poor kid,' not knowing why I was upset.

Everybody piled into the carriages and cars and set off very slowly, not much more than walking pace, into College Street along to Kentish Town then Highgate. I ran after them, kept up all the way till they got to Dartmouth Park Hill. Halfway up the hill I started to flag a bit and Mr Murphy, who lived in the top floor of our house, opened his car door. I scrambled in and went to the burial in Finchley Cemetery.

When we got there, they told me to stay in the car but I waited till they had gone to the graveside and ran over to watch as the men lowered the coffin into the ground. I thought: 'My dad's in there. I've got no dad.' And then I thought, 'He can never hit me again.' The fact is I hated him, but part of me knew he was my dad — no matter what. And I felt so sorry for my mother. She was crying her heart out; on her own now; the breadwinner gone and us kids to look after. My granny put her arm round me and said, 'You've got to give her all the help you can now, son.' That made a big impression on me.

Everybody went back to the house. At the graveside they had all been so solemn, crying, dressed in black, then when they got home they were eating sandwiches and drinking, having a high old time, laughing and joking. I couldn't understand that. It was as if they were making fun of us.

My father had no employment cards, of course, so there was no pension for my mother, no widow's allowance.

Not long after my dad died came my earliest recollection of what became an obsession and my livelihood. Every school ran a Country Holiday Fund; you paid tuppence a week through the year for two weeks holiday in the summer. Thousands of kids from London used to go. Our school sent us to Deal. I only went twice, because I so rarely attended school, but those stays in Deal had a great significance. We travelled down by train; the local teachers met us at the station, and my brother Billy, Jessie Cooper — Jack's grandson — and I were sent to stay with a lady called Mary. Her house was bang next door to the Royal Marines depot and she worked in the barracks canteen. She used to take us in there, past the gym where the marines trained. Seeing those clean-cut, fit young men even when I was so young got me hooked on physical exercise, strength and stamina. We saw them doing boat drills and manoeuvres off Deal beach. We watched them marching on the huge drill square and parading to church on Sundays, navy-blue uniforms, gleaming white cap-covers, belts and gloves, boots polished like mirrors, brass badges and buttons shining, and I thought, 'I'd love to be one of them'. I drank in everything and I still use some of the exercises I saw in their gym in Deal.

Back in London things got bad. I wasn't the only kid playing the hop [truant] to earn a bit of extra cash. The depression was still biting; jobs were scarce and plenty of families were barely scratching a living. Eventually, the Prebend Street rent got too much for us to find week by week and that was the start of the moonlight flits — run up the rent as long as possible and then load all the stuff on a van with a pair of ponies and move overnight to the next address. The rent collector seldom bothered to try and catch up with you; it was more trouble than it was worth, he knew you had no money, so what was the point? The flits meant living in a lot of different places, but I always went back to the turning to play with my mates, the Prebend Street mob. I was the gang leader.

I suppose it was inevitable I should become a fighter. First, because my father hit and beat me so often. And second, from the time when I couldn't talk, only mumble, I had used my fists. All boys fought a bit, but I was a fanatic. I hated getting beaten. Where another kid might surrender if he got a whack in the face, a bust lip and a bloody nose only made me more determined. I always felt great satisfaction when my fists hit someone and the more I got hurt, the more it stung, the more I fought back. When kids called me a dummy, I made sure that was the last time they did. It was frustration, it was feeling unloved, it was a whole lot of things, but I'd taken to the streets early and the streets were hard. Survival was for the fittest and I wanted to make sure I was the fittest. I got a reputation as a fighter, and getting a reputation means that you have to live up to it. There's always someone who wants to prove himself against you. As a result, where some kids only had a few fights, I was always fighting. Not only for myself but for others, too. Jessie Cooper had a lisp so, if the other kids made fun of him, I stood up for him. I didn't think a great deal about boxing, yet, though I do remember in the summer, when it was fine outside we'd be playing in the street and if there was a fight on the radio, you'd hear the commentary coming out of the open windows and act it out. 'Now he's hit him with a left, and a right, he's going down, no, he's still on his feet, another right, a short jab and "ding" saved by the bell.' As for the fighting, I can say now, that the older I got, the logic was to run away, but at the time it was more like a highwayman: 'Stand and deliver.'

It was a dodgy world that we grew up in; a lot of creepy, dirty old men prowling about, haunting the street-corner urinals. We had tramps; one came down our turning regularly, cadged a bit of food. We called him 'the man with 15 overcoats'. He used to doss down under the arch by Cooper's stables. He was harmless but others weren't.

There was a man about 35 or 40 I'd seen several times. He used to push a bike round into our turning. I guess he was eyeing the kids. He wore an unusual cap with coloured stripes across the top — it singled him out. I was about ten.

We were playing in the totter's yard — where there were all kinds of junk — by the canal wall and this geezer peered over the fence and asked me if I'd like to earn two bob. That wasn't to be sniffed at, so I said I did. He took me along St Pancras Way (then King's Road) to a sort of warehouse place with huge wooden double doors across the front with a small wicket gate set in them. He didn't say much. We went in through the small door and he locked it behind him. We were in a yard backing on to the canal. He parked his bike, turned to me and said, 'It's going to be hot work, why don't you take your shirt off? I won't be a minute, I've just got something to see to. You wait there.' I took my shirt off and waited, Then I saw him coming towards me, stark naked, his cock standing up. I dived off but he grabbed hold of me, started slobbering, pushing himself against me. I struggled like a demon, him swearing at me, wrenching at me. Then he punched me, right under the chin, drove my teeth through my tongue. Blood started pouring out of my mouth. That really maddened me. I lashed out and broke free, There was a wall at the bottom of the yard. I ran down and threw myself at it, grabbed hold of the top and clambered over, bleeding like a pig all down my front. The other side was the canal bank. I dived in, swam across and ran back home.

One of my uncles, Jackie Francis, came round and took me off to the hospital. When we got there they said my tongue would have to be stitched and I was scared stiff. I asked if my uncle could come in with me. He was in the Territorial Army and I thought if he was with me, a tough soldier in his uniform, I'd be all right. So, they wheeled me into the casualty ward, laid me on a couch and got the sewing gear out. My uncle sat in the corner saying, 'You're all right, Georgie, you'll be all right.' But when the nurse held on to my jaw and pulled my tongue out for the doctor to push the needle in, my uncle fainted. I just lay there and watched him pass out. A lot of use he was. They gave me eight stitches.

We went back home and by this time word had got out and a few of the men had got together. They told me to show them where this nasty molester had attacked me. They kicked the door in and there he was, cowering in the yard. 'We've come to teach you a lesson, you dirty old sod.' And they certainly did. I stood by the door and watched. I remember Vicky Hanks picking him up, landing him against the wall and whacking into him something cruel. They really paid him. 'Come on, Georgie, your turn, give him a kick for what he done to you.' So I went in and booted him. I really think they might have finished him they were so mad, but a couple of firemen from the station over the road came in and pulled them off; he'd had enough.

I was just over ten, working on the rides at a fair on waste ground opposite Inverness Street in Camden Town, when I felt a bad pain in my gut. I ignored it, I was earning money, I'd keep going. The pain worsened, it got so bad I doubled up and fell off the merry-go-round in agony. They whipped me off to the hospital up Dartmouth Park Hill, but they couldn't trace my mother to sign the operation release form. In the end a Dr Thackeray gave me an emergency appendectomy. I woke up after the operation to find my mother at the foot of the bed weeping. I told her I was all right, but she was in a terrible state. The point is, I was in bed number five, the bed on the right just inside the ward's main doors where they put children, handy for the nurses to keep an eye on. My brother Charles had died in that very bed. He'd swallowed a coin. They cut it out from his throat but, during the night, he'd torn at the wound and bled so much that he died. They tried to revive him, but it was too late.

My appendix had burst in the delay before they removed it and I got peritonitis. Dr Tanner, a specialist, did another operation and for a long while I had two tubes sticking into my stomach which had to be pulled out, cleaned and replaced every morning — very painful. In the 24 hours, the scars part-healed round the tubes and the pus built up so it was murder pulling them out. Because bed number five was just inside the door, they'd come to me first, and if I felt cowardly I'd pretend to be asleep. But that only delayed the inevitable and I had to lie there listening to them going slowly round the ward, knowing my turn would come eventually. There was no escape. I realised then that it was better to face it head on than play for time that was bound to run out. But the wicked scars they left . . .

I told my mother: 'They're horrible scars, Mum, a butcher could have done better.'

She would reply: 'Don't be ungrateful. At least they saved your life.'

After the peritonitis, I stayed in the hospital for six weeks then I went to a convalescent home in Herne Bay for a month. Absolute paradise. A life of luxury. Trolleys going round first thing in the morning loaded with porridge and eggs. Three meals a day. All their clothes to wear — grey shorts with braces, socks and shirts. Underpants. I asked if I could take them home with me; I didn't want to leave. We had trips to the beach — there were about two dozen of us in there recuperating from various illnesses. Two kids were in bathchairs so we took turns to wheel them about. Every evening we had a bath; it was like heaven sitting there in the hot water, knowing you had clean pyjamas to put on and fresh sheets to climb between, instead of the crowded beds with mangy, grimy sheets in the scruffy old turning. They even taught us to wash our hands after going to the toilet. Real toilet paper, too.

The nurses were always so kind and thoughtful. I wanted to go home, but I didn't want to leave. I felt so looked after. That's what I prized, then as now: kindness, thoughtfulness and cleanliness. And Charles Howes was the complete, exact opposite of all three. He was one of the most evil men I've ever known, a cunning, devious, bullying bastard — and my mother married him.

Howes had taken over from my father as street bookie, which is how my mother got to know him. It wasn't long before he shifted into the house, and none of us could bear him. If he'd had a good day he didn't bother us, but if he had a bad day, he'd be counting the money out as he sat in his chair then, suddenly, throw the coins up in the air, shout and swear and go off round the pub, come back hours later the worse for wear — which brought horrible memories of my father flooding back — and he'd rant and spit at my mother which I couldn't bear. He had a mean, spiteful streak in him the full width of his gut. It made me very upset because I had always been so close to my mother; I worshipped her, but he slowly came between us. The worst of it was that, as time went on and I had rows with him, she began to side with him. She had always been devoted to me, but he changed that. She was a small woman, quite slight, and he frightened the life out of her, but when she stood up for him instead of me, I was badly hurt. Besides that, it was little things about him which niggled and built up. His feet stank something rotten. I know people to this day who remember Charlie Howes and say he had the most stinking feet they've ever caught a whiff of. You'd be sitting at the table eating a meal and there would be his hideous ponging feet and socks right under your nose. His body odour was rank, it stank the place through, especially their bedroom — even walking past, the reek hit you. And he used to leave the door open when he was making love to my mother, so we could hear and see. He had filthy habits — spitting into the coal scuttle, so when you came to build up the fire, there'd be gobs of his phlegm on the coal. He was never very clean in the toilet department, either: he was always leaving unflushed crap in the pan. He hated me, of course, but I wasn't big enough to stand up to him — yet. I just threw a plate of fish and chips in his face and ran off. In no time he had run the betting pitch down, loused it up, ruined it. He was no good at it and a lazy bastard into the bargain. Mother kept him, most of the time.

A few people stand out in my life, for the kindness they showed me, especially when it felt as if I was fighting everybody and anybody. One was Sergeant Fitzsimmons at the local police station. In the old days the local coppers knew everybody, all the families in their manor, took an interest in them, kept tabs on what was happening. They weren't enemies. They'd nick you if you were caught out, but they'd just as likely have a quiet word in your ear and put you straight unofficially. After my father died, Sergeant Fitzsimmons always had a friendly word for me, tried to curb my temper, stop me running completely berserk and wild. He was like a Dutch uncle. I owe him a lot, not least for saving my bacon on one occasion.

I was up at the Lido on Hampstead Heath one afternoon. He was there, too. We used to lark about. Later, I went back to the turning to see where my pals were. Billy Sheed's mother told me they were swimming. I was walking along the towpath towards the Con pub where we used to change, when the whole mob ran past me full pelt. 'Come on, George, run.' I watched them go and a minute later up raced a police special in the funny little hat they wore. This one was a bloody nuisance we nicknamed Winkle, always poking his nose in and stirring up trouble for no reason. He grabbed me, all out of breath, and said, 'You're nicked'.

'What for?'

'You stole that bag of corn.'

'I didn't steal no corn, I don't know what you're talking about.'

He hauled me off to the temporary police station in College Street and charged me with pinching a bag of corn from the stables belonging to the Constitution pub and heaving it over the wall down on to the towpath. I kept telling them I hadn't done it. They wouldn't listen and I found myself up in court for stealing. Mother was in a terrible state. Running wild was one thing, now I was turning into a criminal.

The Juvenile Court was in Friends House in Endsleigh Gardens, Bloomsbury. I was in front of the bench, knees quaking, and the chief magistrate asked what the charge was. There was Winkle, sharp nose and piggy eyes, reading out his statement and gesticulating to another special in the court who staggers up with a bag of corn and dumps it in front of the bench. The magistrate peered down at the sack of corn, shakes his head and said: 'Could that boy lift a bag of corn as big as this?'

The magistrate turned to me. I was boiling but who'd believe me? 'Well, boy, what have you to say?'

'The man has made a mistake, sir.'

'Are you saying that he is lying?'

'No, sir, I said he's made a mistake. I wasn't there. I'd only just come down the canal when he arrested me.'

'Can you prove it?'

'I was at the Lido all afternoon.'

'Was anyone there who could say you were there, too?'

'Sergeant Fitzsimmons, sir, from our police station.'

One of the officials piped up. 'I believe Sergeant Ftizsimmons is in the court today, sir, attending another case.'

They fetched him in and I was acquitted. Winkle looked as if he'd really been prised out of his shell: four foot nothing and a hat. You can't trust a special like an old-time copper . . .

Shortly after that I lost Peter. One of the people from the yard took him up to Elm Street churchyard for a walk and he ran off. Whether he got stolen or killed I never found out, but I never saw him again. I was heartbroken. And just before the war broke out, I got rheumatic fever.

It's another disease that was rampant in bad, damp housing, and it's mostly kids who get it. The pain is unbelievable. The joints get so inflamed and tender that even if someone just nudges the bed you're lying in, the pain shoots through your whole body. It can bring on St Vitus' Dance. The worst of it is that an attack can damage your heart severely. In fact, a lot of kids survived the illness but died later from a weak heart. Your temperature goes up to as high as 110°C and you sweat buckets. For the first month in hospital they wrapped my knees, ankles, wrists and elbows in cotton-wool, laid me in a loose flannel gown, flat out in bed on flannel sheets (to soak up the sweat and changed every day), under a metal cage to keep the weight of the bedclothes from touching me. The only treatment was aspirin to bring the temperature down, 'break the fever' or keep it as low as possible, anyway. And you had to lie absolutely still and flat, not even move your head, just stare at the ceiling. The least movement put an added strain on the heart. It was horrible. My tongue was furred over, my face burned, the sweat ran off me in streams and smelled sour, and occasionally my pulse raced so fast I thought I'd shake to pieces. After a month in the local hospital I was taken to recuperate in Queen Mary's Hospital, Carshalton. The pain took a long time to go and when I did eventually manage to get out of bed, I could hardly support my weight. I was tottering about like an old man and it still hurt a lot to put pressure on the joints. But I was so miserable in the hospital, I asked my mother to take me home. They said I wasn't ready to go, but I got dressed and said I wouldn't stay.

When the war broke out, we, as kids, just accepted it in a way adults couldn't. It was a big adventure to us, scallywag time. Life went on pretty much as usual, except that we didn't have to play truant — the schools only opened in the mornings and quite often they sent us home, if we ever happened to be there in the first place. We hopped off to the zoo, the West End, down to the Thames, we got everywhere. If the truant officers did nab us, there was always an excuse. 'We had to stay away — the family's got TB.' Or else scratch the webs of your fingers raw and say you had the itch.

Mary, Billy and I were evacuated, plus Chicky Scotchford and a few more of us, along with hundreds of other kids from London. We all lined up on Camden Road station with our gas-masks and clothes in a laundry sack. About two hundred of us were sent to Bedford, where they paraded us on one side of a school playground with a crowd of grown-ups on the other side: the people who were going to look after us. We were eyeing them up, wondering what we were getting into. They stared at us, not having a clue what they were getting either. In the middle stood a line of trestle tables laid out with corned beef, fruit, dried egg, biscuits, and we had to file past and take one of each. As we went by and got ours I realised they weren't checking, so I nudged Billy and said, 'Come on, let's go round again,' which we did, several times, and filled a sack.

Then we stood in the line again waiting till a lady came up and pointed to Mary and tried to take her off on her own. I wasn't having that. 'You're not splitting us up. My mum told us you weren't to split us up.' And there was a bit of an argy-bargy until another lady, Mrs Lacks, came up and said she'd take all three of us.

The locals were naïve; they didn't know what they'd taken on: a bunch of wild kids from Camden Town. The sweetshop keeper would be standing all polite behind the counter serving someone while we were round the back of the shelves, ransacking the place, cramming our gas-masks full of chocolate, sherbet dabs, sugar chews, sticks of liquorice, bubblegum balls — to sell — then away, in and out like locusts.

Being evacuees, we only did half days at school. But I couldn't read or write so they couldn't be bothered with me. There was one teacher I had a crush on, though, so there was a bit of an incentive to go in, especially for a day trip to a farm out in the country. We saw this teacher sneaking off round the side of the farm buildings and followed her. She'd gone off to meet one of the men teachers. They went into a hay shed and we crept up, got our eyes glued to a vent in the plank wall and watched them perform. I think I felt jealous.

I spent a lot of time hanging round Bedford market. One occasion we nicked some grapes from the Duke of Bedford's estate and flogged them in the market. Of course they all asked where we'd managed to get such nice juicy grapes, but they couldn't prove anything and they were getting them for a good price, so why should they care?

Mrs Lacks found me a bit of a handful and I didn't want to stay in Bedford either. I was getting homesick for my territory. Chicky felt the same — he was my best mate at the time — so we got a couple of bikes to ride back to London. We were all set, and it was like that bit in Butch Cassidy and the Sundance Kid when Robert Redford says he can't swim. Chicky couldn't ride a bike.

'Why didn't you say?' I said.

'I thought you'd thump me,' he said.

'I feel like thumping you,' I said.

So, we dumped his bike and I rode him back to London, 50 miles, on the saddle, the crossbar, the handlebars. It was some journey but we made it. He kept complaining that he had a sore arse and I said he was lucky he still had enough feeling in it to know it was sore. I hadn't.

We flogged the bike and got ten shillings for it. They kept Chicky at home, for some reason, but they sent me back, locked in the guard's van so I couldn't get off the train. But I couldn't settle and, in the end, no place would have me and they sent me home. Billy came too, but Mary stayed on for the remainder of the war and until she'd finished at school. Mrs Lacks was like a second mother to her, it worked out well and she got a good education.

Memories of the war:

Standing by Camden Town tube station when the bank on the corner took a direct hit from a bomb, my pal Morrie Mason copped it — he was blown down the escalator by the blast.

They used the platforms as an air-raid shelter and the stink down there was diabolical. In the well at the bottom of the escalators they had four WC cubicles; queues and queues of people lined up permanently waiting to use them.

When the bombs were dropping, most people took cover — Anderson shelters in their backyard, reinforced corrugated iron hutches in the road, the tube stations. But there were blokes who weren't thinking about getting hurt, even killed, they were on the make, kicking in shop windows helping themselves to what they could grab, lobbing it into a blanket roll and if a policeman stopped them on the street, they say, 'Where's the shelter? I got caught.' There was a coffee shop at 142 College Street which had been bombed out, but the gas meter was still connected. A gang of blokes had the key to the place and used the basement as a warehouse for storing and selling off the stuff they looted.

A young fellow in our turning committed suicide. He'd deserted from the army and barricaded himself in on the first floor of the house. The military police came for him — they're a hard bunch. We watched it all from the bottom of our stairs. They told him to come down and give himself up. He yelled down at them that he'd slit his throat if they came up. They said they were coming in after him. He screamed out: 'I've got the knife, I'll do it, I'll do it.' But they kept going and he slit his throat before they were halfway up. We watched them carry him out.

A few deserters hid out at the Pond. After a while you got to know who they were. They'd be trying to tap the other blokes for money or an identity card. Sooner or later they would get caught — there was nowhere for them to go. Occasionally the CID would come round and you'd see the AWOLs nipping off round the side of the Pond, over the fence and then haring off across the fields to escape.

One day, I saw two guys in RAF uniform, wearing dark glasses feeling their way along the pavement. They fumbled their way to the edge of the kerb, so I went over to help them cross the road. They got very angry, told me to bugger off and pushed me away. That upset me. I was only trying to do them a favour, but someone explained later: 'Don't mind them, George, they're just trying to get their lives back together again. They don't want to be mollycoddled. They're independent. Proud men.' They'd been shot up and badly burned.

By then I was doing a man's job, working for Jack Cooper full time. I'd already been working full time, illegally, since I was 12 on 28 June 1940. My brother Billy was 14 round the same time and he had his School Leaving Certificate on the mantelshelf. I was already big for my age and I looked as old as he did and I wasn't going to be left out, so I took his papers and went down to King's Cross to register for work and get my cards.

Billy was working as a vanboy for the railway on an open cart; 25 shillings a week. My first job was as a commissionaire's assistant at the Aerated Bread Company (ABC bakery) in Camden Town, on the site where Sainsbury's is today. Thirty bob a week, plus commission on the errands I ran for the staff, shopping mostly. I knew Camden Town that well and I could run fast, dodging through the pedestrians, so I got through a lot of extra foraging. Plus, there were rejects that couldn't be sold — cakes, bread, rolls, which I used to collect into a sack, put it by the canal towpath, which was my route to and from the bakery, and go round after work and take it home. That made me very popular with the family, bringing home all that free stuff. I already had a reputation for ferreting.

Every few weeks I had to do fire-watch with three of the men and a fire warden on top of the ABC building. We all slept on the premises and when the air-raid siren went off, we ran up on to the roof and pinpointed fires. Sometimes the incendiary bombs didn't detonate, so we saw them being carted off next day — about 18 inches long, shaped like a torpedo. It was a weird sight, up on the roof at night, pitch dark in the blackout, the bombers droning miles over your head and spurts of flame leaping up suddenly from houses way in the distance, or quite close. The fire warden had to phone through where the fires were to work out roughly which street had been hit.

First thing every morning I had to go out to the front of the main entrance to the building and polish the ABC sign — brass letters on a black background. I was terrified of being spotted and someone reporting me for being underage. I polished that plate as quickly as I could and got back inside. I was spotted a couple of times, but nothing happened until the end of my first year. The authorities discovered that they had two William Francises living at the same address, registered with two different boroughs, both with working cards. I was back in the Juvenile Court at Friends House.

My mother spoke for me. She said I gave all my money to her, which I did. The magistrate listened and I didn't feel at all scared, somehow. You can be terrified of being found out, then when you are it seems like nothing. Besides, I was earning money for the family, not just running the streets which I had been doing all my life. The magistrate said he could see I was helping support my mother, so he bound me over for one month to go to school and get my leaving certificate. When I'd got it, I went to work for Cooper, driving a cart.

It was heavy work, but the casual labour I'd always done, plus the swimming in the canal — from our bridge down to King's Cross and back, then on to Camden Lock and back — had made me fit and strong. The spells in hospital had only spurred me on to physical exercise. Seeing the marines training in Deal had planted the idea, and now I had another inspiration. Regent's Park was taken over as a military base, and the Coldstream Guards, I think it was, from Albany Barracks round the corner, set up an assault course on the grass area alongside the Outer Circle by Cumberland Terrace. We used to go and watch the soldiers training over it; warm-up exercises first, then the obstacles — embankments with steep steps up, ramps to run along, walls to clamber over, ropes to swing on across a chasm, tunnels, ditches, barriers. We went back in the evening when the place was empty and copied them. And I admired them: they were fighters.

Cooper's carman, Johnny Phillips, had died aged 35 from TB. His death upset me badly. I lost a real friend, someone who taught me a lot, a man who had cared for me after the tram accident. I mourned him more than I mourned my father; it's a hard thing to say but it's true. In place of him, Jack Cooper had an Irishman, Jim O'Keefe, about the same age as Johnny, and we got on famously. He lived in our turning, between our house and Cooper's yard. Long dark hair, blue eyes and a lot of gipsy in him; he always wore coloured shirts and a handkerchief as a neck scarf fastened with a wooden ring he'd made himself. He was very clever with his hands, never still, always had to be busy, making things of wood, fixing things. He had a fund of stories about horses. He sang songs, played the guitar and the violin. He was teaching me to play the violin a bit and I had just begun to grasp it. He even loaned me his fiddle to take home to help me on. The noises I got out were a bit screechy, but I was getting on. Then Charlie Howes lammed in. 'We don't want that fucking noise in here.' I told him to mind his own business. He roared back and there was a row. In the scuffle he grabbed the violin and broke it over my shoulder. As if there weren't enough reasons to hate him.

Jim was okay about it; easy come, easy go, but I felt sick. 'Don't worry about it,' he said. 'There are worse things. Take things in your stride.' He always had time for me. A patient, good-humoured, generous man.

It was Jim who took me in hand a bit, taught me in his backyard not so much how to fight but how to win; they are two different things. He'd travelled a lot, worked in fairgrounds, lived rough, good times, bad times, so he had a worldly wisdom that came from wide experience of people and character.

'If you can't win with your fists,' he said, 'win with whatever you can lay your hands on. It's not enough to be a fighter, you've got to learn how to fight. The principle is, "Kick. Bollock. Bite". Use all your weapons: knees, elbows, feet, teeth, anything. And never mind what you're kicking or biting, either. There are lots of mean, evil-minded, dirty fighters around and you've got to be up to any trick they can throw at you and keep a few of your own in reserve. Some men you fight are decent. The vast majority of street brawlers wouldn't know a fair fight from a trip to the moon. Keep your back to the wall if you can, especially if you're up against two of them, in case one of them slips round behind you. Always try to get in the first punch, never wait till they're ready. Get stuck in, the sooner the better. If you're inside and they say "Come outside" forget it: like as not they've got others waiting out there ready to jump you and drop you. Never take your coat off, it leaves you vulnerable while you're tugging your arms out of the sleeves. By contrast, if they take their coat off, hit them when they've got their arms half in, half out. Don't stop and be thinking you're taking advantage, it isn't fair. You are taking advantage and who's to say they're going to treat you any fairer? While you're dallying around to find that out, they've belted you and the fight's over.'

Jim had fought in boxing booths in fairs. One time they set up a fairground in Hawley Road, Kentish Town, and they had a boxing booth there. Any challenger who went three rounds with the fighter won a fiver. The gloves they wore were filled with horsehair and well doctored with the knuckles shining through. I did all right; I won my fiver. Jim trained me well.

When I was about 14, a new kid moved into Rochester Road: Alfie Newton, a tough little Welsh kid, about two years older than me, and when he came round our turning it was inevitable we'd fight. He was going to try to knock me off my perch. There'd be a lot of needling, winding up: 'Go on, George, get him,' and the others formed a circle and we were at each other's throats, rolling about, pummelling and scrapping. It was the toughest fight I'd ever had and it went on for about half an hour. In the end he had me pinned to the floor with both hands and thought he had me. 'Give in?' but I craned my neck up and bit the bottom of his ear off and spat it out. I enjoyed that. He'd relaxed and let me in again. He screamed and the fight was over. We became very close mates after that. About 18 months later, when he was 18, he got into trouble and was given a choice between going to prison and joining the army. He joined up, did his six weeks' basic training in Ireland and went abroad. He was one of the first to be killed.

It's a bit perverse that I battered people, because I'd been battered myself. Fighting gave me my first identity, I suppose, after being kicked around a lot by my father, by other kids, and as I got stronger I fought back and I enjoyed it as I began to come out on top instead of being walked over. And I did get strong, from working in the stables, heaving massive baskets of horse manure about in my hands and on my head. When I went out on the carts to begin with I could only just about drag the sacks of vegetables along the flat buck, but as time went on I was hoisting them up from the ground on board. The first time I took a hundredweight sack of potatoes on my shoulders it nearly threw me over backwards, but I got used to balancing the weight, and balance is crucial for a boxer.

A lot of strength came from handling the horses: getting them in and out of the stalls, hauling on the reins when they were racing downhill, breaking the new horses in. I used to run alongside them, holding them by the halter, up Swains Lane — which is a very steep hill, about half a mile long into Highgate — to see what their wind was like. Down to the bottom and back up again, this time with the cart to see how they would pull. Later, when I ran that same hill for training it really used to get to me, a hard slog; but I never thought twice about it before.

Every morning Cooper's carts went off to his stand in Neal Street, Covent Garden, between what is now Pied à Terre to Shorts Gardens. The pavement was marked out with chalk bays for the various shops, stalls and barrows we delivered to Kentish Town, Hampstead and then back to the yard in Camden. We drove in, me on the van, through Somerstown on to Gower Street, a long straight road, and as soon as we arrived at the stand, around 6.30 a.m., we gave the horses a nosebag and got our breakfast at the coffee stall — sausage roll, bacon sandwich, cup of tea. Then we waited for the porters to barrow the goods up and park them in the bays on the pavement. Opposite our stand, in what's now Red or Dead, was Ellen Keely, a firm that made barrows and trolleys for porters and in their basement was a gym for pro boxers run by Billy Doughty. He always had boxers in there training before first light. And on cold, dark winter mornings, when I was waiting for the carts to load up, I used to go into Doughty's to get warm. Billy got to know me and soon I was helping, handing up the gumshields, fetching, carrying and watching them train. I was only a kid but that was one of the places where the boxing started for me. I learnt invaluable lessons in Doughty's, not that I was aware of it at the time; the professional approach, above all. Cooper would have to come and haul me out, more often than not, give me an earful because they were waiting to get on. But there's no doubt, going in that place planted a seed in me.

In time I was driving one of the carts myself: massive, four-wheeled, flat-back — the buck — with high vertical raves round the sides and front, the driver's seat and footboard about ten feet or more above the ground. The pair of horses was hitched either side to a shaft, the yoke pole — attached to the front-wheel assembly — which turned for steerage, and from their shoulders by traces to the swingle-tree — a crossbar pivoted in the middle to give them free movement. You held the reins bunched in your hands and that gave you most of your control. There was a brake, but it was no more than a lever with a leather-padded block at the end which rammed against one of the wheel rims. The pad wore through pretty quickly, so it got replaced with strips of old traces twisted round. With a full load of three tons, once those horses got steam up you had to work hard to slow them down or stop. Potatoes were the worst — a dead weight of three tons, 60 sacks of King Edwards or Whites on the back of a cart, made a cruel load for the horses to pull. There was a yard off York Way, next to the railway, which used to be all potato firms and as the porters brought the sacks up and loaded them, you could see the cart sinking. The trouble was that the road directly outside the yard sloped downhill and you had to turn right after a hundred yards down another slope towards a crossroads and a blind left-hand turn at the bottom. That was murder.

You gee the team, the horses strain at the cart, plodding along, struggling at the weight, out of the yard and immediately the gradient dips, the wheels start to roll and the horses are going. You know what's in store: you're already hauling on the reins a bit to check their speed, but the hill falls away, you begin to accelerate and there's the right turn almost at once. The brake is near useless once the speed is up, so when you swing the corner your best bet is to run the inside wheel rims along the kerbstones of the left-hand pavement, if there's nothing parked in the way to stop you. All the kerbs round there were rubbed smooth from that. Down the slope, the horses stamping, you reining them in, hanging on for grim death, the road bends to the left and you can see the crossroads. No policeman on duty. If there's a copper you can shout, 'Coming down!' and he'll hold up the traffic because he knows you're not going to be able to stop. The cart is gathering way, wheel rims grinding and bumping at the kerb, and 50 yards ahead of you there are cars or a bus pulling out across the junction, and you're half-standing on the footboard, feet and legs braced, pulling at the reins so hard the horses' collars are riding up past their ears and they're bunched right back against the cart and as a result the point of the yoke pole — sheathed in lead to prevent it splitting — is sticking out a couple of feet in front. Nothing for it but hope you can get round into a space in the traffic, otherwise that shaft is going to drive straight into anything that gets in the way. I saw that happen a few times. Ramming speed, full ahead together. The rule was that horses had right of way.

We had a bloke working in Copper's who couldn't handle a cart that well and one time, when a copper waved him through, he drove straight over the man's foot!

There was another lad the same age as me who worked for Cooper, Georgie Clarke. He took meticulous care of his ponies, plaited their manes and tails, tricked them out with ribbons, polished their hooves, always kept the brasses on his tack gleaming and as spanking bright as the military, very handsome. He made such an elaborate show of them I was green with envy. I was more of a worker. I could break the new horses in, get the young horses trained up to working in the cart by putting them in a pair with an older, experienced horse so that if the newcomer shied at a bus, say, the old horse would keep him steady.

What we used to do for devilment sometimes in the mornings, as soon as we got round the corner into College Street out of Cooper's sight, was to line up side by side and race all the way to Neal Street, like the chariots in Ben Hur. It was early morning so there was very little traffic. Loser bought breakfast. Fantastic, yelling the horses on, neck and neck, squeezing every bit of pace out of them, the empty cart rattling and rolling, wheels rumbling, reins slap-snapping. 'Go! Go!' One trick was to let the other guy ease slightly ahead, hook your wheel behind his and steer him into the far kerb, then pull back and let fly while he's trying to pull his team off the pavement. At the end of Gower Street, across New Oxford Street and into Shaftesbury Avenue and Neal Street, steam pouring off the horses and your heart thumping with the thrill of it. Five minutes later, in trots Cooper, looks at the horses, all lathered and panting, and goes crazy. 'Have you been racing those horses?'

Only thinking of the job, Jack . . . first come, first served.

In winter, in icy conditions, the horses had to have frost nails in their hooves to give them a better grip. But when the wind howled sleet and snow straight down your throat it was bitter cold, perishing up on the hard slatted-wood driver's seat, your only protection an old chaff sack slung over you. The snow soaked it, then the wind froze it to ice and it would be like hardboard down your front with the gale blasting straight through you. Your hands were frozen, the reins turned soggy so you could hardly hold on to them. If one of the horses slipped and fell, you had to rein in as quickly as you could before the other one went over, climb down and get the first one to his feet and press on. The tram lines were a hazard: the outer line had a raised lip which sometimes caught a wheel and made it judder so the cart lurched, the yoke pole jerked into one horse, he stumbled and threw the whole kaboosh sideways. You might even have a horse get a hoof caught, can't get out because the other horse keeps going and the leg breaks: the horse has to be destroyed. Horrible.

When there was snow or ice on the road, at the top of a steep hill you had to lock one of the front wheels to slow the cart. There was a loop of chain hooked onto the front of the cart. You left one end hitched, threaded the other end through the spokes of the front wheel and hitched it back. Then you applied the brake with all your strength and hung on for your life.

In wartime it was a rule that when the air-raid sirens went and bombs started falling, you had to get your ponies out of the shafts and tether them to the back of the cart in case they took fright and bolted. One afternoon I'd parked the cart on the stand and was having a cup of tea at the coffee stall when the sirens went off; we never expected the bombers to come over at that time of day. Anyway, I heard a commotion and looked round to see my cart careering up Neal Street. The ponies had kicked and gone. I chased off after them, all the way round to Cambridge Circus, Charing Cross Road. They were going like the clappers, pedestrians scattering in all directions. In the end they swerved off into Leicester Square and belted straight into the foyer of the Odeon. How they didn't collide with anything or anyone I don't know. I was calming them down, backing them out into the street, when the police steamed up and asked what the bloody hell did I think I was doing and why hadn't I hitched them to the tailboard; didn't I know the rules? And there was a bloody war on. 'I was having a cup of tea,' I said, 'and saw them go.'

I was still making extra money wherever I could. I sang in pubs, requests. Someone'd shout out a title and buy you a snifter of gin. There was a ledge behind the piano where I kept all the tots to sell back to the landlord at the end of the evening — and a glass of water to sip at, pretending it was the hard stuff. I went for an audition at the Butcher's Arms in York Way one time, but got a frog in my throat and couldn't shift it. The guy who got the job was a bus conductor, name of Matt Monroe, the future singing star. And that pub was where I had my first training gym.

One day in early 1944, I was driving the cart round the crescent, and a nice young lady pushing a pram along the pavement caught my eye. She was about my age, fair hair, lovely figure. As I drove past, I gave her a wink and called out: 'All right for you.' She smiled, I drove on and thought nothing more about it.

Chapter Three

Bare-fist Fighter to Boxer to Trainer

By the age of 15 I'd been in a full-time job for three years, so I was pretty streetwise. The hard physical work had broadened me out and made me big for my age and I was mixing with older guys. Also, for the first time in my life, I'd been able to save a bit of money to buy myself some decent clothes — stetson hat, Abercrombie coat with a velvet collar, brogue shoes, black or brown, which were the rage, and if you had a Crombie you'd made it, you were in. We used to take a suit length to a place in Kentish Town to get it made up in the style — double-breasted, high-pinched waist, broad lapels. Open-necked shirt, otherwise in a fight your opponent could grab a tie, throttle you or hold your head where he could hit it.

Our place was the Black and White Milk Bar. They'd come in from America, all done out in black and white tiles, serving milkshakes, knickerbocker glories and ice-cream sundaes. It was a place to meet girls too, though some of the blokes were always on the hunt for trouble, mostly bullies, wanting to show off in front of their mates. Me being quite a bit younger than most of them and looking a bit like a choirboy — fair, curly hair, fresh pink face, smooth cheeks — it was obvious if there was anyone going to be picked on it'd be me. It would start: 'Who are you looking at? You fancy your chances?' I don't ever remember going after trouble, but I didn't run away from it when it came along; only by way of protecting myself. Once one of them said, 'You fancy your chances, do you? Come outside, then.' Outside, a couple of them jumped me. Jim O'Keefe was right. After that, as soon as the challenge came, I hit them straight on the chin and took it from there. It wasn't nice, though I must confess that at the time I enjoyed it. Only winning, mind you. And I admit that from 14 to 17 I was fairly wild. But it was a wildness that I finally tamed; it laid the foundation for my professional life. I even called the large stable of boxers I had my 'Fight Factory'.

One night I walked into the Black and White with my mate Chooky and saw a girl whose face was familiar sitting at one of the tables with a friend. Then it clicked: she was the girl I'd seen pushing the pram along Queen's Crescent. She recognised me, too. Chooky and I sat down at their table and got chatting. Her name was Joan but, the way these things go, it was Chooky who talked more to Joan and I talked to her friend, Ivy. I know I had my eye on Joan, but maybe I was a bit nervous because she had her eye on me, too. I was still playing Jack the Lad, I didn't want to get caught. Chooky walked Joan home; I took Ivy.

That didn't last long. We went up to the Heath a couple of times, which was where you took your girls, but the attraction between Joan and me was too strong. I'd say it was love at first sight on both sides, really. That put Ivy's nose out of joint, but when you're young it's 'easy come, easy go' before you get married — or so I thought. Joan was 16, I was 15, but had the build of an 18-year-old.

One night I walked Joan home and on my way back I popped into the fish shop at the bottom of Litcham Street. It was a tough area round Queen's Crescent. Even the police did their patrols in pairs; there were a lot of spiteful blokes living about the place. And it was definitely not my patch. I suppose a few of them round there had taken umbrage that I was taking one of their girls out. Anyway, I got my fish and chips and came out through the blackout curtain straight into the pitch black — no street lamps on, no house lights, nothing. The minute the door shut behind me some guys pounced on me out of nowhere and beat the daylights out of me, knocked me unconscious and left me on the pavement, pouring blood from a wound in the back of my head. I've still got the scar there. All I heard before I passed out was one of them saying, 'I've done him, Archie.'

I came to and got myself home. I had a fair idea who they were and next night, my head all bandaged up under my cap, I went back with support — Billy my elder brother and Chicky, Chooky's brother, both of whom were older than me, to back me up. I also had Betsy with me: my pick handle. We got to Queen's Crescent and split up. I was walking along when I saw these three guys coming towards me. Archie was with them. I took a firm grip on Betsy and kept going.

'You want some more, then?' one of them said, but I didn't bother to reply. I just laid about them, straight in, didn't give them time to breathe. I flattened two of them and the third ran off. I thought that was probably the end of it, but no.

I was doing a casual job at the time, with a gang digging up tramlines:

part of the war effort — they needed the metal for munitions, any metal that could be spared. First all the railings went, then the tramlines. I'd gone up to the ganger and asked for a job.

'Ever worked a pom-pom, have you?' he said. That was a big pneumatic drill for digging up the sets (cobbles).

'Yes,' I said, never having even had a go with one and he took me on. That pom-pom was murder. It shook your arms and body to pieces and peeled the skin off your hands. So, I was standing there in the road, hanging on to the pom-pom, a thick roll of bandage under my hat, when I saw the same three blokes walking down the street. I put the machine down and called over to my mates on the gang and said: 'Here comes trouble. They're the guys who split my head open.' They didn't ask any questions, just slipped the pick-heads off the handles and waited. That was that. The Queen's Crescent posse changed its mind and legged it, and we got back to work.

It was a hard road, made of concrete sets, that we were working on. Nothing you could do with them. But when we got on to Camden Road, which was made from tar blocks, we sold them on the side as fuel for fires, There was always a bit of bunce to earn. You could flog the copper contacts, found in the central channel under the tram where the electric power linked, for a fair price. And there were fiddles. Cement for the concrete when the road came to be resurfaced — someone might be doing some building repair work on a bombed-out house so a few sacks went missing.

Walking out with Joan got me into trouble, but it wasn't the last I heard of her friend, either. She hadn't taken me dropping her too well and one night I was standing with some pals by the coffee stall outside Camden Road station, opposite the Eagle, where my father used to drink, when a guy in a Royal Marines uniform came up to me and said: 'Are you George Francis?'

'Yes.'

'I thought so. I want you. My name is Speed.'

'Don't mean nothing to me.' Which it didn't. I only found out later that he was Ivy's brother, a good three years older than me.

'I'm not going to waste my fists on you,' he said and he started unbuckling his leather belt. I didn't wait. As he was tugging his belt off, I went for him, caught him off balance before he could pull any strokes and gave him a right caning. It was a tough fight, a really tough fight. But the fact is, if I hadn't been streetwise, he might well have done to me what I did to him. I caught him on the chin, he went down and whacked his head against the kerbstone, knocked out stone cold. I left him unconscious and fled off home. I didn't know whether he was alive or dead.

I found Billy and told him what had happened. He said the police were bound to come after me and he'd take the blame. I was too jittery to say

anything that made much sense and when the Bill did arrive Billy said
he'd had the fight and they took him off. It was ridiculous, they were
obviously going to find out it wasn't him and, sure enough, a while later
they came back with him and arrested me, on a charge of Grievous Bodily
Harm. I was in grave trouble.

I spent the night in the cells wondering what I'd done and what was
going to happen to me. Next day I was bound over while the police
prepared the case and a while later I was taken before the bench at
Clerkenwell Magistrates' Court to answer the charge. Speed was there, in
hospital clothes, a light-blue outfit from the military hospital. He looked
terrible.

The police said that, after interviewing all the eye-witnesses, they had
concluded that it was Speed who had come after me, looking for trouble.
He'd been asking them who I was, what I looked like, obviously it was he
who had picked the fight, instigated it. As a result, they had reduced the
charge of GBH to a much less serious charge of common assault.

Various witnesses came and went and, when all the evidence had been
heard, the magistrate said to Speed: 'You are 18 years old, a Royal Marine
in His Majesty's forces. George Francis is a 15-year-old boy. Plainly you
came to Camden Town intent on finding him and, when you had found
him, intent on causing him injury — perhaps as serious as the injuries he
inflicted on you. Equally plain is the fact that you got a lot more than you
bargained for. However, the law must take its course and I have no option
but to address the charge of common assault and to find Mr Francis guilty
of it. In the circumstances, I order Mr Francis to pay a £5 fine.'

A lot of money, a nice old white fiver, but I was glad to pay and get out.
Had I not known how to fight, I'd have been badly hurt. Speed came from
the Queen's Crescent area and it was a fight over nothing really. He was a
nice enough fellow; got married not long afterwards.

That fight with Speed did shake me, though. It was a turning point in a
way and, once again, I owe Sergeant Fitzsimmons a kindness. He sought
me out after the case and gave me a good talking to. He could see I was off
the rails and heading for disaster and it hurt him. He didn't mince words,
he gave it to me straight: 'George, this street fighting is going to be the
death of you, or else the death of someone on the end of your fists. Pack
it in. I know what's going on with you, but you've got to get your head right
and stop fighting the rest of the world.'

There wasn't much I could say or wanted to say. But he gave me the first
push into the future. 'Why don't you give boxing a go? Come down to the
St Pancras Club with me and see how you get on? What have you got to
lose?'

He wasn't the sort of bloke to take no for an answer; besides, I'd always
been grateful to him for his help and, if you like, I owed him a favour over

the sack of corn business, so I went down to the Prince of Wales Road baths, where the club met, and pulled on the gloves. That didn't appeal to begin with. Being used to bare fists I thought gloves were cissified. And, as soon as I got in the ring I was completely out of order. I was used to all-in, anything-goes, head, elbows, knees, but suddenly it was footwork, dancing, circling, sparring and looking for an opening. And before you climbed into the ring to have a decent go at an opponent you had to be punching bags, skipping, shadow-boxing, That wasn't my way of fighting by a long chalk. I didn't want to chase shadows, I wanted to be thumping someone on to the canvas and calling for the next one. It didn't go down too well.

The trainer came up to me and said: 'Hold on, hold on, you're not in the street now.' But I couldn't take to it and I left after a few sessions.

I was beginning to feel more and more adrift. I'd met Joan, but my feelings for her only added to the confusion somehow. The real trouble was that I couldn't come to terms with the way the family had broken up. I couldn't come to terms with the fact that I had not only lost my father but my mother too.

She was for many years the most important person in my life. I loved her so very much. She nursed all of us when we were ill and sick. When my father was spiteful, she often took the whack from him to protect me. When he died, she was on her own, close to destitute with four kids to look after. She scrubbed steps, she did any job that was going, didn't matter how menial. There was always the threat that we were going to be put in a home. She dreaded the family being broken up and vowed it wouldn't happen, not while she had breath in her body. Her words.

Whenever we asked for something which she couldn't give us, she'd smile and say, 'When my ship comes in.' The times I heard that, 'When my ship comes in.' I used to ask her, 'When's the ship coming home?' and she'd say, 'It's on the way.'

One Christmas Eve I woke up and I could hear my mother crying. I went in to see her, put my arms round her and said, 'What are you crying for, Mum?' She burst out crying even more. She said: 'I haven't got you nothing for Christmas, any of you.' I told her not to worry about it, we were all together, that's the main thing. But we had got her something and next day we handed her a little box. As she opened it up, a big smile spread over her face. It was her own wedding ring. She'd pawned it to get food for us. One of our relatives had told us she'd popped it and was going to lose it because the pledge was up. We clubbed round and got it back for her.

Unfortunately, our family life gradually broke up. My eldest sister Dorothy went her way. My brother Billy too. My younger sister Mary was still in Bedford. That left Charlie Howes, my mother and me. And bit by bit he broke down the relationship between my mother and me. There was something evil about him. Mother was badly scared of him but it slowly destroyed all my respect — for her, for myself. I was getting big enough by now to square up to him, and I knew what would happen, inevitably. But I could see my mother would never forgive me, so I left home.

I went to live in a dingy, poky, cheap little rented room in Varndell Street, off Hampstead Road, opposite the Temperance Hospital. I got very depressed. I felt bad about myself. The fight with Speed only added to that, and even though I'd met Joan I couldn't see any real future. In fact, she was so good and I felt so useless, I didn't feel worthy of her. It all got too much. The family was broken up and we had been so close. I sat in that miserable little room one night when the air-raid sirens went off, a gloomy wailing nose, and suddenly I thought; 'I've had enough.' I filled the gas meter with coins, opened the oven, put a pillow inside, switched on the gas, lay down and went to sleep.

I woke up in the hospital with a policeman sitting at the end of the bed. He told me he'd been making his rounds checking on the blackout and he'd seen a slit of light at the bottom of my kitchen window where I lived. He'd tapped on the glass and shouted: 'Put that light out!' When nobody switched the light out, he went round to the door and knocked, got no reply, smelled gas and kicked the door in. He dragged me unconscious out of the oven and carried me 100 yards to the hospital. It was pure luck. He saved my life.

When I'd come round, he asked me a load of questions — suicide was a criminal offence in those days. I was still sleepy with the gas, mumbling and stammering. When he'd finished, he closed his notebook and said angrily: 'You're bloody stupid.' It must have seemed a terrible waste to him and very selfish, especially in wartime. He wasn't unkind, far from it, but I remember feeling I had let the guy down.

Eventually, I had to go before the Assizes, which they should never have done, me being a juvenile, not yet 16. It meant they couldn't convict me immediately, so I was sent to Wormwood Scrubs for seven weeks' observation and psychological tests.

The observation ward was in a separate block of the prison. Through the main entrance, a long corridor ran left to right with another one stretching directly ahead down to where the padded cells were. I was taken to see the psychologist in his office on the ground floor, to register, then along the corridor to the left a short way and up some stairs through a locked gate and into the ward. They showed me to my bed and left me to it, with the biggest load of weirdos: rapists, child molesters, geezers working their loaf to keep out of the army — one of them had shot himself in the foot, another one had slashed his chest with a knife, anything to prove they were barmy. There were blokes in there for violence, buggery and a whole variety of perversions. I thought to myself, 'Eyes open, George, and keep your back to the wall.' In fact, one of the warders took me on one side and said: 'Be careful in here, and if you have any complaints come and see me,' because I was a boy in with men. And some of them in there were really crackers — two got carted off to the lunatic asylum. And, when we queued up with the regular prisoners to go to chapel, there was always some vicious undercover jabbing and swinging at the 'nutters' who were fair game. It was petty vengeance, needle someone weaker than you.

The ward was T-shaped, a long room with beds on either side opening out in another area at the far end, with a table at the crossing for the screw. At the near end, by the door, were the toilets and washroom. We had a screw on duty the whole time; it was his job to observe everyone in the ward, to see what you did, how you behaved and take notes in his book. When you went out for exercise, the same thing: observation the whole time. In the ward you could roam around, talk, pass the time of day, but the time of day went so slowly it was enough to drive you crazy. I suppose the idea was to set up a dull routine to turn you into an automaton. Not me. If anything, the enforced idleness made me even more fidgety. I did a lot of thinking — about trying to kill myself; my mother; what I was going to do when I got out. I was determined not to stay in this place a second longer than I had to. And I thought about Joan. Having tried to do myself in, feeling my life was all in bits, I began to decide that I had to get the bits back together again, somehow. It was a queer place to do that in.

At lunchtime, the duty guard used to take an unofficial break; he went out of the ward unbeknownst to the senior guard — and left the gate unlocked so he could stand round the corner and have a cigarette, a bit of time on his own before his replacement arrived three-quarters of an hour later. Lunch was a small can with soup and potatoes in the bottom and a helping of duff in the lid. It was the only time I was scared, when we were unsupervised. That's when things happened. The cranks got hold of the homosexuals in the toilets. The first time I blundered in there and saw what was going on, I couldn't believe it. I'd never seen anything like it. I shot out through the gate and found the warder.

He went mad. 'What are you doing out here? You're not allowed through those gates, get back in there, you'll have me fired.' He started hustling me towards the gate.

'You'd better come in here too and see what's going on,' I said. 'There's blokes giving it to other blokes from the behind.'

He came back in, charged into the toilets and gave the blokes a good belting. I was unpopular with a few of the nastier ones for grassing, but most of the blokes didn't like what went on either, but weren't so brash as to speak out.

I made myself useful, particularly helping dole out the meals; anything to keep busy. At teatime there'd be one man carrying two tea urns round, another with a big tin of cobs [hunks of bread] and me following to dish out lumps of margarine from a tray. We worked our way down the ward, then went downstairs to do the padded cells. They had a yellow line painted on the floor in front of them, a danger mark, not to be stepped over without supervision. Every padded cell had two doors: one that opened outwards to an inner door that you could push open from outside but couldn't be opened from inside the cell. The idea was to put the mug of tea, cob and margarine down, push them in through the inner door, then away out of it. One day, in my eagerness, I was dashing ahead with the margarine tray, not paying proper heed to where I was going, across the yellow line, blundering at the first padded cell — the outer doors were opened at meal times — and kept going through the inner door and before I knew what was happening it had clanged shut behind me.

I looked across the cell. Squatting in the corner sat this bloke, huge as a gorilla, trussed up in a straitjacket, glowering at me. His face was black and blue with bruises. I've never seen an expression like it. A mixture of hate, fear and pain all directed at me, as if I'd caused it. I was terrified. He just stared at me. I dropped the tray and stood rooted to the spot, shaking. My bowels went loose and I felt the crap going down my legs. The first time that had happened since I was a kid. I don't know how long I was in there — long enough not to move a single muscle — until the warder opened the door and hauled me out.

'You silly sod, what do you think you're playing at? Pheugh! Is that you?' I couldn't speak, I was shaking too much. 'Go and get yourself cleaned up, and never do that again.'

After a month, the psychologist had you down to his office for half an hour to give you tests. In the weeks before it came to my turn, I learnt all those tests. Every bloke that went down from the ward came back and told the others what they'd had to do: the cards and pictures to look at to say what they reminded you of or suggested, puzzles to work out (which box goes into which shape, etc) and the questions he asked, to analyse your state of mind, your hang-ups. But it was always the same pictures, puzzles and questions, in more or less the same order. The result was that, when it came to my turn to go down to see the psychologist, I knew exactly what was coming: I'd memorised everything.

I walked into his office.

'Good afternoon, Mr Francis. George. You probably know why you're here — a few tests, that's all, nothing to worry about.'

'I know. Only, don't waste your time.'

'What?'

'I know exactly what you're going to ask me.'

'Ah,' he said, probably thinking. 'I've got a right one here.' But then he started on the cards. I told him what he was going to bring out next, then told him some of the questions he was going to ask and his eyebrows went up. 'How do you know all this?'

I explained and we had a long chat. What I didn't tell him was that, one time, the duty guard sneaked off for a fag without locking his observation book in the desk, so someone read out all the comments in there, too. Anyway, we struck up a friendship and before he sent me back to the ward he said, 'I don't think there's very much wrong with you.' I was pleased to hear it; nice to have it official. He asked me if I was bored and I said I was bored rigid; why didn't they give us something to do instead of twiddling our thumbs all day?

'Good idea. Any suggestions?'

'Well, the whole place is filthy; it could do with a scrub out.'

The old obsession with cleanliness. So, two of us did it: we washed and scrubbed the whole place from top to bottom, walls, ceilings, doors, floors.

The second visit to the psychologist he said: 'Come in, George, only this time I think you'd better sit in my chair and ask me the questions.'

The third occasion he said: 'We must get you out of here.'

I was there for six weeks and at the end of the time I was taken in the van over to Stoke Newington to appear before the examining magistrate. I had to collect my normal clothes before I went and there stood the warder who'd yanked me out of the padded cell. He handed over my togs and said, 'Your pants clean, George?' and had a good laugh and as I went through the door, he said, 'Maybe you're not so hard as you thought you were.'

In court, the psychologist said I had been a great help to him — he didn't let on exactly how. He said I wasn't disturbed in the head; that family upsets and losing my father and having to cope with a stepfather I hated had all contributed to making me extremely depressed. He told them I had a quick mind and knew how to use it and there was no way I could be crazy. He recommended me for immediate release, but suggested that it wouldn't be a clever idea to go back home, if there was somewhere else to go I'd be happier and it would give me some breathing space. I'd said that I'd sooner go and live with my grandad out in the caravan at Broxbourne and work on the timber. The magistrate released me on condition I didn't stay in London but went to live in Broxbourne. That was fine by me.

The next time I went inside the Scrubs was on a visit with John Conteh, after he won the world title.

In Broxbourne I became a deal porter, a 'back', because that's all you were, a moving back to carry timber. At first my grandfather tried to put me off. 'It's all men working here. Ten hours a day non-stop, rough old wood, tons of it. It'll kill you.' But I did it and it bloody nearly did kill me, before I got hardened up to the strain. The timber was imported on the lease-lend arrangements for the war. They couldn't store it in London because of the bombs, so it was transported on barges from the dockyards on the Thames, up the river Lea to Broxbourne and beyond to Ware. The 'backs' had to offload the timber and hump it up across the fields and up gangways, 'roads', to build the stacks, some of them as tall as a house. As the stack grew higher, the roads got steeper and you had to clutch tight onto the timber to stop it slipping away, the plank walkway bouncing under you, on up to the top run, shove the timber off for the stackers to lay out and keep on going straight down the opposite side for the next load on the barge. You got a splinter in your hands, in your neck, your shoulder, hard luck; you kept going, round, up, down, round, like ants.

But living in the caravan at Broxbourne was a good time for me. My grandfather was a lovely old guy. He helped me slowly to feel better about myself. He used to speak about my father and he said one day: 'George, you can't hold a grudge against him for the rest of your life. He knew he was going to die; it made him uptight. He was scared. It made him drink more and he picked on you, but he was really lashing out against what the TB was doing to him. It wasn't him; you happened to get in the way. Your real dad was a nice guy, you can take my word for it. He thought the world of the whole family, every one of you. He knew he wasn't the man he used to be. Trouble was, you always were plucky and he was afraid of you standing up to him, silly as it may seem, but thats how it happens. He hit you because he was scared of you, envious of what you had. You were full of life and spirit and his was draining out of him. But you have to try to forget the nasty part and forgive him. He did his best to be a good father and he didn't have the luck: he died before he'd hardly got going.'

Then one day my brother Billy came out to see me, with a visitor — Joan. I suppose I didn't expect she'd want to see me again, but she told me she'd missed me. I missed her, badly. We talked and that was it really. I told her the court had insisted that I stay in Broxbourne for a while, but I could speak to the probation officer and see when it would be all right for me to come back to London. It would probably mean going back home, but I felt I could handle that better now. Besides, I realised that Joan meant a lot more to me than I had admitted and I didn't want to lose her. We didn't make any promises, or anything, but we both agreed we didn't want to spend any more time apart than we could help.

At the beginning of 1945 I went back to London, saw the probation officer and he cleared me to stay. That was the start of Joan and me courting. I was so drawn by her kindness and gentle ways and finding love, being loved was something I craved. We were only young but the bond between us was very strong. She represented someone who might be mine, and I could be hers. That was very important to me, given what had happened.

We'd meet in the evenings. Once a week we went to the Bedford Theatre music hall in Camden High Street. They had a different show on every week: comedy acts, dancers, singers you could sing along with. When I was a kid it had been a picture house — threepence to go up in the gods. Now we were teenagers we sat down in the stalls. It was great entertainment, real old-time variety.

Another night we'd go to the pictures at the Forum, Kentish Town, kissing and cuddling in the back row, seeing the show through twice. A nice, cosy place to spend time in.

The Mitre pub, just round the corner from where Joan lived, was another of our haunts. Harry Darrant was the landlord. We used to sit in his saloon bar with the gas fire blazing, often just the two of us, dragging out one drink of lemonade for an hour and a half, maybe two hours. He never complained. He knew Joan's father, an engine driver. At weekends the saloon would be packed, but during the week it was pretty quiet.

As the warmer weather came we went for walks up on Hampstead Heath, past the anti-aircraft rocket site above Kenwood, over to the Vale of Heath, for a lemonade in the pub there. The war being on, V1s and V2s flying over, you didn't stray far. I know some kids used to go up over the Heath searching for shrapnel fragments and bits of cordite. Highly inflammable stuff and they took it home in their pockets.

I had an idea to join the Merchant Navy. The Royal Marines was out, I was underage, else I'd have joined them like a shot. But I had listened to the reports of the Russian convoys on the radio, the merchant ships sailing through the Baltic, in the ice and storms, German submarines lurking, and the newsreaders saying how it was the toughest assignment anyone could imagine. That's what I wanted to do. I wanted to be a tough, macho man. I wanted to do something for the war effort. At one point, early on in the war, we had been lined up for evacuation to Canada, and I was looking forward to that sea trip more than I can say. Then it was cancelled because of the U-boats in the Atlantic, and that was a huge disappointment. I had always wanted to go to sea, from the first time of seeing the marines at their manoeuvres on Deal beach.

Anyway, I went in to see the probation officer and told him I'd like to try for the Merchant Navy. He said he thought that might be just the ticket. He got me the forms and a few weeks later I was accepted for training on the TS *Trinton* moored on the Thames.

They gave you an introductory course in all the jobs you'd be expected to do on board ship, and then assessed your abilities to decide which suited you best: deckhand, able seaman, engine room, 'sparks', navigation, steward, waiter. Then there were the regular skills everyone had to have; lifeboat drill, rowing the boats, compass reading. I found a lot of the study quite difficult, but I came out tops in rowing and I'd have been happy to do whatever they put me to . . . go to sea and see the world.

I enjoyed the training on *Trinton*, but something else was gnawing at me. I had realised, over the past few months, how long I had been starved of affection and the one person who had given me affection was Joan. I felt alone in the world, no family, but there she was. I became obsessed with her in a way, very possessive and jealous. I craved love and she was offering me love. If we got married she'd be someone of my own, my own family, I wouldn't have to look for family where there was none to be found. She had become my hope of everything, and I asked her to marry me. She said 'Yes'.

It was a bit of a shock all round. I was still not yet 17 and I offered about as reliable a future as a husband as a Russian convoy did of a pleasure cruise. Joan's family were nice, friendly, decent people. Her father was a steady, fair man. Joan getting married was a bit of a disaster for the family. Their lovely, well-educated daughter, a sweet Catholic girl, who would almost certainly have gone on to be a secretary or something in that line, marrying a wild kid who could hardly read or write, with not much sense and less money or prospects. That's how it must have seemed to them. But we wanted to get married and we got married in Euston Town Hall, in May 1945.

After the wedding party Joan and I walked back to Agar Grove. We were going to live with my mother until we got ourselves sorted out. It wasn't a very clever idea, but we had no choice. I can still hear Charlie Howes shouting to my mother: 'Don't worry, Rose, they're only kids. It'll all be over, they'll be back to mother in next to no time.' But 53 years later we're still married.

We lasted only two weeks with them, though. There was an almighty row and my elder sister, Dorothy, said we could move in with her for a while. When we arrived, with what few things we had, she had a Yank with her, Johnnie Butkus. He was a nice guy, gave me a pair of high-ankled, rubber-soled, US Army-issue boots. They were perfect for working on the timber barges.

Johnnie went over in the D-Day landings and then back to America. He and my sister wrote to each other for a while, there was a real bond between them. But, in the way of things, he got married, she got married — twice, actually — both her husbands died. She became matron of a school in Borehamwood and, after she retired, she decided to go off and tour the USA. She even went to the town in North Carolina where, years before, Johnnie had lived and she bumped into him. In 1990 they got married. After all that time. She told me: 'It wasn't meant to be when we first met, I don't know why, George, but we still felt the same when we met again, so why shouldn't we have our happiness in the end?'

I carried on working on the timber for a while: walked along Agar Grove to Camden Town; trolley-bus to Manor House and on to Tottenham Hale for the 7 a.m. train to Broxbourne. The train used to be packed with girls working in the munitions factory out at Brimsdown, near Cheshunt. Coming home I was often so tired I missed Tottenham Hale and woke up at Liverpool Street, not knowing where I was. Money was very short.

Although Dorothy helped us, the rest of the family were very stand-offish and I got very disillusioned with them. Joan and I had our backs to the wall and we needed help. I don't mean hand-outs, but it was as if they didn't want to know. It was as if because I had been a wild kid I wasn't worth a farthing, that getting married was stupid so why should they bother? Before the year was out, Joan was pregnant.

We'd gone back to my mother's — they had moved to College Street — and I got struck by rheumatic fever again. The first attack had left me with a dodgy heart, so this time it was even more serious. It was awful. I lay there, thinking about it. Joan had no one to turn to. No one in my family came to visit her to see if she was all right. They didn't help, they didn't even offer help. She came in to see me and sometimes we just looked at each other, wondering what we were going to do. Then visiting hour finished, she'd say goodbye, cry, as often as not, and I'd watch her go feeling more miserable than I could believe.

As soon as the pain eased off a little bit, I thought, 'I can't stay here', and I told the nurse to bring my clothes because I was going to discharge myself. Of course the sister said, 'You can't do that, you'll end up dead.' But I said, 'I'm sorry, I can't help it, I've got to go' and I went.

I dragged myself round to see my uncle, Alfie Bing. He was a ganger on the timber gangs working down in the City Road docks of the Grand Union Canal. I told him I was desperate. So he put me to work. How I got through, I don't know. I could hardly bear to put my feet on the ground. My joints hurt so badly it was agony to move, let alone heave massive baulks of timber about. Gradually the pain eased off. Then, after not much more than a week, Alfie came up to me and said: 'Sorry, George, there's no more work.' But I heard a whisper that there was a barge coming into the wharf the next day and I went down. There were blokes working. I went up to Alfie and said, 'If you can't give work to your own flesh and blood, who can you help?' He didn't say anything, just turned away and I thought, 'That's it, I'm never going back. I'm never asking this lot for a favour again,' and I walked out. I went back to work for Cooper, but his trade was dropping off, lorries were becoming more and more popular, and the money was terrible. I stuck it as long as I could.

At the age of 17 years six months I was called up for medical examination, like everyone else, for the forces. I went along to the military clinic and the MO gave me the once-over and said: 'Mr Francis, I'm afraid I am going to have to mark you C3 [the lowest grade]. Entering the forces is out of the question. I'm very concerned about the condition of your heart. I need to write to your doctor.' Shortly afterwards, I received a letter from my doctor saying that he wanted to see me but I didn't go. I knew what he was going to say: no heavy work and plenty of rest.

At the end of the war, if you weren't educated but were physically strong, you went where your muscle could count. The places to find work were at London Docks and Covent Garden. I'd turned my back on the timber gangs and in any event the work was gradually shifting back from the river Lea to the London Docks, and they were bringing in new, massive cranes, so the timber porters had very little future. All they seemed to get was a hernia or a rupture — a lot of blokes had haemorrhoids from straining their backsides — and a tired old age for seven quid a week. Besides, the dockers were very close-knit. It was nigh impossible to get your ticket if you were an outsider, only the dockers' families could bring in new men. The other most lucrative way of turning physical strength into money was in Covent Garden, the only trouble being that the porters were almost as close-knit as the dockers. Still, I knew the place inside out after working for Cooper, and I thought, 'If I can get an in, I can work my way up to being a porter.' I'd try anything, give anything a go, work my heart out. I wasn't prepared to go on slogging away for no money, and with our daughter Mary growing fast and Joan pregnant again, I had to do something to heave myself up.

First, you had to have a recommendation. I had the luck to know one of the top union men, a guy called Paddy. He'd said to me: 'Why don't you come and work at the Garden? I'll recommend you.' It seemed like a good omen and I went for it. He got me a union card and I had my first job as an empty man at Tommy Wharton's, along Dean Street, just by Cooper's stand. I had to work for a dreary old sod called Fred. He wore the same threadbare brown smock day after day, a greasy trilby hat and a sour, gloomy expression on his sour gloomy face. He was a jumped-up, humourless, sharp-nosed, snide little Hitler. The first morning I walked in, I took one look at him and knew we weren't going to get on and we didn't. I hated him and he hated me. The other three guys who worked there weren't much better. They were like imbeciles, no drive, no go, no decision, no bottle or spirit in them. They did their work, stopped for a sandwich and went back to work as if nothing had happened. It would have been funny if it wasn't so depressing spending time with people who had no interest, enthusiasm or ambition beyond one day's end and the next day's start, if they could tell the difference, which I doubt. They were like robots, zombies, doing a dull job that seemed to have taken them over completely.

I got the job collecting the empty fruit and veg boxes into the warehouse because it was the worst job going and no one else wanted to touch it; but it was a start. I was working in Covent Garden, and I was determined to get my porter's badge. Getting that badge was the big thing in your life, you were in and nobody could push you out.

Around about this time we moved into the first place of our own in Dale Road, a couple of rooms right at the top of the house where Joan's mother and father lived. The street tapers away to nothing against the wall over the railway lines, the outside wall of the house went right down to the tracks. All day and night we had vile sulphurous smoke from the steam engines belching up at our windows. The curtains rotted, the place reeked of burnt coal soot. The roof was in such bad repair that we constantly had water running down the walls from the ceiling. There was no bath, no toilet, no kitchen. You had to go to the bottom of the stairs, three flights, for sanitation. All day and night we had the noise of engines shunting trucks backwards and forwards in and out of sidings; squealing brakes, hissing steam, clanking buffers.

The only good thing about that place was that we didn't have to share it with anyone, except us: me, Joan, Mary and Billy — who was born in 1948.

On the way home from the market I often looked in at Doughty's gym and I suppose the idea of boxing was beginning to take hold of me and in 1949 — through a lucky coincidence — I went back to the St Pancras club.

Working as a staff man I'd occasionally have slack times and have to search out casual labour wherever I could find it. I happened to be doing a fortnight of orange-grading down at Fresh Wharf by London Bridge. If a freighter coming in with a cargo got caught on a low tide, you had a couple of hours to kill and several days I strolled up to the Old Bailey to sit in the gallery, never dreaming that one day I'd be down in the dock fighting for my life. Anyway, we were sitting around on the wharfside, and one of my mates got into some argy-bargy with a docker, the docker suddenly lost his temper and knocked my mate down, spark out. That lit my fuse and I waded in and gave him what for. One of the blokes in the crowd watching — and nobody intervened, a fight livened the day up — was a docker, Harry Gibbs. He'd been a PoW in Germany, always a boxer and, by this time, an international boxing referee. He came up to me afterwards. 'Why don't you come and learn to box?' he said. 'You'd do all right in the ring.'

I said I'd given it a go but didn't take to it.

'Which club?' he asked.

'St Pancras.'

'Well, there's a coincidence. I'm the trainer down there.'

And that's how it started. I went back to the club and Harry took me over, turned the wildness into skill and technique, concentration and cunning. He trained me to keep my cool, to focus the aggression and, above all, to restrain my emotions. If you carry any of your anger and hostility from outside the ring into it, you've got no chance. In the ring — the four corners of truth — you have to learn how to be cool, calm, collected under the enormous pressure of a bout, and to keep the same concentration as when we were sparring. And I had to learn what I had never been able to take before: to take punches and bide my time, instead of just charging in and battling to avoid getting hurt. Also, with gloves on, you couldn't hold on to your opponent like you can with bare hands when it is possible to more or less immobilise him. But they say that a boxer will always be a decent match for a street fighter, and it's true — with or without gloves on. Harry taught me tactics, funnelling all the brute violence into technique: jabs, driving in like pistons, with the whole weight of the upper body behind them instead of the mauling, flailing, all-out swarming, smother-attack windmill I'd been used to. He was an amazing bloke. Under his tutelage I had to unlearn what had become second nature through all the years of brawling and absorb a new science. And that aspect intrigued and excited me: the fact that you weren't just plunging in, that you had to use your brain. I was always streetwise, now I learned to be ringwise, to use wits as well as brawn. But the best thing about Harry as a teacher was not only that he could teach but that he made me want to learn. He inspired and motivated me. A trainer may have all the expertise in the world, but if he can't motivate his boxers then it's worth next to nothing.

The training sessions lasted from 7 to 9 p.m. and often Harry would be in the ring, sparring with the boxers the full two hours. He was a very fit man, physically strong and mentally sharp; extraordinary powers of concentration, to spar with a whole string of boxers, each with a different style and different strengths. He planted such enthusiasm into me. I was a light-heavyweight but I was that keen, I'd take on any weight: middles, heavies, seniors.

There were four rings in the club and I bounced round all of them. 'I'll take him ... I'll fight him,' I'd say while scrambling through the ropes like on the army assault course. I felt at home. Kick — bollock — bite for survival had been replaced by something which became very precious and central to my life. The team spirit in boxing, whether one to one, or as part of a boxing stable, is what I'd been hankering for, subconsciously, from the time when I was a kid. A loner then, a loner still.

But it was great just to walk into the club, meet the other guys, get changed, chatting away, then box together; or get into a coach with the whole team and go off to bouts. Only amateurs can give you that real team spirit in a crowd and I loved it. I took to it, like coming home. Most important, too, boxing gave me a sense of fair play. In the streets, it's crush or be crushed; in the ring, you shake hands before a fight and you shake hands after. I didn't find that easy at first, acting friendly with someone who had just beaten me. It went against all my first instincts. But gradually I saw it as part of the whole code that Harry drilled into me. Sadly, for me, Harry left St Pancras after a year to join another club. There were two other trainers to coach me along: Harry Harris and Joe Birkett, a wonderful old boy who had trained boxers all his life.

We fought for prizes — crockery, electrical goods, watches, clocks — lots of clocks. Generally I took any prizes I won to Len Fowler's shop at the top of Neal Street. He sold trophies — such as statuettes of boxers with fists poised — and he'd give me a price for the goods I wanted to trade in. I got a crockery set in a bout against some university students, I think they were from Oxford. They were fit, strong, natty fighters and they never gave up, and the support they had — the spectators would bring the roof down, cheering their blokes on. At the dinner afterwards we sat opposite our opponents and they delivered the prizes we'd chosen earlier and took none themselves. Very gentlemanly. They also said boxing was a brilliant relief from book study.

At one show I fought in I was in one of the two lines for the medical tests (which we all had to have before stepping into the ring) and when it was my turn I walked around the screen and came face to face with Dr Dean, my doctor from Malden Road. He went crazy, asked me what did I think I was doing there and that I knew damn well that I shouldn't be boxing with a rheumatic heart. He gave me such a filthy look, I thought he was going to fling me out. I said I was fitter than I'd ever been in my life. He calmed down and glanced me over. 'Well, in all conscience I can't permit you to box, you'd better go into the other queue.' Which I did, got passed as fit and won my bout. As I walked out, after collecting my trophy, I winked at Dean and he gave me a broad smile.

In those days Covent Garden was always alive at any hour of the day or night. The actual market packed in trading around 4 or 5 p.m. when the BRS lorries drove out across the country. By then the pubs and restaurants were beginning to open for the evening, people finishing work were stopping for a drink on their way home and the theatregoers were trooping in; it was a Mecca for them as it was not only handy for the West End theatres but also for those in the Strand, Drury Lane and Aldwych. Add to this the editorial staff from Odhams Press during the day and the printers by night, plus the Masonic Hall in Long Acre, and the hotels and restaurants dotted about all over, the place was on the go.

The firms were in shuttered alcoves under the canopy of the Jubilee Hall — where the shops and stalls are in the modernised piazza. All around the hall in front of the outside firms ran a covered pavement, the 'run'. Beyond that were the open cobbles, where the lorries drove up, parked and waited to be unloaded by the pitching gangs who lined up to whip the boxes off the tailboard as quickly as they could go. Then they would deliver them to the staff man — that was me, temporarily — for stacking in the firm. Of course you had to keep an eye on what was coming in, where it went, how many boxes of this, that and the other. Time was money and you didn't waste a second.

The first lorries from the farms and market gardens rolled in from 10.30 p.m. onwards until beyond midnight, when the staff men opened up the firms. From that moment on the market was a hive of activity, with upwards of 1,000 people working through the night until 6.30 a.m. when the porters started barrowing the produce and another 1,000 or so day workers took over the running of the market.

By now I'd started on night work at Medlock's. Their stand — where Ponti's and half of Haagen Dazs is today — was on the outside of the run, with all the rest of the English firms, who mainly dealt in the heavier fruit and veg. Inside the hall were the small firms dealing mostly in light, imported stuff and smaller packages — mushrooms, tomatoes, apricots, hothouse grapes, soft fruit etc.

Basically, my job was to pile and sort the goods as the pitching gang heaved it off the lorries: unload one, once he had driven off and along came the next; unload him. It was non-stop until they'd all been through. It was up to the staff man to keep track of everything: different varieties of potatoes, apples, tomatoes, counting the sacks of greens, turnips, swedes, cabbages. Tallying the bananas, oranges, lemons, grapefruit. The sorting was incredibly difficult: for example, the tomatoes would arrive as 1,000 trays from five different senders in Jersey, all to be classified by grade and sender, into different stacks, keeping them roughly the same height with enough space between them to move — but not so much that they'd be in the way of the porters. And while you're puzzling that out, there would be more lorries drawing up with more stuff to unload and sort. Apples, say, which were never marked; they came in wooden bushel boxes. A grower might send seven different varieties of apple in the same load. You took the box from the pitcher, gave it a shake to see what sort they were and what grade — Cox's, for instance, either bests, seconds or drops (the windfalls which came packed in straw) — and the skill to do that came from an eye trained over months.

When the buyers came round, from about 4 or 4.30 a.m. onwards, they wanted to see all your produce to check the quality and freshness. The veg would be lined up neatly, the best at the front, with sprigs of parsley to make the stuff eye-catching, irresistible. The fruit stacked where it could catch the light.

At 4 a.m. the firm's salesman arrived; he was a vital man. He settled prices with buyers and that called for a lot of experience, canniness with figures and market skill. He had to weigh prices against the need to shift the stuff when it was fresh. Anything left over got gradually more stale and less saleable, which meant money lost; but, ask too cheap a price and there'd be little or no profit. Salesmen and buyers played a cat-and-mouse game.

Smart buyers got in early and snooped about to see what was in short supply; that gave them the chance to shave prices. For example, if there weren't many carrots around one morning, but Wilkinson's happened to have a glut of 250 bags, then the buyer would be glancing over the other stuff at everything but the carrots. He'd be sniffing the greens, peering at the cauliflower, humming and hawing about the potatoes, and then he'd say, almost throwaway: 'Those carrots don't look too bad. How much, Alf?'

'Ten bob a sack.'

'How about those swedes?'

And so it went on, till the buyer had made his list and then he would say as an afterthought, 'I'll give you eight bob a sack for the carrots, all the lot.'

Now, the salesman had an option: shift all the carrots at a low price, 20 per cent under the asking price, or hold out and risk being left with some. If he did sell just to be shot of them, the buyer could depend on making his two shillings per sack extra if he'd cornered part of the market in stock which was scarce. Or the salesman might smell a rat and decide he could afford to wait; though he was on commission from the suppliers — on every box or sack he sold, his firm owed a percentage of the profit to the farmer. No sale, no cut.

I had been reluctant to go on nights, but I got fed up with the other job after a few months and decided to give it a go; all towards getting my porter's badge. Two old guys, Ned and Ted, in a nearby firm had been working in the wonderful world of nightwork for 30 years; they were fantastic to me. The shows of fruit and veg they put on were brilliant, and it was they who taught me. Where some guys only opened one sack and pulled out the best from that one, I'd tip out four or five and take my selection. The better the show you put on, the more likely buyers were to stop and look. The more buyers you attracted, the quicker the stuff sold, and the quicker it sold the fresher it was, so everyone gained and you kept your customers happy. The show might be a pyramid of cabbages six feet high; an arrangement of sacks with the tops neatly furled back showing turnips, swedes, potatoes. By the potatoes I would place a plate of them — cooked — for the buyers to taste. We also specialised in celery: huge bundles, 12 or 18 per roll, and they would be all filthy with black soil, if they came from around Manchester — the sooty earth was excellent for celery growing. Cos lettuce was another speciality. The dirt clinging to the vegetables was not a bad mark: people liked to see the soil, they didn't want it cleaned off, it gave the produce the stamp of authenticity. Of course, that meant when you heaved loads of celery off the lorry, you'd get covered in muck. Also, the soil kept the stuff moist and cool — there were no cold stores in those days. It wasn't until Tesco's opened a warehouse in the market and started pre-packing their stuff that all the farmers began to wash their stuff before they delivered it.

Ned and Ted may have been working for a rival firm, but they spent a lot of time coaching me. Of course, they had an ulterior motive: they wanted to make sure of me, so I wouldn't go spilling the beans about them piling spare fruit and veg into unlabelled sacks.

'It's like the three monkeys, George,' they said to me. 'Hear no evil, see no evil, speak no evil.'

Those guys pulled all sorts of strokes. For example, as the pitching gangs unloaded boxes of apples they scraped a few off the top, riddled the box to make it look full and slipped the surplus into a spare box. By the end of the offloading they had a few boxes to themselves. Or they would slip the string on a large sack of spring greens, lose a few, shake the sack to rearrange it, lift more greens up and butt their tops out, refasten the string and, by daylight, they had a whole consignment of extra greens.

Sometimes when you arrived at midnight, you'd hear hammers banging, like in a carpenter's shop. A crate of apples had got dropped on the ground to crack the bottom off; out came a few, ruffle up the straw and nail back the broken slat.

Tomatoes came in cardboard 'handles' or 'chips' — a box with two compartments divided by a central carrying handle — which would sell at 12 lbs. So, if they weighed a few handles and averaged them out at 13½ lbs, say, they could milk four from each, which would never be missed, and end up with a surplus to sell at half price for a straight profit. Offer a buyer 20 'chips' at full price and 20 at half price with a sales ticket for each to keep the records straight and they were quids in. Or they stashed the extra 'chips' in discreet places around the market and sold them on to a greengrocer or a driver who'd come in early and was looking for some bargains.

An articulated lorry might draw up at 6 a.m. with a load of 400 trays of tomatoes. The pitching gang would unload them and the taker-in would count off the trays. Any broken or slack (not full) had to be marked down. When the 400 trays were sorted and stacked, the driver signs for 30 slack trays, whereas there have been only three. He has to be straightened out, generally with beer money of up to a quid, which was a fair amount in those days, or a cotchel, the standard currency of exchange in Covent Garden. A cotchel was a bag of mixed fruit and veg. It had originally meant a remnant of goods — usually grain left in a sack, or else a portion of a load left over. Everybody went home with a cotchel, and one guy I knew used to exchange his for turkey legs at the kitchen of a local restaurant. One morning he was walking up Bow Street with his bag when a plainclothes policeman stopped him, searched his cotchel and found the turkey legs; pulled him into Bow Street and had him sitting in a room for ages, wondering what's going to happen to him. In the end the copper let him go, he probably only wanted to put the frighteners on him. Anyway, a few weeks later he steamed into the market in a flaming rage and said: 'Those rotten plainclothes bastards, you know what they've done? I just went round to get my turkey legs and there were none left. The coppers had been there first getting theirs.'

Once I saw a high-ranking policeman from Bow Street station, which was opposite the market, come in one night and, walking past a stand near me, he tossed his bag in, a big, black holdall, and said to the staff man, 'See you later.' When he came back, the bag was full of lovely stuff — fresh fruit and veg, handed over without a word. The same bloke strolled up to Medock's one night, lobbed his bag in and said, 'See you later.' I filled the bag with swedes and turnips; it was so heavy you could hardly lift it. He never came back to me.

Another bit of villainy: a lorry rolled up with 250 sacks of Jersey potatoes on it. The staff man told the driver they were so crowded and he'd have to wait till they were clear, and he was sent to park up in the Strand till they were ready. Some geezer overheard this and a bit later wheeled his trolley down and said to the driver, 'The foreman sent me. He'll be down shortly but he needs 20 bags now,' and then he hands over any old ticket he's got in his pocket. On goes the load, off goes the guy. Another guy who's had the tip rolls up with his trolley and off goes another 20 bags. Later, when the foreman brings the lorry in to unload it, he says, 'You're 40 bags light.' The driver tells him two of his blokes came down and took them.

'Not my blokes, mate. You've been done.'

There was fiddling, but only a small percentage; it was no den of thieves. There were night men who had their own greengrocery shops, run by their wives and family, making a nice profit at either end of the buying and selling. Regular fiddlers never got greedy and didn't get nicked; the 'mountain goats' who moved faster than everybody else. The fact is, you had to keep your wits about you. I became a sort of cowboy: I could sleep under the gaslights with one eye open. If I could finish by 4 a.m. I'd take a nap, nod off at the tall desk, sitting on a stool, slumped over. However, with all the stuff laid out on the stand, and the piles of boxes and sacks so tall you couldn't see over the top, anyone could mosey up and nick a box; you had to be vigilant. You had to have eyes up your backside; especially when the Mau Mau were operating.

The Mau Mau were a bunch of four scavengers who prowled the market, hunting for 'overs', night men working fiddles. Any fiddled stuff had to find a buyer and the Mau Mau (called after the bandits in Kenya) were ready to buy. For example, because farmers tended not to cut or harvest on Sundays, in a lot of firms the night man didn't arrive till around four or even five o'clock on Monday morning. That left his stand empty. It so happens that a lorry does come in with a delivery; the driver rumbles round the market like a tourist looking for his spot, one of the Mau Mau sees him and asks which firm he's after. The driver looks at his docket, reads out the name. The villain says, 'You're all right, son, it's just round here.' The whole place is empty and quiet. The driver asks where he should put the load.

'What have you got?'

'Fifty bags of greens.'

'Here'll do, on the pavement. I'll give you a hand.'

So the driver and the con offload the stuff, the driver pushes the invoice through the firm's letterbox, thanks the bloke for his help and off he drives, away home nice and early. The guy sees him off, gives a whistle, the rest of the Mau Mau arrive with their lorry, pitch the load onto the back, sweep up the pavement to clean up every trace and store the stuff in an empty warehouse for sale. The night man arrives, finds the ticket and thinks the driver must be parked up somewhere; tells the governor when he comes in but, by that time, it's fairly obvious that the load has gone missing. Ructions. I could never afford not to be on the stand.

You usually got breakfast at the coffee stalls or the cafés which opened at 4 a.m. When you were pressed, you sent a driver over for a jug of tea and a handful of bacon rolls, to help you out. It was in the driver's interest because the sooner you got his stuff cleared, the sooner he was away. And drivers at the back of the queue used to come up to help unload the lorry at the front. Speed was of the essence to everyone. It was a beehive, everyone mucking in to help — if a porter's barrow tipped over, other blokes helped him set it to rights and reload. The quicker you cleared work, the sooner you had a break. The pubs opened at 5 a.m. for the porters to wet their whistles before they started work, but there was always a mixed bag of people in them: printers from the newspapers in Fleet Street, nobs and debs in their finery on the tail-end of an all-night spree — the men in evening dress, the women in ballgowns, sports cars parked up. The nobs would stroll around the run, curious to see what was going on. Often there'd be a cast of actors in the pub, waiting for the first editions of the papers to read the reviews. If it was a rave notice, there'd be drinks all round. The pubs served coffee as well as drink and food: egg on toast, light snacks, anything that was quick and easy.

One Saturday lunchtime I was taking Mary, who was now five years old, to a children's party in Hampstead Road. She had her pigtails all done up in bows — Joan's mother used to do that, to make her look special. We got the bus from Queen's Crescent to the stop outside the pie and mash shop by Camden Road station and were just going to cross the road for the next bus when Mary said: 'Look, there's Granny Francis.' She was on the far side of Camden Road, outside the Eagle pub. I called out, 'Mum!' and I could see she'd heard me, but she ducked her head and scurried off. We went over and caught her up. She wouldn't look at me, and then I could see why. Her face was black and purple with bruises. She started crying. I knew. I went cold inside, and the heat rose.

'Has he done that to you?'

She nodded. She was on her way back from Clerkenwell Court with a separation order.

'It's all right,' she said. 'The rent book's in my name, so they said I can stay in the house. He's been seeing the barmaid in the pub. When I confronted him he went berserk.'

'Where is he?'

'No, Georgie, you don't have to do anything.'

'Where is he?'

'He's the foreman on the site up the road.'

'All right, you get off home.'

I took Mary on the bus, left her at the party, came back and walked up Camden Road to the building site. It was 1 p.m. and they were knocking off work. I could see Howes up on one of the scaffold landings with some other blokes. He saw me and turned away.

'Charlie,' I yelled, 'I want you.' There was a dead silence. Then he said something and the blokes with him laughed, and he swaggered down, full of himself, to the ground level. All the other blokes milling around the site.

'You fucking great bully. You're all right knocking little old ladies around. Let's see how it is when you're up against someone who can stand up to you.'

I took him apart. I whacked him about so hard he went down and I went after him. I kept whacking him. He'd broken up our family and now he'd beaten up my mother. I hit him smack in the face: 'That's for mother.' I hit him again: 'That's for Mary.' Again: 'That's for Billy.' This wasn't like going into the ring — this was revenge. All my old instincts flooded back. I knew what I was going to do and I let nothing get in the way. I put every ounce of hatred on the end of my fists and laid it into him, stuff welling up from years back. And then I grabbed his arm and pulled it right behind his back and said: 'You'll never hit her again you lousy bastard.' Then I broke it.

If the other blokes hadn't pulled me off him, I think I might well have killed him. But they did, and it was enough to give me a pause for breath, to think I'd done enough. The new instinct took over, luckily for me, luckily for him.

I went straight round to where they lived in Agar Grove. I went through

79

the place and got all his bits into a couple of his grubby old cases and flung them out into the front garden. Mother, her chest all bruised and her face black and blue, was sitting in the kitchen. I sat with her till the police arrived in a squad car. I answered the door. They had Charlie in the back of the car, his arm in a sling. The sergeant came in.

'Are you George Francis?'

'Yes, I am, only before you say anything else, come with me.' I led him down the corridor into the kitchen. 'This is my mother.'

He looked at her. She was sobbing. He saw what had happened. He shook his head. 'He did that to you?' he asked.

She nodded. By this time, the others had brought Charlie Howes in. He was shitting himself. The sergeant turned to him. 'You did this?' He was so shocked his voice was shaking.

Howes mumbled something.

'I take that to be yes. Well?' the sergeant asked.

Howes nodded.

'Right.' The officer took a deep breath. 'If Mrs Francis wants to press charges against you, she is perfectly entitled to. She can take out a summons here and now. As far as I'm concerned, though, this is a domestic and I'm having nothing to do with it. Only, if you want to press charges against Mr Francis, here, you have every right in law to do so. Go ahead. It wouldn't be my advice, because I don't think you've got a leg to stand on. But if you want to, feel free.'

Howes didn't want to know. He mumbled something and left. When they'd all gone I told my mother never to let him in the house again. Two weeks later she took him back and that's when I started to drop out of her life, really. If she could forgive him, I couldn't see any future in our relationship. It was a mistake, but I couldn't see any other way.

It was 1951. We'd been living in the Dale Road rooms — little better than a slum — for five years. Our third child, Danny, was born and he was about six months old when things finally came to a head.

Billy had been constantly ill from the start. At 11 months, he caught bronchial pneumonia and it was touch and go for a long time. And he developed an abscess on his appendix at the same time. The pain of that made it impossible for him to cough up the phlegm on his lungs. It was winter, the fog and the smog came as well as the smoke from the railway, and he couldn't bear to be outside. He'd cough and cough and cough. It wrenched him apart, it wrenched Joan and me apart. There was nothing we could do for him. The hospital did teach me to lay him face down across an orange box to help ease the pain of coughing so he could dredge the filthy muck up from his lungs, but the abscess was getting worse and worse, and he was screaming with pain.

He caught pneumonia again two years later and we had to take him back to Great Ormond Street Hospital, where he'd spent weeks of his life already. Joan would sit by his bedside, hour after hour. Professor Moncrieff told us we had to get him out of London till his lungs could recover, otherwise the pollution would kill him. So I borrowed a friend's motorbike and sidecar, bundled Billy up and drove him down to a rest home for kids by the seaside which was run by Auntie Copper. Billy stayed there for six weeks and got better and had a lovely time. Auntie Copper was a marvel with kids; warm-hearted, patient, friendly. She had a donkey, Pepo, to take them for rides and when Billy came home he was a changed boy. He was rarely ill after that, though the hospital told us we nearly lost him several times. Then, having always been healthy, Mary got ill.

It all started when one of her teachers at the Grafton Road school gave her a goldfish in a bowl and she was so excited that as she ran home to show us, she tripped and fell. The glass bowl smashed and the broken glass gashed her hand wide open. She lost a mass of blood and nobody found her or did anything till a railwayman who lived nearby whisked her into the hospital. Casualty bandaged her up to wait for stitches and while she was waiting for them she caught whooping-cough from another kid in the ward. Billy caught it from her and they both got so sick — convulsive coughing, day and night, terrible wheezing to catch their breath — they had to be taken off to the isolation hospital in Chingford. As Billy had had pneumonia it hit him very badly.

Joan was in bed with Danny and when the medics came up she went mad. 'Don't take my children, don't take my children away from me.' The whole thing was horrible. I went with them, following behind the fever ambulance, windows blanked out like a prison van. I had to leave them there: strictly no visiting. Their little faces looking at me, begging, 'You're not going to leave us, daddy, you're not going to leave us?' But they were contagious and I had to. I was allowed to take them fruit from the market, but that was all. I couldn't go in to see them. Nearly two months they had to stay there. Just before they came home, the ceiling of one room fell in. The plaster had got so damp it caved in. All we had was the soot-ridden old laths and rafters over our heads.

The kids did come home, eventually, but they weren't cured. The coughing started again and we were at our wits' end.

Joan's mother said the best thing was for me to take them on the Thames steamer down to Margate for the day and give them some sea air.

We got to Tower Pier and on board the boat. It pulled away under the bridge and the kids started coughing. There was no disguising it; once you'd heard those whoops and barks you know. Everybody ran away from us as if we had the plague. Someone told the captain and he came down. Luckily, he was sympathetic. 'Look,' he said, 'I can't stop the boat, but you'll have to get off the main deck. We'll give you some blankets to wrap the kids up in, and go up front and get the fresh air in their faces.' It seemed to help.

At Margate, I took them round everywhere. I bought them sticks of rock, gave them rides, everything you do at the seaside, but I was on edge the whole time. Whenever they let rip with a cough, people backed away. I couldn't stand it.

About four o'clock, we walked down to the pier, but a bloke said: 'If you're thinking of catching the boat, you're too late, mate.' That was the last straw. I picked both the kids up, Billy under my arm, Mary over my shoulder, and hared off down the pier. As I ran, they bounced about and the bouncing brought on the coughing and then they started vomiting on to the boat, and I made my mind up about their future.

I found out where the offices of the NSPCC were, dressed Mary and Billy in their best clothes and took them down there. We waited and went in to see the fellow. I didn't waste time on pleasantries. I said: 'The kids are sick the whole time, we're living in a place not even a dog should live in. It's killing me. I love them to death, but I'm leaving them here. This is the address. I've had it.' I walked out. Mary clung on to me and Billy clung on to Mary. The guy called after me, 'I wish I could help.' I kept going.

When I got home and Joan found out she went mad, screamed and hollered, 'I want my children', over and over again, till she was exhausted.

That evening, we were sitting there, Danny in bed. She refused to speak to me. There was a knock on the door and the man from the NSPCC came in with Mary and Billy. He took one look at the room: ceiling down, damp running down the walls, the air thick with steam, smoke and coal dust. He just shook his head and sat down and mumbled: 'Oh, my God! Oh, my God!'

Within a week he came back to tell us he'd found us a council flat on the Hilldrop Estate, Leith House, off Brecknock Road. We moved in straightaway. It was paradise, compared to what we'd had for the six years we'd been married. A bathroom, with a bath, kitchen, bedrooms; a sitting-room. Warm. Dry. It was fantastic. A fresh start. We could hardly believe it. We stayed there 20 years.

Because of the boxing, I was taking my fitness very seriously. I did train a bit in a professional boxing-gym in Earlham Street, Covent Garden, but my main training-ground was the fields and the Pond on Hampstead Heath. And there was another reason for going over there when I got back from work in the mornings. I used to feel so tired, very often I slept way past my stop and woke up when the bus got to Tufnell Park or Archway. The only compensation was seeing the other poor blighters all trooping off to begin their day's work, when I had the day free. Except that, come ten o'clock that evening — I can always remember it — hearing the chimes of Big Ben introducing the ten o'clock news, and groaning because I had to get up, only an hour to sit with Joan, have some food and then catch the late bus into the market. Sleeping during the day — not only with our kids racing around, but the other kids in the flats — it was nearly impossible. So, as soon as the warmer weather came, I used to go off to the Pond and sleep under one of the chestnut trees by the Pond. A group of gays used to congregate there; I got friendly with them, one in particular, Gersh, a nice guy, friendly, a regular at the Pond. We often met at the café down the road for a cup of tea at 8 a.m. then walked up the hill together to join the others. I'd take them some fruit from Covent Garden and they kept watch over me while I slept. They got really fierce if anyone made a noise and woke me up.

After a couple of hours' sleep I did my training: running, weights, skipping, shadow-boxing, swimming. Then I could sleep a bit more. Training wasn't the only reason for going over there. I love fresh air and sunshine — the winter you can keep, for me the best season is summer and I lap up the sun, every beam, every ray of it. Night work is deadly unhealthy. Many blokes doing night work hardly see daylight at all during the winter. It gives them a ghostly pallor. Their eyes get crow's feet from creasing up in bright light. And broken sleep wears you down, taps your energy. The Pond had a major part in combating the effects of night work. The life up there grew on me and I got addicted to the cold-water swimming, the fitness, fresh air and the friendship. The place became a second home.

I was getting better in the ring and I won a few trophies: a novices cup; a cup for the best punch of the night (I knocked out my opponent in 28 seconds from the bell — including the count — in the first round). Those two trophies were stolen in a burglary from my house a couple of years ago; that felt horrible. They were of sentimental value only to me, useless to anyone else, but mementoes of a time that was very important to me.

One night at the club, neither of the regular instructors turned up. One was at a boxing show and the other, a guy called Kerr, had been taken ill and never did come back. Everyone was standing about, twiddling their thumbs, not knowing what to do. I hated wasting time, so I pitched in, got things going, got them sparring, sorted out the evening's training and this went on for a couple of weeks. One of the club's committee men, Ernie Tillinghurst, an international amateur referee, took me aside at the end of a session and told me he'd watched me working. He said: 'You seem to have a natural gift for teaching.' I laughed: 'I'm an old gang leader, that's why.' We chatted a bit and the result was that the committee offered me the trainer's job at a pound a night. Extra money. Great, I thought, not imagining that would make any difference to my boxing. But when I lined up to box at a show one night, an official called me out and said: 'You've taken money for training. That means you have to be classed as a pro. You can't box as an amateur.'

It was a bad blow, I didn't know what to do. Boxing had done so much for me; I didn't want to give it up. On the other hand, I did have a real taste and a feel for training the others. And it was money which I could ill afford to lose. So I gave up competition boxing. That didn't keep me out of the ring. I did what Harry Gibbs did: I sparred with my boxers. I sparred all night. I got more boxing than I had ever got before. Then I persuaded the club to start a Friday session as well as the training on the other two nights. I ended up with an extra £3 a week; very handy.

I never set out to be a trainer. I became one pretty well by chance. But I found my calling. Perhaps I knew, instinctively, that I was never going to get to the top as a boxer, and turning more to training relieved me of having to pursue an ambition which I didn't feel entirely comfortable about. I was a handy enough boxer; strong, aggressive and certainly fit enough — up to a point. But I think it was the knowledge at the back of my mind that rheumatic fever had impaired my natural power, that when it really mattered in the ring, I wouldn't have the reserves to draw on that stopped me as a boxer. I've never shirked a physical challenge, I've always been able to drive myself hard. But boxing is a physical and psychological challenge like no other. It takes you into areas of stress you couldn't imagine possible. Maybe I realised that when I compelled myself to exceed normal limits, I would break down. Or, perhaps, I had the sense that my technical skills as a boxer weren't top grade. There is, after all, a big difference in being able to do something to perfection yourself and moulding perfection in someone else. I have only to compare my own talents as a boxer with those of the brilliantly talented men I've trained to prove that. I took to training as if I'd been preparing for it my whole life; not that I was aware of the talent before. That's what makes it so much of a stroke of luck, those official trainers not turning up that evening. It changed my life, though I didn't know it then.

There was another advantage in being the club trainer: I could get into the ring as soon as the session began and stay in there till the end — two hours sparring with the kids I was training. I loved that, it was perfect for me. It meant I got all the boxing and the training too, instead of having to wait my turn outside the ropes in a queue for ten minutes with the trainer, like the rest of them. It not only gave me the chance to get fitter and fitter, it drew me out, introduced me to the same buzz I'd had, in such different circumstances, with the Prebend Street mob. The buzz I still get every time I go into the gym; whether it be training Frank Bruno as world champion, or training him in the bleakness after defeat. The buzz of doing what you do best, 100 per cent, even when everything seems to be going wrong, against you, pointless. The buzz that keeps the blood pumping, the mind working, the spirit singing the same old song: 'Never give up.'

When the Prince of Wales baths were modernised, the club moved to Holmes Road School, where the evening institute held classes. I did their boxing trainer's course, passed with distinction and became one of their instructors, working with the St Pancras club. That qualification entitled me to £2 a night for twice-weekly sessions. The girls had cooking classes in the same building so, after training, the boxers crowded in there to eat the grub. Being the instructor, I was asked to judge the cooking competitions. And it was there that I met a man who had a huge influence on me, the most inspirational man in my life: one of the institute board, Monty Barnes. He served on a lot of council committees, too. He was a guiding light, and he encouraged me in what became my life's work. But, before that, he urged me to get an education. He said: 'You're an instructor here, why don't you take advantage of the other courses?' I'd left school more or less illiterate, and though Joan helped me I still couldn't read that well, and my writing was never great. Monty fixed things with the principal, Mr Edwards, and I joined up: English, history (I loved that), arithmetic — useful when it came to working out how much I ought to be earning. Boxing had converted my wildness to skill; those institute classes made me feel less and less of the slum kid I had always felt myself to be. Silly things helped; like having to keep an official register of the boxers every session, marking them present or absent in the book; that made me feel very grand.

I became more and more enthusiastic about training. I wanted my guys to do well, so I gave them extra training, off my own bat. Every Sunday I held a club meeting up on the Hampstead Heath running track, near the Lido. I took a big basket of gloves up so they could spar on the grass oval in the centre. Crowds of walkers used to line the railings to watch. I also took the boxers into the Pond enclosure to train. One day I was in there putting them through their paces when the governor of Pentonville Prison happened to be there. He was sitting on the bench in his vest and braces, asked me how I was doing and did I fancy coming into the 'Ville to do a spot of training with the prisoners — they weren't allowed actual bouts. I was ready for anything, boxing had more or less taken me over and I agreed.

I took two classes a week in the prison yard — the gym had been bombed out during the war and there was a shortage of carpenters among the prisoners so it was still a wreck. A few of the warders had been keen boxers, and I knew them — they used to be judges at the amateur shows. My class started off with 18 prisoners, but I got it up to 50. They loved it: hard physical exercise in the fresh air, anything to get out of the rotten stuffy cells. It gave them a goal inside gaol. One day I arrived with a bunch of skipping-ropes to take in. One of the warders looked at me and said: 'Are you crazy? You can't take them in. They'll be knotting them together and out over the wall quicker than you can ring the bell.'

It was a hard place: they still had hangings there. But, although I started out with a warder supervising the sessions, in the end we were left on our own, which was great for the prisoners' morale.

At first I missed boxing in the shows; the adrenalin pumping through you in the dressing-room, walking out through the crowd, getting into the ring, hearing the applause, people shouting for you (and people shouting for your opponent). That's what fired me up to box in the first place. All the stirring-up trouble when I was a kid was only a way of drawing attention to myself. But in the boxing-ring, I found myself, I was on stage. I could excel, instead of being a bloody little nuisance and people would applaud, cheer, clap. Not a dummy any more. I missed that. But when any of my young boxers — poor kids, a lot of them in trouble, like I'd been — were hauled up before the Juvenile court, I went down in my club blazer to tell the panel I'd sort them out. I'd been where they were, so I knew what problems they faced. I knew how to draw them out of that slum mentality a lot earlier than I had managed. I could see the difference it made in them, the pride, when they pulled on the club strip, knowing they were part of the club, part of the team, boxing and behaving so as not to let any of the others down.

And I found a new buzz: watching the kids I'd trained go into the ring to fight. The top guys in the club and the new kids, it was the same for me. That was the vital thing about the club: they were all your boxers, St Pancras boys, and you supported them all alike, regardless of their standing. I ran with them, sparred with them, skipped with them. I never asked them to do anything I wasn't glad to do alongside them. If they won, that was great. If anyone lost, I told the guys who'd won to make a fuss of them, build their confidence back. With strong team spirit, everyone tries that bit harder, the best to excel, the slower ones to catch up, and no one feels left out, even when things aren't gelling for them. Everyone trained hard: the internationals and the three-round novices, and the trainer's job was to back them, support them all equally. It's not easy, especially when everyone naturally crowds round the stars but, at the same show, there might be a mum and dad watching their lad have his first fight . . . and he's one of tomorrow's fighters. There was no room for ego trips. In a group of boxers I was training, there'd always be stars and plodders. The parents of the stars would think I was a brilliant trainer; the plodder's people would think I was useless. You're only as good as your pupil. You can't give him what he hasn't got; all you can do is draw out what he has got and perfect it, if he's willing to work and learn.

On club evenings, I went home at nine o'clock to snatch a meal and then straight out to catch the 290 night bus down Camden Road. There was no doubt the nights were grinding me down. In 1953, Coronation year, after seven years' night work, the kids growing up and hardly a chance to see them except at weekends, the sleep I did get in the day always interrupted, I got rheumatic fever for the third time. They took me into UCH again. I was desperate. I had to get back to work. As soon as I could bear to put my foot to the ground, I discharged myself and went home. Joan told me I was mad, but we needed money, so there couldn't be any argument. I staggered out to catch the bus, and while I was waiting at the stop Dr Dean chanced by and gave me a hell of a wigging. I told him I had to get in to work, we were skint. He drove me straight back to UCH. It was the saving of me. I used to have terrible sore throats, so severe I couldn't breathe or talk, and nosebleeds. The consultant suggested taking my tonsils out. They removed my tonsils and I never suffered that illness again.

When I did come out, I talked things over with Joan and told her the night work was killing me and it wasn't doing her or the kids much good either. I said I'd try for a day job and went in to put the problem to Mr Mayer, who was a really kind gentleman and boss of both Wilkinsons and Medlocks. He asked if I'd consider going to Wilkinson's as second to their senior staff man, Arthur Vaughan, for the same money. I jumped at it. No more nights, and Arthur was a terrific guy: he taught me a lot. Five years older than me, he lived just down the road from us in Tufnell Park. He really took me under his wing and helped me with a mass of things, explaining, working problems out and thinking out what was best to do instead of just leaping in head first, which — being impulsive by nature — I tend to do. He educated me about money, too. 'Don't just think about today,' he used to say. 'Earn money and save it.' I opened a building society account, planning for the future, aiming for something further than one day's end.

One day he came in to work and said: 'Ever been abroad, George?'

'No, I never have.'

'If you fancy it, get saving, and we'll go, me and my missus, you and Joan and the kids. Near Rimini, Hotel de France, bang on the beach, 50 quid a week, all in.'

It was fantastic. Hot sun, lovely sandy beach; we had a great time.

I worked with Arthur at Wilkinson's for three years. My dream, though, was still to get my porter's badge, to change a flat rate £8 a week for whatever my muscle and drive could bring in. But when a porter retired his badge went to one of the established families. There was no way in. I'd see guys who'd hardly been in the market five minutes getting their badges. Arthur had no desire to be a porter. 'Hauling barrows is for mules,' he said.

I checked the TGWU rules. If we could get a minimum of 40 (if I remember) or 50 union members to agree to hold an emergency meeting that was official, any resolution passed would be binding. I did the lobbying and got the numbers, all hush-hush, and we called the meeting, in a hall in Lamb's Conduit Street. I told them: 'When the vote comes, keep your eyes to the front, don't look at the opposition.' I didn't want them intimidated.

News got round and the meeting was packed. The two committee men who presided called for order and the resolution was put. There was some discussion, as there had to be, and the chairman announced the vote: whether porters' badges should be given strictly on seniority of employment in Covent Garden. There was a terrific atmosphere. The established families wanted to keep their grip on the old closed shop and if they won this they'd have plenty of time to organise themselves a second time round. My heart was beating that fast. All the guys I'd talked to had told me: 'I'm with you, George, you can depend on me.' But support has a way of evaporating under the bright lights of a hall, with officials sitting at a table and the opposition ranged round the place in numbers.

The vote came: those in favour? A sea of hands. Everyone had stuck. Those against: no more than a scattering. We'd won, badges could be earned. A lot of the old families hated me for that. But three months later I got my porter's badge and started with the firm next to Wilkinson's, Victor Torf's. Their governor, Stan Phillips, was one of the best salesmen in the market; and the more a firm sold, the more work a porter got.

It was a great moment when I stepped between the shafts of the barrow for the first time, hooked the trace-rope round my middle, monkey's fist knot through the eye, and hauled off my first load. It was a flat-backed barrow with two wheels, standing legs and long handles. The trace-rope helped in the pulling and the balance. I used to haul 14 hundredweight plus. It wasn't long before I got a reputation for being fast — and the nickname 'Greedy Bastard'. I had GB painted on my barrow . . . Good Boy. We relied on tips, and if buyers knew you were dependable, they'd ask for you especially. Soft fruit, for instance, needed quick shifting as it was in the days before fridges. If anyone needed a load done first he'd say: 'Get George for this lot.'

The system was: buyers left orders with the salesmen at all the firms they visited and by six o'clock, when the porters started, every firm would have lists of orders to be taken to various points in the market, where the lorries were waiting to drive the stuff away. Earlham Street and Neal Street was known as Darky's, after a cart-minder who worked there for years. The cart-minder patrolled the stands where the lorries were parked to see that nothing slipped off the back of the vans while they were waiting for the remainder of their load. At Christmas time, for instance, a bag of Brazil nuts could go — 30 quids worth.

On every item on your barrow you earned porterage — threepence per hundredweight sack of potatoes or a big case of oranges, twopence per 28-lb sack, a penny per tray of tomatoes etc. It was all recorded on tickets from a salesman's book covering a sale; these went to the cashier who took money from the buyer. Then the ticket went back to the foreman who gave them to the porter. He got them signed by the customer when he delivered the stuff. Every ticket was totted up in the cashier's office on Thursday, and on Friday you were paid. From six o'clock every morning, the race was on. Load the barrow, take the strain, get it rolling and go.

Bow Street was a long uphill drag and a lot of the porters stopped halfway for a breather, but I kept going. Easier than stopping and starting again. From Jubilee Hall to Darky's all the runs were a steepish climb and often the place was so overcrowded you had to weave in and out, shouting, 'Coming through!' The smooth pavements were faster, but if the way was blocked up James Street, I'd bump the barrow off the kerb onto the road, dig the balls of my feet into the cobbles like a sprinter and sweat up the slope, pulling my 14 cwt of goods. I went for broke. If someone was holding up the traffic and there were four or five barrows waiting, it was the first one to spot the gap who got through. Sometimes it was amazing that anyone could get through, the place was so crammed with lorries, horses and carts, buyers milling about.

When the barrow was really laden it was a job to shift, so old Billy Neal the foreman used to give us a push. He was in charge of loading the barrows, giving out the tickets: 'this to Darky's ... this to Long Acre ...'. He was about 60 when I knew him, very tough and wiry, tremendously strong, feared no one, wouldn't be bullied and a great sense of fair play. He'd put his shoulder to the back of the barrow to help you get rolling. 'Come on, George, dig your toes in,' he'd urge. And we'd grunt into motion up James Street. Halfway up, where Floral Street crosses, are two pubs on the corners, Nag's Head on the right, White Lion on the left, and as we gathered speed up the slope, Billy would peel off the back of the barrow straight into the pub for a tot of whisky — he'd buy a bottle at the beginning of the week, and it was his fuel, it kept him going. Ran in, downed the glass and out again. He had bronchitis; the whisky gave him a kick-start.

As lorries took over the market gradually began to seize up, with massive juggernauts and artics longhauling from the continent, arriving in Covent Garden and getting stuck because they couldn't turn the corners. You had to heave your barrow up on the pavement, go down one-way streets the wrong way, anything to keep moving, non-stop. Time meant money. All weathers, rain, snow, sleet, soaked to the skin, numb with cold, your fingers stiff on the handles of the shafts: 'Coming through! Coming through!'

There was a trick we played on new porters in winter. Down towards the Strand, outside a hotel we called the 'News of the World', the dossers used to string up a length of rope every night over the heating ducts set into the pavement which blew hot air from the kitchens. They'd hook their arms over the rope and hang from their armpits to sleep in the warm air, six or seven of them in a row, like corpses hung out to dry. We'd send the new blokes down there in the dark . . . waltzing round the corner and they'd come face to face with a washing-line of stiffs.

In May or June of 1957, not long after I became a porter, we went on strike against a new scheme to unify labour in the market. Pitching gangs and staff men were all to be rated as porters. Previously, porters had been the only trade to earn money above their basic retainer, now everybody in the market was to share porterage from now on, regardless. We were out for five weeks and the confrontation got nastier and nastier and, to our disgust, the union went to an industrial tribunal and the strike ended. We had lost; we had to go back to work and accept the new work practices. From now on everyone was a porter and no matter how much you loaded your barrow and how fast you pulled it, the porterage went into the general kitty. The most humiliating trick of all was that they were going to install time clocks. We didn't need the kind of school-teacher control, shoving us on to a common-or-garden workers' ant-hill. I felt let down so I tore up my shop steward's card and went back to work none too willingly.

Things gradually got back to normal, as they do, and life went on. That was until 1961 when a cruel blow struck. I was over the fields, running back to the Pond, and saw Joan. She never came over to the fields but she was waiting by the entrance, looking very grave. I asked what was wrong. She started to cry and said: 'It's your mother. She's been killed.'

I suppose my immediate thought was that Howes had murdered her, but no, she'd been knocked down: it came out at the inquest. She had been walking home from the Old Street works with a friend and as they were crossing the road she saw a young kid on a motor-scooter racing towards them. She yelled: 'Watch out!' and pulled her friend out of the way. The scooter swerved but too late — it collided with her, knocked her into the air, threw her over backwards, her head crashed on to the pavement and split open. She was killed instantly, only just over 50 years old. Died doing somebody a favour, which was typical of her.

I went to the mortuary to identify her body, and it felt like the worst thing that had ever happened. She lay there on the slab, her head battered and caved in and smothered in blood. I managed to hold on to myself for that, but just before she was put into the ground I broke down, went to pieces a bit. She was a sweet woman, none sweeter, who had never done anybody any harm in her life, who had done her best for us kids, been widowed and had to cope on her own and then been treated like rubbish by our stepfather. It made me bitterly sad — she'd never had very much out of life and for it to end like this ... And where was Howes? In Brighton on holiday at the races for a week while she worked to support him.

When he arrived back and I gave him the news of her death, he just said, 'Oh', without any emotion and went back to where they lived and ransacked the place, took every bit of my mother's things that he could sell, jewellery that would have gone to my sister, the lot.

My last words to him were: 'I'll let you come to the funeral, and I'll pay for that, but if ever you see me again, cross over.'

After the fight with him, I had seen less and less of my mother, especially after they moved from Camden Town to Pitfield Street, down near the city. We never fell out exactly, but I found it difficult to accept that she had taken Howes back after what he had done to her. I could have made more of an effort to go round, to try and be closer to her, and of course I regretted it when she died. That swept over me at the graveside, thinking how badly I had failed her by not seeing as much of her as I could, even if that was only because of Howes.

I talked it over, years later, with a priest, and he told me such feelings were natural; that however often I had seen her I would still believe that I could have done more, that in a weird way it was as if I felt responsible for her death. He assured me that I would have felt guilty about her no matter what. It's a bitter loss and grief is a bitter emotion. She was a wonderful mother; the sacrifices she made ... what more can I say? I owe her more than I could ever repay.

Every summer at Covent Garden we had the market sports day for charity. Freddie Mills, world light-heavyweight champion 1948–50, opened it one year. The whole place was packed. Pubs bulging. Money collectors going round rattling their tins. Porters racing round the square with 20 or more baskets on their heads. There was a barrow race with half a ton of potatoes, a race with a sack of potatoes on your shoulder, tug o' war. And the winner was awarded a small prize — bunch of flowers, basket of fruit. The governors put up a prize, too.

It was a happy place to work, in spite of the pressure. On Friday lunchtime, when we got our wages, most of the week's work done, everybody was in a happy mood and the buskers came round. It was a sort of daytime party.

Whenever the work was on, though, the pressure was relentless. One time I nipped into the café for a cup of tea and a sandwich, which you were allowed to do every two hours, and parked the barrow outside. It wasn't unknown for other porters to borrow a barrow for five minutes to do a quick job, for example, on the way back from a nut turn [carrying a tower of light trays, like mushrooms, on your head]. When I came out of the café, my barrow had gone. There would be hell to pay if I went back to the firm without a barrow. Then I saw one of the other porters offloading 15 crates of oranges from my barrow. I was so livid, I ran over and flung the whole lot off, lifted the barrow and tipped it over. He came back at me: 'Come on, lay off, I thought I'd get it back in time, keep your hair on.' But I was that fired up I'd lost my temper completely and it ended in a fight. Stupid, but in a market there's a strict pecking order; if you're soft, you'll get swept aside, land up empty-handed. You have to be fair, but hard enough so that nobody mucks you around. If things did boil up and there had to be a settlement, you went down to Brewery Yard, ten o'clock in the morning, for a 'straightener'; there might be 200 guys to watch. Fair fight — fists only — and shake hands at the end.

I went round the market recently and, out of curiosity, scribbled down a few of the old rules, orders and byelaws of Covent Garden Market, 1924, which you can see painted on the board opposite St Paul's church.

> XVI No person shall shell Peas or Beans or trim Vegetables, shake Nuts, peel Walnuts or Soft Fruit in, or over any of the footpaths in the said Market or fight or create any riot or disturbance or use indecent or obscene language or hawk, carry about or cry an article whatever for sale in or stick up any Bill of Placard on any part of the said Market.
> Penalty: Ten Shillings
> XVII No person shall sleep or lie down on any Stand, Footpath or Gangway in the said Market or on the said Terrace or Steps leading thereto.
> Penalty: Five Shillings
> XIX Every person who shall be detected in purloining any Fruit, Flowers, Vegetables, Roots or other things in the said Market or in wilfully cutting, breaking or injuring any Sack, Bushel or other package belonging to any other person shall forfeit and pay the sum of Forty Shillings.

The friendship and brotherhood of Covent Garden was very strong. There were lazy blokes — 'laying back in the shafts' as we said of one pony in a pair who let the other one do all the work. But it was a true union brotherhood and, if you were prepared to graft, you took home good wages. For the first time in our married life Joan and I had some leeway. Putting some money by meant we could give the kids extras and we could go on holidays. We were happy, even comfortable. Until one Saturday night in November 1962.

Chapter Four

On Trial: The Old Bailey, 1963

Saturday, 24 November 1962. We were in bed, fast asleep. We were woken by a big crash; a muffled noise of intruders in the flat. Voices in the passageway, getting louder. We thought: 'Burglars'. Footsteps stopping outside the bedroom door. Then the door was flung open and the lights went on as three men in raincoats burst into the room.

One of them barked: 'Are you George Francis?'

'Yes, I am. What's going on?'

'You'll find out. We've got a warrant to search this place.' He waved a piece of paper.

'Get to it,' he said, and the others set off through the other rooms in the flat, ransacked the cupboards and drawers. They searched the place from top to bottom, inside out. A whole hour of it, rummaging through our stuff. The main guy even rummaged through my clothes, including a pair of trousers hanging on the back of the door. He pulled out a wad of money — £231 in notes. He smirked. 'Get your clothes on, you're coming down to the station.'

I can't describe the shattering effect of them bursting into our home while we were in bed asleep; the bewilderment, disbelief and fear that paralysed Joan and me. She was beside herself. The kids were huddled in the doorway, looking scared and baffled. They watched as I walked between two plainclothes detectives to our front door, the front door they'd pushed in, and along the open balcony, down the stairs and into the waiting police car. It was unreal.

Even as we drove away, I'd looked up and seen Joan haring along the balcony. She'd raced round to my brother Billy's place — a mile or so away up Dartmouth Park Hill — to tell him what had happened. I kept thinking: this is a nightmare. It's a dreadful mistake.

At Paddington Green station, I was taken into the interview room and left for quarter of an hour with a stony-faced PC standing in the corner.

Then two of the detectives who'd barged into the flat came in and started questioning me.

Where had I been on the evening of 17 November between 6 and 8 p.m.? Where had the money in my pocket come from? I told them it was savings, my savings from wages.

So it went on, the same questions over and over again.

Then: what did I know about a grey Ford Thames van? Did I know anything about a lock-up garage in Highgate?

A sort of memory stirred, but I didn't say anything.

The interrogation went on and on, the same questions over and over again until I was dizzy with it. I began to think I was crazy. I didn't know what they were talking about. Two hours, three hours, I don't know, I lost track. finally the two men left. After a while, sitting there on my tod, the third detective came in, asked if I'd like a cup of tea and was altogether friendlier. He didn't ply me with questions, he just chatted, said he knew how I must feel. At first I thought he was only buttering me up, softening me to put me off my guard, but I really think he believed there had been a mistake and they'd got the wrong guy. He'd been friendly to the kids and Joan.

Eventually, I was charged with stealing and being in possession of a stolen van.

They took me outside to a car compound and showed me a small, grey Ford Thames van.

'Do you recognise this vehicle?'

'I've never seen it in my life.'

'Look at the number plate.'

The number was 7302 MX.

'The van's a ringer,' one of them said. 'It's got false plates.'

'I don't know anything about false plates.'

'False plates you collected.'

Suddenly the penny dropped; I felt sick. The whole thing was a ghastly mistake, but I could see where it had been made, partly . . .

Three or so weeks earlier I had had to take a couple of days off work with a swollen ankle, twisted while I was training. I went back towards the end of the week and worked Saturday morning, 10 November.

I got to work, picked up my *Boxing News* — I always got it from Mitch who had a newspaper stand near Medlock's. He started work at 4.30 a.m., a chirpy, happy-go-lucky bloke, full of beans. He did a paper round as well as running the stand — never stopped singing. We used to call him our dawn chorus. His wife said that during the war, when he was in the navy, he missed his train back one time and the ship sailed without him and went down. He'd never stopped singing since.

About 10.30 a.m. I called in at the coffee stall for some breakfast before getting off home. A couple of blokes came up, I recognised them: they'd bought tickets for a few of my boxing shows, good seats, good customers. I didn't know their names. We chatted about boxing. They praised my fighters highly, seemed decent enough guys. They asked me if I'd give them a lift up Gower Street on my way home, I said sure. We finished our coffee and I went and fetched the van and we set off. Near the Euston Road, one of them asked if we could stop off and collect something from a firm just round the corner — Hill's Patents.

We got to the place and the guy sitting in the back of the van leaned over and said something to his mate in the front who turned to me and asked if I'd slip up and collect a pair of number plates, for a Mr Brown, prepaid.

Up a staircase, into a store with a customer counter. The bloke serving went off, searched along a storage rack and came back with two number plates — both with the number 7302 MX. Back to the van and we went our merry way, up through Kentish Town, right along Leighton Road to Leith House in Brecknock Road. Halfway along I saw one of my boxers, Alan Cherry, walking past. I slowed down and gave him a shout. 'How you doing?' he called back, and I drove on. At the end of the road, quite near home, the guy in the passenger seat said: 'I tell you what, George, you wouldn't mind giving us a lift to Highgate, would you?'

'No, of course not, only you should have said earlier, we've come a roundabout way.'

I parked the van outside 103–07 Highgate North Hill and they got out and asked me if I minded waiting. I was in no rush and I was quite happy to get stuck into the latest *Boxing News*. They were gone about 20 minutes, came back all smiles and thank-yous, they asked me if I could drop them at a tube station on the way home, which I did.

I sat in Paddington Green all day, another night, and on Monday morning I was taken to the Magistrates' Court. Joan and Billy were there. The charges against me were stealing and receiving and being in possession of a van. I was allowed bail — the police could keep you in custody for only 72 hours anyway before arresting you in those days, and I hadn't been arrested, only charged. I was ordered to appear in an identity parade at Paddington Green police station the following week, on Tuesday, 27 November.

I didn't know what an identity parade was. The magistrate explained.

The day of the ID parade, I put on a favourite shirt — bright red — told Joan I wouldn't be long, that this would clear me, the mistake would come out. I left the flat, drove my van across to Paddington Green, parked outside, went in and reported to the front desk. One of the duty men took me along to a big room where about a dozen blokes were standing in a line; plus a number of uniformed police, including the detectives who had grilled me, and they told me to join the line. After a bit of a wait, several people were led into the room. One by one they were ushered slowly along the line, looking at each of us standing there. Then a man came in, walked down the line, stopped in front of me and stared me in the face. Suddenly, he leaned forward and poked me with his finger; I was dumbstruck. He went out, one of the detectives came over and asked if I wanted to change positions in the line because I'd been identified. I saw no reason to — I'd done nothing wrong.

Another man came into the room. He walked down the line, stopped by me and walked out. He whispered something to the detective, walked back and stood in front of me, staring at my chest. I tried to catch his eye, but he wouldn't look up. After a long hesitation, he stabbed me with his finger and walked away. Sweat ran down my sides. The detective stared at me, nodded and smiled broadly. There was a buzz of talk round the room. I was marched off to a room and charged with the theft and possession of a grey Ford Thames van and for robbery with violence on three occasions, in August, September and November 1962. All the police in the room were aglow, chuffed and full of it: they'd got their man.

The bizarre thing is that although I was upset, I still wasn't really worried. I thought the whole thing was so ridiculous that the chances of them proving anything against me were nil.

The only person I could think of who might know what to do was Monty Barnes. I gave them his name and address, after which they escorted me down to the station cells where I spent the night. Next morning, I was taken to a small court where I was remanded in custody. From there into a Black Maria to Brixton prison.

As the screw took me to my cell, I said: 'I'm innocent, I haven't done anything.'

He said: 'That's what they all say, everyone who comes in here.'

The cell door clanged shut behind me. Silence broken by muffled noises from behind the thick brick walls and solid iron doors. A stale, unwashed, mouldy smell — damp blankets, the reek of urine from where the slops bucket stood in the corner — the fug made worse by the sickly heat of painted lead central-heating pipes along the wall of the cell. There was no escaping that horrible prison smell. Even when I got out and scrubbed myself from head to foot and changed clothes, the stink of foul air, body odour and grubby bedding filled my nostrils.

We had an hour's exercise each day, tramping round in pairs, in circles in the prison yard. There were some real hard-boiled criminals in there, you didn't know who you'd be talking to and I didn't want: 'Oh, you're in the boxing game, are you?', and the banging on about this fighter and that fighter. I wanted distraction, not reminders of what I might be losing for good, all for no reason.

Joan came to visit me every day and the first time she brought Monty Barnes: I never needed his advice more.

He told me a positive ID gave the police a very strong case and I had to have the best barrister money can buy. It would cost an arm and a leg, but being innocent was no defence if the prosecution won the verdict. He said: 'Bill Hemming's your man. If he can't get you out of this, no one can.'

Bill Hemming, a police sergeant's son, had started working life as an ordinary PC, got promotion to the Flying Squad then, in 1944, aged 31, decided to become a barrister and was called to the Bar five years later — the first policeman ever to be called. His experience as a detective made him unique among barristers. He knew police methods and was brilliant at rooting out details which other lawyers overlooked. The snobbery of the other barristers made life hard for him; they referred to him as 'only a policeman'. Incidentally, John Mortimer based Rumpole partly on Bill Hemming.

Monty went off to see if he could secure the man and the following day his solicitor arrived to interview me.

Maggie Laville, a judge's daughter, hadn't actually qualified as a solicitor — she always said she was far too lazy to bother about doing the exams — but she had a great reputation. She was clever, meticulous, full of energy, a real little terrier. She'd worked with Bill Hemming from his early cases. She knew exactly what he needed to build up a case and worked flat out to get it.

The first thing she said was: 'What on earth possessed you to wear a red shirt to the ID?' I told her I hadn't thought anything of it. But I must have stood out like a tomato in a bowl of gooseberries. Truth is, I felt the police had linked me with those false number plates and they wanted a conviction.

Maggie explained the procedure. There was no police bail in those days so I could expect to be in custody for some time, until my application for bail could be accepted. Then I'd have to appear in court every seven days for renewal of the detaining order.

I stayed in Brixton till 6 December. It was miserable. I was so used to working in the open air, training across the fields, going to the Pond, working with my boxers in the gym, so being cooped up for 23 hours in 24 was grim. They were soul-destroying hours those spent lying on a narrow bed in the cramped four-by-nine-foot cell. If you slept during the day, you couldn't sleep at night and lying awake in the hours of darkness, with a 40-watt bulb burning overhead, is sheer frustration.

One time, travelling in the prison van, I was nearly sick: a drunk had been in before me and peed and vomited over the floor, the stench was dreadful. I said to the screw through the grille; 'I'm sorry, but it stinks in here, I can't stand it, I'm going to throw up.' He turned and sneered at me: 'Stink, does it? Have some of this, then,' and he sprayed a can of air-freshener right in my face.

The psychologist in Wormwood Scrubs, all those years before, had once given me a piece of paper on which was written:

Even in times of poverty, sorrow, pain or frustration, life remains a gift to be cherished and celebrated. Appreciate this and you see a way forward when all seems hopeless.

I kept it for years till it was worn through and eventually lost. I sat there in Brixton and I looked at those words. I thought: 'Well, that's what I have to do, even if I don't believe it any more.' And I'm not sure that I did believe it. Nothing seemed real any more. Then Joan would come and visit me and for a while it all seemed back to rights; until I realised she was going off home and I couldn't go with her. I could hardly bear to ask how the kids were because I missed them, I missed them all so badly.

Even after I was bailed on 6 December I still had to go to court every week while the prosecution prepared their case. Finally, on 19 December, the court fixed criminal proceedings for 3 January, when the prosecution would parade their witnesses against me and the magistrates would decide if there was a case to answer. Shortly before the committal, Maggie Laville took me to see Bill Hemming.

He was an impressive figure, about six feet tall, broad shouldered, burly, darkish hair slicked down with Brylcreem, frank grey eyes that looked straight into yours. One of those people you have to meet only once, never to forget. I took to him instantly. A man you could trust. We shook hands, he squared up to me and said: 'I am going to make one demand of you at the outset and I want you to accept it honestly. Whatever you say, I will defend you — that's my duty as a barrister; we work on the taxi-rank principle: next in line gets the fare, but I have to have your assurance that you will never lie to me. If you do, about any detail, however seemingly trivial, our whole case is jeopardised, the defence goes to pieces, do you understand?'

I replied: 'I'm not going to lie, I've got nothing to lie about.'

He told me: 'I must warn you that the prosecution will do everything in their power to prove that you did. For instance, the matter of the life savings . . . that won't do.'

The money the police found in my trouser pocket that Saturday night hadn't been savings as I had told them at first. I owned up in the Magistrates' Court that Monday. My brother Billy, who had a greengrocery stall in Inverness Street market, had given me the money, part of his takings, in the Buck's Head that evening, I'd gone into a funk when the police quizzed me, like a scared kid who's done nothing wrong and tells the grown-ups what he thinks they want to hear.

'It was a mistake.'

'We can't have any mistakes. Robbery with violence is a serious charge.

It's also pretty unusual. Not very popular with criminals, you may be surprised to know. So the police want this one, they want it badly. You've been picked out by two people in an ID parade.'

At the committal, a cold, wintry Thursday, third day of the new year 1963, I appeared alongside a man I had seen at the ID parade. There were three charges:

Firstly, on Tuesday, 1 August, at 10 a.m., Hildebrand Jeweller's in Marylebone High Street had been robbed by a gang of men who drove away in a Jaguar car, number plate 6061 MM. A false plate bought a week earlier by a man calling himself Mr Brown of New North Road, Islington, from Hill's Patents. I had been identified as the man standing by the Jaguar. Another witness said he heard one of the robbers saying: 'Don't hit him with that, George, you'll kill him.'

Secondly, on Thursday, 20 September, at 10 a.m., Mr Van der Linden of Noor Foods, Welwyn, was robbed of a £2,055 payroll as he returned from the bank in a van with his wages clerk. The gang drove a yellow Triumph Herald — abandoned after the robbery — and a maroon and grey Zephyr, number 321 XEV. False plates bought by a Mr Jackson of 28 Bride Street, Islington, on 27 August from Hill's Patents. I was identified as one of the gang, wearing a white coat, who had hit Mr Van den Linden with a piece of timber after trying to smash their van windscreen with the same piece of wood. The other guy was also identified as taking part in this raid.

Thirdly, on Saturday, 17 November, at 7.10 p.m., there had been a raid on Murray Bros., Butchers, of Church Street, Paddington, by robbers masked with silk stockings, carrying crowbars, driving a Zephyr — later found abandoned — with the number 557 RPK and a grey Ford Thames van, number 7302 MX. The Zephyr had been stolen as 773 LLK that same day; the van as 599 EXR on 31 October or 1 November. The plates 7302 MX had been ordered by a Mr Brown of 22 Bride Street, Islington, and picked up by me the following day.

The man behind the counter at Hill's, Brian Allen, had become suspicious about the addresses in Bride Street given by the Mr Jackson who ordered the 321 XEV plates. He knew the area had been badly bomb damaged in the war and told his boss who informed the police. The two numbers given in the street no longer existed. The police already had the same car registration number, given to them in a statement by a witness of the Welwyn robbery. The police traced the number, found it was false and checked with Hill's and when another set of plates was ordered by a guy purporting to live in Bride Street, the police were ready waiting as I drove up that Saturday morning. They followed my van to the lock-up garages in Highgate and later searched them.

In garage 11, rented to a Mr Watson of Royal College Street, with the account requested to be sent to 28 Bridge Street, they found a grey Ford Thames van, number 7302 MX; the motor used the following week in the Paddington job. They also found a Zephyr wheel similar in colour to the car used in the same robbery, the correct number plates of the van, and a rent book for a lock-up garage in Camden Road. On a second visit to the Highgate garage, two days after taking me in, they found it empty.

At the garage in Camden Road they found a Jaguar car with 6061 MM number plates, a security wrist strap, similar to one lost in the Welwyn hold-up, a cosh, cloth cap, two brown smocks or boilersuits (from the Paddington job) and various items belonging to the owner of the stolen van.

Bill Hemming stressed: 'George, you must understand that even if you're innocent, a case can go either way. There is a strong case against you, especially on the third robbery; two separate IDs; a lot of evidence, some of it circumstantial, maybe, but — above all — we have to secure your alibis, and that's where Maggie comes in. She'll go through everything with you, every minute of every hour when those robberies were committed. I'll sift through what she gives me and add what I can. It's going to be a slog for you, but better that than go ill-prepared into the witness-box. And as I've told you: no dodgy witnesses. The alibis have to be cast-iron. One single falsehood and the prosecution will tear us to bits; one flicker of doubt and the whole case collapses.'

So it began. I traipsed back and forth to Maggie's office. She asked me where I was, what I was doing and when, who saw me, who else was there, their names and addresses, over and over again, the same question; where were you at . . .? It's a lot harder to remember for certain than you may think. Some of the people I asked to testify for me refused: the fruiterer I bought a hand of bananas from on the way home on Saturday 17 November, and a typical response was from the guy who saw me and waved from the balcony of Leith House as Joan and I walked over from the car: 'I'd like to help, George, really, but not in court, it's not fair to ask me. I know I saw you and I think I know what time it was, but I'm not absolutely sure. What if they turn me over?'

Bill said he could have subpoenaed them, but there was no point; we needed solid testimony not witnesses who might crack and get confused when the prosecuting counsel got to work on them.

Charlie Dear, a mate of mine at Covent Garden, went to the timekeeper and asked for the entries covering the morning of the Welwyn robbery. The entries either side of the date were there, that date had gone. The bloke in charge of the time clock never liked me, because I was the shop steward and always fought a hard fight for the union, and he went red as a beetroot when I asked where the record had disappeared to. I'm not saying the police got there first, but it was a terrible blow to me.

Bill Hemming asked me to drive him round to the lock-up garages in

Highgate so he could see for himself; he took some photographs.

Needless to say I had to give up work and this put the family under a considerable strain, as if there wasn't enough anxiety already. When the date of the trial was set for the beginning of March, it came as almost a relief. At least we'd get a decision.

The Old Bailey warder led me up the steps into the dock; a single chair for me to sit in. To my left, in two rows on benches, sat the jury. To my right, the seats for Bill Hemming and Rodney Bax, and directly in front of me was the high bench where the judge, John Maude, sat.

I know what it's like to be in a boxing-ring, a lonely, lonely place. That dock felt worse. Here I was helpless, totally dependent on someone else, impotent, my hands tied. There were occasions I felt like a dummy again, the tongue-tied kid who couldn't control himself; except that now I had to concentrate all my energies on maintaining my calm. Bill had impressed on me the need to hold myself in, to rein back my frustration. He knew I was a talker so he told me: 'Yes and No, George. The more you say the more ammunition you give them to attack your defence.'

In boxing parlance: keep your gloves up close together, no chinks.

Rodney Bax called his first witness.

BAX: Mr Hildebrand, when did you arrive to open your shop in Marylebone High Street?

HILDEBRAND: About 10 a.m.

BAX: What did you observe in the street outside?

HILDEBRAND: I saw men washing a car.

BAX: What did you do when you entered your shop?

HILDEBRAND: I opened the safe. Three men came into the shop, one of them carried a bucket and a scrim and asked me if he could clean my car. Before I could answer, they attacked me, pushed me into the back office. I heard one say: 'Don't hit him with that, George, you'll kill him.'

BAX: What was 'that'?

HILDEBRAND: A piece of timber.

BAX: Did the man referred to as George hit you?

HILDEBRAND: No. He waved it at me.

BAX: He threatened to hit you?

HILDEBRAND: It felt like that, yes.

'Don't hit him with that, George.' Very convenient, I thought. Why didn't he add surname, address and telephone number to make absolutely sure? Bill said it wasn't worth pursuing — it was almost certainly a police verbal and better to leave the jury to make up their own minds than push them, which would give the impression of giving the point more weight of importance than it merited. More witnesses.

BAX: Mr Lewis, according to your statement, you were in Marylebone High Street, in your shop, at around 9 a.m?
LEWIS: Yes. I saw two men cleaning a car. One of them had a bucket. I spoke to them. I asked them if they'd clean my car.
BAX: What did they say?
LEWIS: One of them, the tallest, said: 'Your car doesn't want cleaning.'
BAX: Do you see that man in court today?
LEWIS: Yes. It was the accused.

* * *

BAX: Miss A. What did you see?
MISS A: About 10.45 I looked over to Hildebrand's across the street. I saw possibly two men in a Jaguar car outside the shop, then two men walking out of the shop. They got into the car and drove off along the street.
BAX: Did you take the number?
MISS A: It was 6061 MM.
BAX: I refer to exhibit three, photograph of the false number plate with the number just given by the witness.

Bill cross-examined her.
HEMMING: Miss A, you say you saw two men in a Jaguar outside the shop and then two different men emerging from the shop?
MISS A: Yes.
HEMMING: So your account and that of Mr Hildebrand are not cinematographic?
MISS A: I'm sorry, I don't know what that means.
HEMMING: They don't exactly agree.
MISS A: No, I suppose not.

Bill Hemming then called John Flynn, my sister Dolly's son, an RAF corporal at Uxbridge.
HEMMING: You saw your uncle on 21 August, the day of the first robbery, in the morning?
FLYNN: Yes.
HEMMING: But you knew of no charges against him till November, so at that stage you didn't know whether the robbery had taken place in the morning or the evening?
FLYNN: No.
Bax pitched in.
BAX: Something of a coincidence that you happened to be on home leave on the morning of 21 August — convenient for an alibi?
FLYNN: It happens to be true.

BAX: You also say in your statement: 'George was asked to go to an ID parade and he didn't know what it was.' Did that surprise you, the fact that your uncle didn't know what an ID parade was?
FLYNN: I suppose so.
BAX: Do you know what an ID parade is?
FLYNN: Certainly. But I'm in the RAF police, you'd expect me to know.
JUDGE: I'm not sure I know what point you're trying to make, Mr Bax. Whether or not the accused did or did not know what an ID parade was, he attended it, after all.
BAX: Yes, my lord.

My alibi for that morning of the first robbery was questioned from another angle. I had gone to the doctor with a bad back later that afternoon. I did miss some work with it and it was still niggling me when I went back to the same doctor on 27 August. Bax asked him his medical opinion on the severity of my bad back.

DOCTOR: I thought he was making rather a fuss about nothing.
BAX: Did you refer him to hospital?
DOCTOR: Yes, I did, in the end, but I had the idea he was just trying to secure an excuse for not going into work.

Bill Hemming gave him a fairly rough ride. He was only a young guy, a bit too full of himself, wanting to make an impression and the police were obviously puffing him up. He was their witness, ever so eager to please.

The prosecution moved on to the second robbery at Welwyn. The Van der Linden factory accountant described what had happened.
ACCOUNTANT: I left the firm's premises in a mini van driven by Mr Brewster at 9.50 a.m. on 20 September. We collected £2,055 plus a few shillings from the bank and put it in a metal case. I didn't use the wrist strap. It was an oversight.
On the way back, a yellow Triumph Herald car drove slantwise across our van and forced it onto the wrong side of the road. Mr Brewster braked hard and tried to reverse, but there was another car drawn up behind, a maroon Zephyr. A man in a white coat got out of the Triumph and ran towards us waving a big piece of wood. He smashed our windscreen three times but it didn't break. Mr Brewster tried to drive off but the yellow car suddenly reversed, mounted the pavement and banged into us. I got out of the car and tried to run away to the rear of our van. A man confronted me. I said, 'What do you want?' Then I got hit on the head from behind and dropped the bag with the money in it. I tried to tackle one man in a white coat but he retreated from me and motioned to another man

behind me. I turned round, saw the bag and picked it up.

Then the accused, George Francis, hit me on the hand with a piece of wood. I dropped the case and sat on it. They hit me seven times, one blow broke my glasses. I know who hit me, that man in the dock and the other man who appeared at the committal proceedings. I cannot say who the others were. They all had nylon stockings over their heads.

The judge stepped in.

JUDGE: You say that all these men who attacked you wore nylon stockings?
ACCOUNTANT: They did.
JUDGE: And yet you recognised Mr Francis, the prisoner, even though he wore a nylon stocking over his face?
ACCOUNTANT: I'd recognise you with a nylon stocking over your face.
JUDGE: I see. I think we must pour cold water on the evidence of this witness.

My alibi for the Welwyn job depended partly on a guy called Stevens who was doing some decorating for us in the flat. He arrived at about nine-thirty in the morning; I hadn't got home from the market yet, but Joan was in. I got back early afternoon, three o'clock or so, and went to bed. Stevens finished his wallpapering by around 5 p.m. and I believe I got up for a cup of tea. When Bax cross-examined me, I told him I'd never been to Welwyn in my life.

BAX: You used to work for a firm called Roberts, I believe? Loading timber onto barges?
FRANCIS: Yes.
BAX: But Roberts has its headquarters in Welwyn.
FRANCIS: I only worked for them in the depot at Broxbourne.

The other prosecution witnesses gave slightly differing accounts of the Welwyn raid. One woman said she couldn't remember seeing any masked faces at all. But it was the stupid remark made by the accountant about recognising a face masked with a stocking that threw the case sideways and that was more or less the end of the Welwyn charge.

Then they turned to the Paddington job of 17 November 1962.

BAX: Did you know the name of the man who asked you to take him to the garage in Highgate?
FRANCIS: No.
BAX: But you recognised him?
FRANCIS: By sight, yes.

BAX: You say he offered you £5.

FRANCIS: Yes, he gave me £5.

BAX: A rather expensive car hire. I mean that it would have been cheaper to take a taxi, wouldn't it?

FRANCIS: I suppose so.

BAX: And was there anything wrong with him, was he limping, for instance, that made it difficult for him to collect the car plates himself?

FRANCIS: No.

The judge intervened.

JUDGE: Mr Francis, you portray yourself as a helpful man, a man who will do people a favour, why did you not take the false plates into the lock-up garage yourself, having been so kind as to collect them from upstairs at Hill's?

FRANCIS: They didn't suggest it, and I was very keen to have a look at *Boxing News*, it's our weekly bible. I'd bought it the night before but hadn't had a chance to look at it.

Bax continued with his questions and I sat down feeling wrung out, bled white. It was always the same.

Bill cross-examined one of the policemen who had followed my van to the lock-ups.

HEMMING: You say that you observed my client entering the lock-up garage number 11 at 103—07 North Hill, Highgate, from the road.

DETECTIVE: Yes.

HEMMING: And garage number 11 is in the near left-hand corner, at seven o'clock, as it were?

DETECTIVE: Roughly, yes.

HEMMING: And from the corner of the driveway of the road, you observed my client in the garage area leave his van, walk into garage number 11 with the plates and emerge without them?

DETECTIVE: Yes.

HEMMING: I would like to show the jury a series of photographs, if it please my lord, taken from various angles in North Hill, Highgate, of the view into the interior of the garage area in question.

The photographs proved that wherever the police had stood, there was no way they could possibly have seen me get out of my van and go into the garage; the van itself simply was not visible from the road.

The lady from the estate office which rented out the garages said the man who paid the rent on them wasn't in court. A woman from Hill's said I was not the Mr Jones who had ordered the plates. The Mr Jones she remembered had pimples on his face.

The link between me and the garage was getting thinner, but it was only a tiny part of the charge against me. I had yet to establish an alibi for the time of the robbery a week later. There was some disagreement about the timings. George Watts, Joan's brother, said I arrived at his house to collect Joan at five-thirty but that usually I came earlier, nearer five which was when the football results started on the radio.

The judge asked me how long it would take me to drive from Leith House to Harrow Road, where Hildebrand's, the Paddington job, was. I told him about 20 minutes, which I had checked at Bill Hemming's suggestion. As Bill pointed out, if all the timings were half an hour out — beginning with when I arrived at the Watts' house — then as far as the police and the prosecution were concerned there was time for me to have got to and from Hildebrand's and be at the pub to meet Billy; especially as one of the pub witnesses mentioned a time of seven-forty in his statement — was I there then or not? The pub landlord, another Chandler brother, wouldn't testify: his licence was his livelihood and he couldn't risk losing it. If he came out against the police that made it precarious.

As Bill told me: 'What happened usually isn't at issue. The fact is, you are asking the court to believe that this Saturday you were half an hour later than usual. Why? That half an hour late makes the rest of the testimony look fabricated.'

Joan went into the witness-box.
HEMMING: Did your husband say anything about the money found in the flat coming from Billy?
JOAN: I can't remember. Billy often asked him to look after the stock money.
HEMMING: How much did it tend to be?
JOAN: Anything up to £200.
HEMMING: So the £231 found in your husband's pocket by the police wasn't an exceptional amount of cash to have in the house?
JOAN: No.

Bax's turn. He quizzed her about the diary she kept — she never wrote much in it: the kids being ill, a win at bingo, that sort of thing. Even quite humdrum stuff, like visiting her mother's, going to the cemetery to visit my mother's grave. Unfortunately, there were no entries between 14 and 25 November. Bax pressed her on that, but what was there to explain? Then he asked about me coming to collect her.
JOAN: We had a cup of tea about five-forty My brother, George, was checking the football results, with the radio. My husband came in to collect me and get the scores.
BAX: Before your brother had taken the results? During? After?
JOAN: I can't recollect.

Doubt can work both ways: if the jury isn't sure, they can decide you're telling the truth because knowing all the times exactly looks suspicious. But, whenever Rodney Bax stood up, put one foot on the bench and started grilling the witnesses, my heart sank. It all sounded so convincing. And he had an annoying habit of standing in front of his seat with one foot up, while he flicked the queue of his wig. That used to grate on my nerves. It gave him such a cruel air, such a look of calculating arrogance.

BAX: About the money the police found in the possession of your husband when they came to your home on Saturday evening, 17 November, you say you knew nothing of any money being given to your husband until he appeared in the Magistrates' Court on the following Monday?

JOAN: That's right.

BAX: In that court, your husband's brother, William, said that he had given a sum of money to your husband the previous Saturday night.

JOAN: Yes.

BAX: And you said that you had given him some money also.

JOAN: Yes, but not then.

BAX: When?

JOAN: In September, £300 to put away for me in my savings.

JUDGE: Mrs Francis's nest-egg, if I recall.

BAX: Thank you, your honour.

BAX: What did you know of any robbery?

JOAN: Nothing.

BAX: Didn't you make a statement to the effect that you had been to see Billy about the robbery?

JOAN: I went to see Billy straight after the police took George away. They'd said something about George committing a robbery between 6 and 6.30 p.m. and Billy said he couldn't have done, George was with him. I said he'd been with me.

BAX: You couldn't agree on the times.

JOAN: It was only half an hour.

BAX: That will be all for the moment. Thank you, Mrs Francis.

A bit later he came back to the money the police had found in the flat.

JOAN: George did tell me he'd earned a couple of bob on a job that morning. He seemed annoyed it had taken him rather longer than he expected.

BAX: A 'couple of bob'. Could you be more precise?

JOAN: Five pounds. It's only an expression.

When Bax asked me about our savings book, the judge stepped in.

JUDGE: How is it that the police did not find this savings account book, Mr

Francis, although they searched your flat pretty thoroughly?

FRANCIS: I keep it hidden. Only Joan and I know where it's kept.

JUDGE: May I suggest that you bring it into court so that we can examine it?

Next day they read out all the entries which showed I'd been putting money by regularly — exactly what Arthur Vaughan had encouraged me to do when I first started in the market.

Nonetheless, the police impounded the £231 they had found in my trousers pocket and didn't return it till after the trial. Bax quizzed my brother Billy about it.

BAX: In your statement to the police at Paddington Green station you said nothing about giving any money to your brother, the accused. Why not?

BILLY: They didn't ask me.

BAX: Did you give your brother that £231?

BILLY: Yes. I always do. I reckon it's safer with George.

BAX: You didn't agree with him during a visit to the police station to say this to provide an alibi?

BILLY: I wasn't allowed to see him.

BAX: Why should your brother change his mind about the origin of the money?

BILLY: Because he didn't want to involve me, I suppose.

BAX: But you are involved.

BILLY: That doesn't make us guilty, does it?

JUDGE: Please confine yourself to answering questions put to you by counsel, Mr Francis.

BAX: Mr Francis, in your first statement you said that you went to a pub for a drink that night about five-thirty. You played cards with Mason and Chandler and that your brother George arrived at about six and left again between six-thirty and six-thirty-five. Other testimony, taken afterwards, states that your brother came in nearer six-thirty. Which is correct?

BILLY: I told the police, I wasn't sure.

BAX: After you had made your statement?

BILLY: Yes.

BAX: I put it to you that you went to the pub in order to give your brother an alibi.

BILLY: No, I didn't. I always go, to see the people I see every week.

BAX: And you went to see those same people — Mason, the Chandlers and so on — after your brother was arrested to tell them what time it was important to provide him an alibi for?

BILLY: No, I didn't. I just said tell the truth.

It was all true, yet the way Rodney Bax was hammering at it, it all sounded very thin. Other witnesses climbed into the box and gave their version of the same events. The more versions I heard, the harder it was to believe we were all talking about the same evening. And when Bax was grilling me about the time I'd been in the pub, the judge chipped in.

JUDGE: Mr Francis, one thing puzzles me: you say that you are a TT.

FRANCIS: A what, sir?

JUDGE: You don't know what TT stands for?

FRANCIS: No, sir.

JUDGE: Teetotal. You don't drink.

FRANCIS: No, I never have.

JUDGE: And yet you went into the pub to meet your brother and to have a drink?

FRANCIS: Lemonade. It's what I've always drunk when I've been to a pub, which I do rarely.

And after that day's hearing, one of the Bailey warders said: 'You made a mistake with old Maude there, saying you were TT. He's in the beer business, married to one of the Guinness heiresses.' I said: 'Thanks for cheering me up.'

Rosie Carruthers was a friend of Joan's family for years and she always came to visit us at Leith House on Saturday night. She came on the tenth, when I collected the false plates, on the seventeenth when the Paddington robbery was committed and on the twenty-fourth when they arrested me.

BAX: What was Mr Francis doing?

CARRUTHERS: Eating his tea. He had haddock and eggs and I said, 'That's a coincidence, I've just given my husband haddock and eggs for his tea.'

JUDGE: Haddock and eggs. Very nutritious, I imagine.

CARRUTHERS: It's my husband's favourite.

BAX: Was Mr Francis watching television while he was eating his tea?

HEMMING: My learned friend is leading the witness.

BAX: What else was Mr Francis doing when you arrived on Saturday the seventeenth?

CARRUTHERS: Watching *Bonanza* on the television.

I grew to hate the sound of *Bonanza*. Bax kept on and on and on at me about *Bonanza*.

BAX: What do you remember of that particular episode?

FRANCIS: I came in near the end of it, but the kids filled me in on the bits I'd missed.

BAX: And what do you remember of the part you did see?

FRANCIS: The last quarter of an hour, 20 minutes.

BAX: How come you remember that programme in such detail?

FRANCIS: Only because you're asking me and I knew I had to try to remember everything in as much detail as I could.

BAX: What was to stop you learning up on that particular programme, to provide yourself with an alibi?

FRANCIS: Nothing at all, except that I didn't.

BAX: And what of the previous week's episode? The ensuing week's episode? Do you remember them in as close and exact detail?

FRANCIS: No, because I don't have to.

He made me go through it all: cowboys riding the range, who shot who, who said what, where, when and how. Who won? All to prove I'd been where I said I was. I felt a complete idiot.

One day Bill Hemming dropped a bombshell: 'George,' he said, 'I'd like your children to go into the witness-box.'

I could hardly believe my ears. 'No way,' I said. 'No way.'

'Listen, George, I understand your feelings, believe me, and you must know I wouldn't ask you to do anything I didn't think was crucial to the case. I really believe the kids will not only be first-rate witnesses, I believe they'll stand up to Bax a lot better than you imagine.'

In the end I agreed. There was Joan to convince, of course, but we had both got to the stage where it seemed so horribly possible that I wouldn't be acquitted and the nightmare of that injustice was more than we could bear. Every morning we caught the bus to Holborn Viaduct and went for a cup of tea in a little café near the Bailey, about nine-thirty, to be dead on time for the court. We'd sit there till it was time to walk the hundred yards along the road to the Bailey. Joan was a pillar of strength and support, you couldn't have a better second in such a ghastly fight as we were going through. And she'd hold my hand and say: 'You'll be okay. We'll be all right. It'll come out.' But there were times, when the day before had gone badly, when even she would say: 'How can they convict you of something you never did? You were with me.'

At the time the children appeared in the witness-box, Billy was coming up for 17, Mary was nearly 16 and Danny was 13. One by one they were called to give evidence. Bax grilled them in turn about 17 November. Billy maintained that I had gone round to the Watts around five-thirty; that for me to go at five wasn't usual. The missing half hour again. He stood in the witness-box as cool as you like, answering the questions. At one point Bax nearly lost his rag.

BAX: Mr Francis, you keep giving me the same answer, almost parrot fashion. Why?

BILLY: Because you're asking me the same question only in different ways.

Mary, like a lot of girls her age, kept a diary. But some entries were put in after the date, some before the date, some on the date.

BAX: Miss Francis, this entry, 'Larry phoned'. Is that a significant entry?

MARY: Larry's my boyfriend.

BAX: I see. And you recorded his phone call.

MARY: What's wrong with that?

BAX: Nothing, nothing at all.

JUDGE: Is this getting us anywhere, Mr Bax?

BAX: I hope so, my lord. Another entry here, Miss Francis, for Saturday, 17 November, seems to have been written in blacker pencil than the other entries. If I may read it to you: 'Daddy in bed'. Why is it in blacker pencil than the other entries? Was it made after the date?

MARY: No. I just use different pencils, that's all. Whichever one I find.

There were times when Bax was needling at them, Mary in particular, when I could feel my temper rising. I sat in the dock, my fists clenched, sweat rolling down my neck, my heart beating that fast I might have been sprinting up Kite Hill, as this barrister seemed to be calling my kids liars. I had a lump in my throat, tears in my eyes. I wanted to shout out: 'Leave them alone.' I wanted to leap over and scrag him, tell him to lay off, they were only kids; what right did he have to accuse them of not telling the truth? More than once Bill Hemming caught my eye and shook his head, hardly so you'd notice, but an icy stare to remind me: 'Leave me to do the job, George, however bad you feel in the dock, try and stay calm. You mustn't do or say anything while you're in court. The judge is looking at you. The jury see everything. You have to impress on them that you have nothing to fear, that you're innocent whatever the prosecution says or seems to say. And that goes for the witnesses, too.'

It was very hard to stick to. Then came Danny, 13 years old.

DANNY: That Saturday was the same as most Saturdays. I think Dad went later that day, but it did not strike me as wrong.

BAX: How much later?

DANNY: Not much. Just a bit later. He usually gets back for *Bonanza* and he missed some of it. That's all.

BAX: Is it unusual for your father to miss *Bonanza*?

DANNY: Well, he likes it. We all watch it.

BAX: That's not what I asked. Is it unusual for him to miss it?

DANNY: Quite unusual.

BAX: And did you tell him what had happened?

DANNY: No. [Murmur round the court.]

BAX: I see.

DANNY: Billy did.

The station sergeant at Paddington, Capel, was called to make a deposition.

Bill Hemming asked him one question. Someone, surely, would know if I had received a visit for example from my brother?

CAPEL: It's possible. But there is no record.

HEMMING: So you said. [He paused.] On the matter of the ID, if I may quote from your statement: 'The ID was fair, I'm bang to rights on that.' Aren't all ID parades fair, then?

CAPEL: I hope so.

HEMMING: Why stress that this one was, then? Were you feeling elated?

CAPEL: I was simply stating the obvious. That's all.

One of the policemen who took me in for questioning claimed that my hair was a different colour since the time of the last robbery in November. He insisted that it looked a lot blonder, I must have dyed it to disguise myself. The judge ordered me to be examined by a hair specialist in Bond Street that evening. I went to see him, he cut samples of my hair, probed the roots, analysed and fiddled about, a whole hour, in total silence. It was weird. The next day he appeared in court.

JUDGE: In your expert opinion, was Mr Francis's hair dyed blond?

SPECIALIST: If the hair had been dyed blond, it would have been dyed with hydrogen peroxide, a form of bleach. The hair grows at a rate of a centimetre per month, on average. Given the time span of four months since the last robbery and this trial, that would produce a length of a little less than two inches. Clearly, this man's hair has not been cut very recently. If he had used peroxide to lighten the hair colour, there would be evidence of the bleaching at the tips. There is none.

JUDGE: Thank you. You may step down. So much for the dyed hair theory, Mr Bax.

It was very clear that the police were determined to pin at least one charge, if they couldn't get all three against me. Every morning as we waited — the witnesses, jury and me — in the long corridor outside the courtroom, the police dragged in a cardboard box crammed full of the coshes, bits of timber etc which they'd found in the lock-up garages. It got to be almost a pantomime turn, so much so that one of the jurors said: 'Here comes the box.' One morning the guy carrying the box dropped it, on purpose, you could see. It made a terrific noise that echoed round the vaults of the building. The bits and pieces of lumber fell out and scattered over the tiled floor. It was too obvious, they were trying to shake my nerve, as if it needed any more shaking. Merely watching those coshes being handed round the jury and them glancing over at me, imagining me laying into Hildebrand, was enough to put my heart in my mouth. Needless to say, Bax had delved into the records and brought up my conviction for the fight with Speed; to prove I was a violent character.

There were times when I really thought I might just hop it, run away, go abroad, anywhere to escape, leave everyone, Joan, the kids, my family. I don't think for a minute I was ever close to doing it; only in the turmoil of your mind these crazy notions swim up and stare you in the face. It was all so terrifying. One nervous guy who'd been in the Buck's Head nevertheless agreed to go into the box on my behalf. He was very scared; he said just going to the Old Bailey brought him out in a rash. I really appreciated the fact that he was prepared to go through with what was obviously a horrible ordeal for him to help me. He gave his evidence, left the court, trembling from head to foot. Joan went up to thank him and he said: 'I was petrified and I've done nothing. I feel so sorry for George. I wouldn't go back in there for £1,000.'

Before the summing up, Rodney Bax came over to the dock and said to me: 'Mr Francis, this is nothing personal, but I am obliged to ask for you to be remanded in custody again while the judge sums up. There have been a number of people on trial who have absconded before the verdict lately. I'm sorry I have to do it, but the law requires it.'

'I'm not going to abscond, I've got nothing to hide,' I said.

'I'm sure, but it's my duty and I am sorry for it.'

I went back into Brixton and started to sweat.

On one journey in from Brixton, in the prison van, I'd been handcuffed to Gordon Goody, on trial for the Heathrow Airport robbery, the one they used to finance the Great Train Robbery later that year. We sat there listening to the screws beefing on about how hard, boring, crap-awful their life was. Goody turned to me and said: 'Listen to them, all they can talk about is the nick. That's all they've got in their lives, the nick, the bloody stinking nick.' Then he leaned over and smiled and said: 'You poor stupid bastards, ain't you got no life outside the nick? Can't you talk about anything else?'

Bill gave his final speech, Bax gave his and the judge started his summing up. I know from boxing matches how important the last round can be; that's what sticks in the referee's mind. His speech seemed fair; he even brought old Rosie Carruthers in — 'Nor must we forget the testimony of Mrs Haddock and Eggs.'

The jury retired. I went down to the cell below the court to wait the verdict. Four and a half hours. Joan's sister had given me a rosary. I prayed. I made all manner of pledges to the Almighty if he'd get me out of this hole. I faced 15 years in prison. I fished for any bit of comfort and found none. The jury came back and I was led up into the dock.

CLERK OF COURT: Members of the jury, have you considered your verdict on all three counts of armed robbery and the two lesser charges of stealing and being in possession of a van?
FOREMAN: We have.
CLERK: How do you find the prisoner?
FOREMAN: On the lesser charges, not guilty. On count one, not guilty. On count two, not guilty.

My arms were shaking. I was sick with nerves.

FOREMAN: On count three, the robbery in Paddington, we cannot agree.

I looked over at Bill. I couldn't believe it. His face showed no emotion. There was a long pause before the judge spoke.

JUDGE: The third charge of robbery with violence being not proven, I have no option but to order a retrial.

In those days the jury had to agree unanimously. How had they split? Eleven for and one against? One for and the rest against? I felt sick and hurt. To come so near and miss at the last. We'd have to go through it all again with the whole weight of the prosecution bearing down on that Saturday evening; and it would still be ten to 15 years if I was found guilty. Another £2,000 to find to pay for the retrial — multiply that by about 14 for today's value. My brother Billy steamed round the pubs in Camden Town and raised it in not much more than a week.

In the second trial, before a different judge, Bax informed the new jury that this was a retrial, something he wouldn't ordinarily have done. In any retrial, witnesses called from the first trial are bound by law to repeat the evidence they gave earlier. However, it soon transpired that the police had produced new evidence. It was brutally clear that having got hold of me they had no intention whatsoever of letting me go.

One of my witnesses had been Charlie Francis, no relation, a plumber who saw me going into Leith House on Saturday evening. He knew the time because he'd been doing a job down in Clapham and got back late. He wasn't exactly sure when they got home, but he knew he'd left the site just before six that evening. His apprentice, Robert Kendrick, would confirm the time.

Between the trial and the retrial, the police got to Kendrick and put the squeeze on him, and Kendrick went along with it. He said he might have got the time, even the day, wrong, after all, and made a statement to that effect, but he was never produced in court. Charlie Francis said he knew the day because they'd been installing a new hot-water tank; he had the dated invoices, signed and paid for. There was no refuting that. He presented the receipts.

Then the police sprang another surprise trap: in their fresh investigations, they had revised the timing of the robbery at Paddington — it was entirely possible that it hadn't happened as early as seven-ten but perhaps half an hour later.

Bill Hemming stood up. 'Is all this new evidence necessary? It is a little minnow you have here, a tiddler.'

The judge agreed. He said he thought the police were straining for a conviction. 'Really, you are acting as if this man were accused of murder.'

The last night in Brixton, before the verdict, I hardly slept. It was cold, March winds gusting round the roof eaves. When day finally broke, the skies were overcast and grey. I climbed up and stared out of the small window of the cell, down into the courtyard of the prison. I could see a line of prison vans and prisoners being led out on their way to different courts, different verdicts. Some would be back, others would go free. I had always thought that anyone who landed up in court, for whatever reason, would get their just deserts, guilty or not. Now, I couldn't help but wonder. I saw those guys way below me and knew that some of them must be in the same boat as I was.

The door opened, my turn to be handcuffed and led down the stairs to the open yard and into the van. Over the years I had been schooled to control my fear in the boxing-ring, but this terror was something different and I couldn't shake it off. I felt then, and I feel today, that I would rather go into a cage with an armed killer or a vicious animal to fight for my life than go into the dock at the Old Bailey. At least there is a danger you can confront, you can pit yourself against the creature that's trying to destroy you, you can do something. In the dock you are powerless, dependent. So many factors can weigh against you.

A second time I found myself in the cell below the court. I asked the warder: 'How do you think it will go?' He said: 'You can never tell with juries. I've worked here eight years and you can never tell.'

Time passed. The warder brought me a cup of tea. I couldn't drink it. I thought about those two guys who had fitted me up with this whole disaster.

One moment I was sweating, another moment cold shivers coursed down my spine. At last the door opened and the warder appeared: 'Time to go up, they've called you.' He led me along the corridor to the dock entrance; up the short flight of steps into the dock and, for the last time, I faced the court, the judge, the jury. The warder leaned over, squeezed my hand and whispered: 'Good luck, son.'

I didn't know which way to look. I darted a glance at Bill, but he was staring directly ahead, his face gaunt and expressionless. I didn't dare let my eyes stray over to where the jury sat.

'Court will be upstanding.'

I got to my feet and my knees were shaking so much they nearly buckled. I grabbed hold of the rail round the dock and hung on. The foreman of the jury stood and said, in a voice I will remember till the day I die: 'Not guilty.'

I just about collapsed. Talk about relief, it was fantastic, it was like nothing I have ever experienced before or since. It was over. I hardly heard the judge say: 'Prisoner at the bar, you are now free to leave.'

'Excuse me, sir,' I said. 'I know I can go but can you tell me if there is some way I can be compensated? I've had to use up all my savings. I've had to give up work. I've earned nothing for months. All my life savings have gone, just about.'

'I'm very sorry, Mr Francis, and I do appreciate what you say, truly. However, if the courts had to compensate every individual who was acquitted the whole system of law would collapse. I'm afraid the fact is that there was a case to answer. Your costs will be paid from central funds. As for compensation, I fear there is none.'

That was that, but it was of no consequence compared to the feeling I had when I walked down into the huge entrance foyer of the Old Bailey. There stood Bill and Maggie. Bill said to me: 'You look ten years younger than you did in the dock.' And then we were walking out into the fresh air. At the top of the steps down into the street, Bill turned to me: 'Remember,' he said, 'it's always best to be on the outside of this place looking in, rather than inside looking out.' And there was Joan, the kids, Monty and the others, and members of the jury waiting to shake my hand.

The police came round and gave me the £231. They weren't apologetic, but they'd cooled down. The hunt was over, for the time being. The police in Bow Street were always on the prowl for villainy of one sort or another, and there were some rotten apples in Covent Garden. A bit like the goons in the PoW camps, convinced there was always mischief afoot under their noses.

If any benefit did come out of the trial, it was the privilege of knowing Bill Hemming and Maggie Laville. They were true professionals; they left no stone unturned, no lead unexplored. But more, they carried me through the whole ghastly ordeal with such care and patience and strength. I couldn't have survived without them. They were terrific people, too. We clicked.

Maggie told me afterwards that they'd worked on scores of cases, but only in two were they both totally convinced that for their client to go to jail would have been a horrendous travesty of justice, and mine was one.

Bill is dead now, but Maggie still has the Larousse cookery book she bought with the nice big white crisp old £5 note I gave her a short while after I walked free.

'What's that for?' she said.

'For saving my life.'

Inevitably I'd lost my job at Torf's — I couldn't expect them to hold it for me — but the first Monday I went back to the market I struck lucky. There was a vacancy at Howgego's. I picked up where I left off. Howgego's started at 6 a.m. like everyone else, but they shifted their stuff so fast we were generally done by ten or 11 o'clock. It was gruelling — what we called 'out and home' — but it suited my style and it was great to be free so early for training over at the Heath or the gym. Not only training, either. There's a bench among the flowerbeds in Golder's Hill park where I spent a lot of hours reading and tuning up my education. That was my ideal: fresh air and sunshine, working or relaxing. I still go past that spot on my long walks across the fields; the lawns are carpeted with daffodils in spring, the best display for miles.

I was soon back in the groove at the Market but it wasn't as easy to shrug off the effects of the trial as I'd hoped. Bill advised me to keep a diary, just in case; writing down my alibis every day was a constant reminder of the nightmare. And where before I'd do anyone a favour, I rarely did so again. My mother died doing someone a favour. Those men who fitted me up had spoiled what I hope was a decent and open side of me.

I was loading crates of oranges one morning when a dick from Bow Street approached me to ask if I'd go in an ID parade, they'd pay me half a crown and see me all right. I didn't think for a second and said yes, then suddenly my gut clenched, my whole body went taut and I reared up. I told him I wouldn't go in an identity parade if they paid me all the money in the Bank of England and told him to get the hell out of my way. To say he was taken aback is putting it mildly.

Matters came to a head, though, when a plainclothes man took me into Bow Street for enquiries. He shoved me in a room, kept me waiting for ages, then came in and said: 'Where were you last Thursday at 11 o'clock in the morning?'

I couldn't believe it. Where were you at . . .? Except that I had written records of exactly where I'd been and when. I told him the same place I always was at that time on that day: adding up my tickets at the cashier's. He said they'd check. I told him, feel free. He took me to the cashier's, checked the records and asked several porters to vouch for me and told me I could go. I was furious.

'Oh, no,' I said. 'I'm coming back with you.' I marched upstairs at Bow Street and confronted the CID guys, sitting mob-handed behind a desk. 'How dare you pursue me. You have no right to haul me in on nothing better than having my name on file. It's a bloody liberty. In front of my boss and workmates. It's humiliating.' Then I stormed out. They'd had a crime on their patch and it bugged them like hell. They'd decided to give me a spin.

When I got back to the market, Joan phoned in a terrible state. Seven policemen had come to the flat with a search warrant and turned the place over. I went home, tried to reassure her and then I wrote to Scotland Yard, my MP and the Home Office, a really bitter protest about the way the police were harassing us and that was the last time they bothered us.

My mates at the Pond did a lovely thing. I arrived there one Sunday and they all crowded round, slapping me on the back, cheering, shaking my hand. It was a fantastic reception, but the surprise was to come. When I got back home, one of the men, 'Swiss' George, had been to give Joan an envelope full of money. The boys had had a whip round.

Chapter Five

The 'Who Wants Them?' Brigade

For most of my career I have been associated with black boxers. This may not seem unusual now, but in the early 1960s it was more or less unheard of. In those days, the last thing a trainer or manager would do if he wanted to make a professional go of his career would be to actually choose to train and manage black boxers, the 'who wants them?' brigade.

Black boxers had no fans. Black boxers couldn't get fights. Black boxers not born in the UK were debarred from contesting British titles, even if they had fought for Britain.

The passport tells the beginning of the story. Issued to Mr Basil Sylvester Sterling, then eight years old, four feet four inches tall, from King's House on the island of Jamaica, and signed Hugh Foot, Governor-in-Chief in and over the island and its dependencies. The standard promises are made:

Request and require in the Name of Her Majesty all those whom it may concern to allow the bearer to Pass Freely without let or hindrance, and to afford him [added in ink] every assistance and protection of which he may stand in need.

It was 3 December 1956. A few months later, Basil 'Bunny' Sterling arrived in England, a skinny little kid with a quizzical look as you can see in the old-style oval passport photo. Across the bottom of it, in purple ink, is the stamp which makes this a different passport. The holder of it might, in theory, be able to rely on 'every assistance and protection' like any other British citizen who held the navy-blue book given to them by Her Britannic Majesty. The one thing he couldn't expect was to be allowed to regard himself as a citizen. The stamp which stencils the lower part of the photo reads: Immigration Department.

Bunny's parents were already 'domiciled' — as the bureaucrats put it — in the United Kingdom. They'd been among the first families to come to Britain after the end of the Second World War, Commonwealth citizens

119

who'd done their bit in the fighting and who came to the mother country in search of work. They found work, menial work, mostly. Bunny lived with relatives in Jamaica, came to England and discovered boxing. But for talented young black immigrant boxers there was a big problem. They might think of putting themselves forward for championship fight, but because they were born outside the UK, even though in a Commonwealth country, no immigrant was eligible for a British professional title. That made any progress through the professional ranks virtually impossible.

The British Board of Boxing Control reasoned this way: it was okay for a man of non-British origins who had been born in the UK to box for the British titles, but if the sons of immigrants were allowed to box and win a title, the strong chances were that they'd go back to their original home — Jamaica, Canada, Australia, South Africa, wherever — and arranging any defence of the title would be a nightmare. The usual course would be a mandatory defence after six and 12 months. Voluntary defences were permitted as well, naturally. This ruling didn't apply to amateurs, but anyone with ambitions in boxing would be looking to the professional arena. Even more important, though, in the eyes of the board, was that the British titles were in their control and they wanted to keep them in their control. Fair enough, in principle, but the practice was very far from fair. To put it crudely, they argued that if a boxer not born in the UK, and therefore with no clear-cut loyalty to the UK, were to win a title, that title would be in danger of being smuggled out of the country.

Recently, a politician came up with the idea of what he called the 'cricket test', which just shows how little we've learnt about the kids of the second and third generation of immigrants who came to the UK after the war. Which side do you support in a Test match, he asks? Meaning, what about the children of West Indian parents, for example? Kids like Devon Malcolm, the England Test cricketer, I suppose. Or Linford Christie, Olympic, Commonwealth and former world champion. Or Frank Bruno? Frank Bruno was born in Britain, and being British is a matter of fierce pride with him, as deep as anybody's, probably deeper. Witness the T-shirt he sometimes wears:

> True Brit
> Born British
> Raised British
> &
> Proud to fight
> for
> Britain

What a lot of people didn't understand 30-odd years ago, and still don't understand, is that most of the black immigrants from Commonwealth countries who first came to Britain certainly didn't regard this country merely as a land of opportunity. They came to work. Their loyalty to Britain was, quite unjustly, questioned as a matter of course. Out of prejudice some people wrote off their good faith — accused them of wanting to take without giving anything back. What made them any less generous than the native inhabitants? They came and Britain welcomed them, after a fashion. The opportunity — to carve out a new life here — was offered, but it seemed to have an awful lot of terms and conditions attached which no immigrant could possibly meet. I was painfully aware of this in my own field. A great world champion like Randolph Turpin, born in Leamington Spa, top amateur who became a top pro could be claimed as British born; a potential champion like Bunny Sterling had no chance by the old rules.

I set out to try and change the restriction. It was just me. Common sense was beginning to shine through what was a very old Empire sort of attitude. The fact was that there had not been many immigrants to the UK up till the immediate post-war period. This goes some way to explaining the prejudice against black boxers which I'll come to later. In America, the blacks had been part of society, even if not a particularly free society (they were allowed to fight in the US Army but not in regiments with whites), for a century or more after the Civil War. They still weren't integrated in the southern States, nor were they given much tolerance or respect in the northern States, but they were free, in theory at least. Their young men had begun to turn to sport as a way of bettering their lifestyles, getting out of the ghetto, attaining some status which the colour of their skin would otherwise deny them. The hunger for respect drives the poor and disadvantaged hard; I know it myself. The blacks in America used their talent to break through the closed ranks of white society. Those talents were, in the early days, exclusively in the field of entertainment and sport. One of the great early American cycling champions was the black track sprinter, Major Taylor. In his day, 1901, sporting prowess was about the only way a black could hope to cross the racial barriers and for a long time it continued to be. Black entertainers were still lumped in together as 'nigger minstrels' required to perform the cakewalk and bogus antics, slave spirituals and clown about like poltroons to amuse white folk.

Gradually, though, black sportsmen began to emerge. Black baseball players made their mark. Black footballers, black athletes — remember the sensation that Jesse Owens caused at the 1936 Berlin Olympics, when Hitler went into a rage seeing a black beating the pure Aryan sprinters and long jumpers out of sight to take four gold medals? Black jazz musicians had been around a while, of course. And black boxers came to dominate American boxing, and therefore world boxing. Joe Louis, Jersey Joe Walcott, Ezzard Charles, Archie Moore . . . the list goes on. The black supremacy in the heavyweight division didn't go unchallenged: Rocky Marciano, Gene

Tunney, Jack Dempsey interrupted it, but the white champion — though not so much of a rarity as nowadays — was finding winning tougher and tougher.

It's hard, perhaps, to appreciate how recent it is that black boxers have made their mark in the British ring. Nowadays, you look around at the champions and so many of them are black, at every weight. In not much more than one generation they've come to the fore. But when Bunny Sterling arrived in the UK, black boxers were the rarity. There was a trainer/manager/promoter one-man band operating in the '50s and '60s, and a man who taught me a lot about the business, who did handle black boxers: Jack Burns. Probably the first to do so; but he did his own promoting so he could put his boxers into his shows. He sometimes had three shows on in a week — mostly at swimming-baths, which was the way then. During the winter, they'd board over one pool in the public baths and put on various sorts of shows, and Jack Burns would stage boxing contests; men would pay to come in from passing by off the street, on the off-chance more often than not.

I worked with Jack, off and on, the first year I became a pro manager. There was nothing he didn't know about boxing, as a sport and a business, and his experience was invaluable. One time he offered me a purse for a match and I said: 'Come on, Jack, I want more than that.'

He gave me a look, smiled and said: 'Yes. I got it. I taught you — now you're getting smart.'

That winter I fell ill with meningitis: racking head pain, it was agony. They took me into UCH and gave me a lumbar puncture to draw off the fluid from my spine. I didn't know at the time what a dodgy operation it was, they hadn't much experience of it then. They did tests, couldn't work out what had happened, took the samples to the School of Tropical Medicine and found I had a form of the disease connected with rats. I told them I had been handling a lot of apples, so maybe they had come from rat-infested barns. I've never eaten an unwashed apple since.

They put me in a separate cubicle at the near end of the ward, where they usually put people who haven't got long to live. I was pretty well out of it for nearly nine days, not knowing where I was, who I was, what was going on, and whenever I did wake up there was that blinding pain in my head. When I did eventually come to, I heard angelic voices singing. I looked down at my body and I was dressed in a long white robe; I looked up and saw white walls close round me. Then, through the window from my cubicle into the ward, I saw a group of women, cloaked in red. The pain in my head had gone. I stared at them, over the white covers of my bed, and thought: 'Angels! I've arrived. This is it: heaven!' Then I picked out the words: 'Not in that poor lowly stable, with the oxen standing by, we shall see him but in heaven . . .' It was Christmas Eve. The nurses had turned their capes inside-out and come round the wards carol singing. The white robe I had on was a theatre gown: apparently they'd been getting me ready for a second lumbar puncture. I didn't know whether to laugh or cry.

Next day the surgeon came into the ward to carve the Christmas turkey and he came and stood by my bed, looked down at me and waved his carving knife. 'You're lucky,' he said, 'today was going to be your day, but we changed our minds.'

They kept me in another ten days and I went back and took him a bottle of champagne with a note: 'To the best lumbar puncturer in the business.'

It took me a long time to recover. My head felt soft as a boiled egg. I had no confidence, hardly even to stand up, let alone walk. I did go back to work, but I was all over the place. The barrow felt completely out of my control as if it was going to fly out of my hands any minute and there was nothing I could do. It took me a long time to get fit again. Of course there were stories go around that the meningitis was a result of boxing — you getting any weakness in the head, the slightest untoward pain, and they'll say that.

One evening at the St Pancras club, the door opened after the session had started and a black boy walked into the gym. The room went quiet. He was the first black kid who'd ever showed his face in the place. The reception wasn't warm from the other lads. In fact it was distinctly cool. A couple of them started murmuring, saying things like 'We don't want any of you lot in here'. The usual unthinking garbage. But I beckoned him in and frosted out the hostility. Anybody wanted to box, I was there to help him box.

'What's your name, lad?' I said.

'Lennie Gibbs, mister.'

'Call me George. You wanna learn how to box?'

'Yes. Please.'

'All right. You've come to the right place.'

And that was that. I drew him in. He joined the club. I treated him with respect, as I treated all the kids, and won his respect. He turned out to be a great little fighter — our top guy. More than that, we got on very well together. I mean, it may seem a trivial example, but one time he was due to fight and badly wanted to go into the ring, but he had a boil on his leg. He came round to me and said: 'George, I don't care how much it hurts, but you've got to squeeze the pus out of this boil. I want to fight.' That took some trust.

I had always been drawn to black guys, somehow. Ever since being pals with Darkie Frank in the turning. And Paul Robeson. I saw him in *Sanders of the River* and I can't explain it easily, but I had a feeling about that man which went beyond admiring his marvellous bass voice — when he sang

I got goosepimples. But it was more than that: he made a tremendous impression on me; he became my idol and I had a secret longing that he'd have been my dad. However stupid it sounds, that's how I felt. There seemed to be such a warmth and understanding in the man. I guess it was just me reaching out for what I had missed in my own father. And it was the fact of him being black and therefore knowing what it was like to feel yourself pushed out, kicked out, treated with contempt. Robeson had a dignity and nobility about him that stood up against all the injustice and lack of respect and put him head and shoulders over everyone, his enemies particularly, in the most inspirational way. When he was being hounded by the anti-Communists — McCarthy and his crowd — I was bitterly upset. Here was a guy who happened to be black — but, so what? Who believed in equality for all, in justice for everybody before the law and called for a decent way of behaving towards the rest of the human race, whatever their colour, and what did he get? Abuse and harassment. But it didn't finish him off: he kept his faith, he kept his honour.

That's by way of some explanation to how I felt an affinity with Lennie when he came into the gym that day; it certainly made a huge difference to our relationship, as if I could sympathise with his situation in the England of that time, without him having to say a word. There wasn't so much prejudice in boxing; it was more out on the streets. Nevertheless, the prejudice was there and, of course, it caused problems for the black kids. In the early days, they were outsiders trying to break in and that's a lot how I felt about myself.

Lennie was destined to be my first pro fighter. And he did something which in no small way changed my life, the way these things happen, quite by chance. He got on well at the club and he wanted to share the good experience he was having with his friends. One night he brought a little pal with him, a gangly 15-year-old kid with a straight look and an air of poise, who lived round the block from him. That was one of the ways that the boxing clubs helped with social integration and I believe played an important part in breaking down the racial prejudice that existed. Those young boxers learnt how to treat each other with fairness and respect and that attitude spread outside the ring, into their homes, onto the streets. You couldn't be a club comrade with someone you were going to spit at and shout abuse at outside the club, on the grounds that he had black skin: it was too ridiculous. Anyway, Lennie turned up that night and introduced a new kid to the club: Bunny Sterling.

Bunny was a natural. A born athlete with a smooth grace of movement, reflexes as quick as a seagull in flight, innate strength and stamina, quick feet and a fast-thinking brain. He was not only a gem to teach and train, he was a lovely person right from the start. We clicked. The best of it was that because I had him from the beginning, as a novice, I could teach him good habits from day one. So often it happens that as a trainer you take over a new boxer who's got into bad ways and you're having to spend time undoing sloppy bits which have grown up with slack training elsewhere. Putting bad habits to rights is a near-impossible task and doubly time-consuming, as well as being a real bind. Within three years it was quite obvious that the amateurs wouldn't be able to contain Bunny's talents and ambition. He had found boxing and taken to it as smooth as silk. His natural flair had fired a determination to be more than just another talented boxer: he wanted to be the best. A modest, unassuming guy in one sense, he had a deep self-belief, too, and a very keen estimation of his own worth. I respected that: there's a big difference between mindless arrogance and calm self-esteem. Bunny knew he was good but he didn't jabber about it, he wanted to prove it, where it counted — in the ring. And by some kind of destiny, I can't help thinking it was that, right from the start, his professional career and mine began more or less at the same time.

I've already described Monty Barnes as the most inspirational man in my life, and so he was. He not only steered me towards a crucial decision — turning professional — he encouraged me to take what seemed like a huge step at the time. If I had known what lay in store to begin with I might never have gone pro. Hungry years. But I have never regretted a minute of them. The gratitude I owe Monty stems from knowing how badly I would have regretted not taking that decision to go it on my own.

One day after a training session at the St Pancras club, he called me to one side and said: 'George, you'll never get rich staying with the amateurs. I know you want to make money, who doesn't? Besides, you've gone as far as you can go on this side of the game. Go where you can get something back, some return for your work; further yourself, make something out of the training business. You obviously love it, you have a gift for it, you owe it to yourself to give it a go. You've got 60 lads here; it's probably the biggest club in England and that's largely because of you; they come here to be trained by you. So think about the pro game.'

Of course I had thought about the pro game, but never really very seriously. It was a huge step to take — a gamble; training guys whose ultimate ambition had to be a world title. Putting my training skills on the line, finding out just how good I really was. But Monty's confidence in me rubbed off. He had found me Bill Hemming; now, perhaps, he had found me another life-saver. In 1965 I applied for, and got, my professional trainer's licence. I remained the St Pancras trainer. In those days there were plenty of pro trainers training amateurs, for no extra money beyond what the clubs paid them, but in 1966 we heard the Amateur Boxing Association was going to bring out a new ruling to forbid any trainer with a pro licence from going up into an amateur boxer's corner. Now, one of the main points of looking after my boxers was as cornerman, and if I couldn't go into the corner I couldn't do my best for them. It would mean leaving the St Pancras club. The new rule would allow me to train before the fight but not help during the fight. It was a short-sighted idea, and amateurs would be the losers. I had no choice. I left St Pancras. It was impulsive, perhaps, and I don't regret it now, but at the time it was a hard choice and a major blow. It meant giving up a monthly pay cheque and a whole string of boxers to train — for what? One boxer and ten per cent of nothing very much. The one boxer was Lennie Gibbs who had gone professional with Terry Lawless and wanted me to train him. It didn't look at all promising but Monty encouraged me: 'If you don't try you'll never know, and if you don't go how can you try?' Well, it's easy to say yes, the hard bit is keeping on saying yes after the decision is made. I hated leaving, and the irony is that the new ruling was never adopted.

A while after, *Boxing News* reported that the St Pancras club had gone badly down, dwindling in numbers. Jim Burgess, the club secretary, gave the reason: 'We couldn't get a trainer of the calibre of George Francis, simple as that.' Although the club's decline saddened me, Jim's words made me very proud. And under the guidance of Ron Smith the club is thriving again. Meanwhile, back to the real world.

Lennie Gibbs was a great little fighter and we got on well together. He had a nice string of eight or nine fights with Terry Lawless, won eight and then went on ice. Because he'd won so many bouts, no one wanted to match him.

As it was getting harder for Terry Lawless to find Lennie fights, plus it was a long trip over to the gym in Canning Town, I asked Lawless if he'd release Lennie and let me take him on myself. He was co-operative and I applied for a manager's licence. First thing, I heard the Board wouldn't take kindly to the fact that I had been tried at the Old Bailey, acquitted or not. They thought of me as having form, and there was some delay because of that. Finally, though, I was called for interview by the Board and there sitting at the table with the rest of the licence committee was their legal adviser, Victor Lissack. I knew him well. His office was above Torf's warehouse on the corner of Floral Street and Bow Street, directly opposite the Magistrates' Court. I often used to find him somewhere to park his car, shift a lorry or a cart out of the way, when I worked for Torf's. And we'd exchange comments on the famous trials going on in the court across the street. So, an ally, I thought; until he leaned over the table and said to me: 'I think we know each other, Mr Francis, but the one thing that interests me is this: how do you think your financial situation is conducive to your being a professional boxing manager?' I was speechless. Fortunately, the Board overruled any objection he might have made or implied, and gave me the licence. The only one who asked any under-the-counter questions and I'd been doing him favours for years. But I was a pro manager, and I was about to sign my first champion.

Bunny was 17 and wanted to turn pro with me as his manager. I agreed at once. Because I'd trained him from the off, he was a very pure, skilled fighter. So, now I had two black boxers, I added Mick Oliver — a white heavyweight — and found myself with an empty fight card. No promoter wanted Lennie Gibbs, my most experienced guy, nobody had heard of Bunny, and Mick Oliver was the only man they'd place and how many tickets did I want? I told them I had three fighters. They told me to forget my black guys, only the white man would sell tickets ... possibly. And I should explain why that was.

In those days black fighters didn't draw any support. They were unknown. They didn't put bums on seats and because boxing is a business as well as a sport, promoters weren't interested in giving ring-space to boxers who, as they put it, brought only their bag [no supporters] with them when they came to fight. It wasn't prejudice against them being black; it was that they were unknown, outsiders, simple as that. You put on a show, you've got to make a profit otherwise you go out of business. No one supports outsiders. I found it offensive, but it was fact.

And even if black fighters did get taken up and put in a show, they tended to be overmatched — an easy win for the white guy and no rating for them. Getting into the ratings was crucial; if they weren't rated, the public got no chance to change their mind about them. They continued as outsiders, no-hopers in the opinion of most people. That was the way it worked. Match a white guy against a black guy: the white guy has plenty of support, so his manager sells armfuls of tickets; the black guy has no support: his manager sells none. The white guy makes a good move in the ring, the audience go berserk, roars of applause, cheering and encouragement. Not a murmur for the black guy. But with the crowd loud and strong behind him, the white guy catches the referee's eye, makes him believe he's carrying the fight, even if the black guy is really on top, even by a long, long way. I learnt all about the injustice of that with Bunny Sterling.

I worked very hard with promoters to place Lennie and Bunny and eventually got Bunny a fight on 13 December 1966, in Shoreditch Town Hall against Joe Devitt (who later became one of my trainers), someone I'd never have chosen, but it was a fight. The purse was £30 and my accounts book shows: stoppages — second, 10/-; bandages, 10/-; £29 to Bunny Sterling. And what I wrote, time and time again, in those early days at the bottom of the page: 'Nothing stopped by manager.' No travelling expenses; we went by bus. That was mostly the case in the early days. My guys were earning so little in the ring that I didn't like to charge them the normal percentage. (Usually a manager negotiates the deal with the promoter for a purse; then, after expenses, the boxer takes 75 per cent and the manager gets 25 per cent.) In fact, I was subsidising my stable with the money I earned as a porter. That didn't please Joan. She said to me: 'You give up good extras from St Pancras and now you're supporting these boxers from your Covent Garden wages. It doesn't make sense.' Nor did it, I suppose. They say: 'Show me a successful businessman I'll show you a ruthless bastard.' The fact is, I was still thinking as an amateur.

Bunny lost that first fight, which made him easy meat, so that loss brought him two more fights; which he also lost. Three fights, on bad decisions, but no one wanted the white guy to lose. One of the fights, against John Kramer, we were so blatantly robbed that Kramer's manager, Sam Burns, came up to me after the fight and whispered in my ear: 'I'm sorry, son, the referee must be pissed.' Whether he was or not, he gave up his licence some time later. Still, a loss is a loss and it can shake your confidence — especially on a wrong judgement — not so much in yourself or the fighter, but in the possibility of ever breaking through the system that's keeping you down. Like the fight with Ron Smith, an international southpaw in the North-west London divisional championships. Bunny fought brilliantly and lost over three rounds: a bad decision. As we were walking away from the ring, wondering what else we could possibly do to win — boxing like a dream and winding up in a nightmare — Mickey Duff saw us and called us over. I hardly had the patience to be civil. Mickey gave me a wry smile and said: 'Know why he lost, George?'

'He didn't lose — it was bad judging. Smith's an international and Bunny's a newcomer. The punters probably reckon an international like Smith has more experience than an unknown like Sterling.'

'No, no, George, you're wrong there,' and he reached down by his seat. The championships had been held in a hangar at the RAF base in Stanmore and in military style (if it moves salute it; if it doesn't whitewash it) they'd tarted up the place and someone had left a bucket of whitewash. Mickey sloshed the brush in the stuff and said: 'That's why he lost — he needs some of this; he's the wrong colour.'

His idea of a joke which Bunny found about as amusing as losing. But I know Mickey. He's a smart businessman and we couldn't quarrel with what he said: we had to look the facts in the face, sadly. We plugged on in the gym over the Butcher's Arms in York Way, where I had failed that singing audition years earlier.

Bobby Neal had a school of boxers there, a lot of fine fighters, so my three guys sparred with them and got a lot of experience and stimulation. Working at Howgego's meant I could be at the gym by three o'clock to open up, warm the gym, get things buzzing, train my guys and clear the place ready for when Bobby Neal's men arrived. We had free use of it for that very reason, and it was a great place for us.

ABOVE: A very young George Francis surrounded by relatives (l to r) Auntie Eileen, Uncle Lenny, Auntie Annie and his sister Dolly. This photo was taken at 11 Prebend Street, Camden Town, in 1931

TOP RIGHT: George with his wife Joan on holiday in Italy with their friend Arthur Vaughan

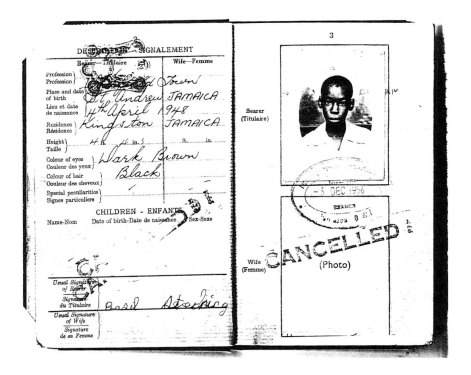

Within the passport:

DESCRIPTION — SIGNALEMENT

	Bearer—Titulaire	Wife—Femme
Profession / Profession		
Place and date of birth / Lieu et date de naissance	St Andrew JAMAICA 14th April 1948	
Residence / Résidence	Kingston JAMAICA	
Height / Taille	4 ft. 4 in. 5	ft. in.
Colour of eyes / Couleur des yeux	Dark Brown	
Colour of hair / Couleur des cheveux	Black	
Special peculiarities / Signes particuliers		

CHILDREN - ENFANTS

Name-Nom	Date of birth-Date de naissance	Sex-Sexe

Usual Signature of Bearer / Signature du Titulaire: Basil Sterling

Usual Signature of Wife / Signature de sa Femme:

3

Bearer (Titulaire)

- 3 DEC 1956

CANCELLED

Wife (Femme) (Photo)

OPPOSITE PAGE, TOP
Lawyer Bill Hemmings

LEFT: Members of the Francis family unloading timber from a barge on the canal

RIGHT: Porters working in Bow Street, Covent Garden

THIS PAGE, ABOVE: Bunny Sterling's passport – Bunny became the first immigrant to win the British middleweight title

RIGHT: George and Bunny celebrate after winning the European title

TOP LEFT: Boza-Edwards boxing in Lusaka, Zambia, with George in the corner

TOP RIGHT: George, John Conteh and friend after the fight against Jorge Amarda

ABOVE: John Conteh with his wife Veronica and Joan Francis, celebrating after his win against Chris Finnegan

LEFT: George at his baptism party in Mexico

George training Boza-Edwards for his title fight against Rafael 'Bazooka' Limón (LEFT), and lacing his gloves just before the fight (ABOVE) while boxing journalist Peter Batt looks on

George with Frank Bruno at a training camp in Tenerife

ABOVE: bandaging Bruno's hand at Highgate Pond
BELOW: with Frank during an early-morning training session in
Arizona, USA

George Francis, manager and trainer of boxers

Slowly the breakthrough started. I got Bunny a fight; he won it. Then eight more fights which he won, though there was one of them I didn't see because I was in hospital.

It had happened in winter. I loaded my first barrow of the day and set off into the pitch dark to run it round to the buyer's stand. As I steamed along Drury Lane, dodging past various carts and lorries parked up on one pavement, I saw a pair of headlights about 50 yards in front: a car driving straight for me. There was no way both of us were going to squeeze into the narrow gap, no way I could stop and go back and no way I had time to think of what was going to happen before it did and I woke up in a hospital bed. Relatively undamaged, by an amazing stroke of luck — shunted off the road by a tram, now a car, what next? I'd probably be safer in the ring.

Bunny was making strides now. For a while it had been touch and go whether he'd keep the determination and pride going in the face of what looked like stonewall opposition, but he had a keen will and it paid off. His next step ought to have been to fight for an area title, except that to qualify as a contender, you had to have been born in England, and Bunny was Jamaican. Now, that was ridiculous. For example, Lennie Gibbs had fought for England, but hadn't been born here — like Bunny he came from Jamaica. So, I put it to the Board of Control that if they could let a boxer fight for his adopted country, they ought to allow him to fight for national titles. They made a ruling which opened title contests to all registered boxers in England, and Bunny set his sights on the southern area title. I'd got him a job to help him out financially, in a metal-working shop, but they had him sweeping floors so he ditched that. His real ambition was to study law, that's what he was aiming for; but more of that later.

By this time my stable had expanded; Ray Brittle and Bernie Terrell had joined me. Ray Brittle didn't stay long in boxing. He had a carpet business which took more and more of his time until he had to choose and gave up the ring. Bernie Simmons, alias Terrell, came to me by accident. I had gone to an amateur show hoping to sign another boxer but he said he wouldn't sign with me unless I signed Bernie too. I wasn't that keen, but I agreed and the irony was that the other kid failed the pro medical, so I was landed with Bernie whom I hadn't wanted in the first place. I gave him the *nom de plume*, after another fighter called Bernie Terrell, because he was a fireman at the time and they weren't allowed a second source of income. The reason I wasn't so keen on him was that I'd watched him box and he had flown in for two rounds going like the clappers and then faded to nothing, a pushover. So I told him he'd have to improve his stamina if he wanted to get anywhere, and that meant early-morning runs across the fields. He was hopeless. He had less wind than a burst balloon, plodding along like a broken nag, no speed, no go, stopping for rests. But he kept at it and within a year he was the best runner in the stable. And he'd lost none of that two-round frenzy, either. A real banger: he could punch all right and, more significantly, he was a crowd-pleaser. People loved to see him in action.

Bernie and I drove to Shoreditch Town Hall for the area championship fight. It's a cramped place, more like a cockpit than a boxing hall; you can feel the crowd breathing down your neck all the way into the ring, even in the ring. It makes for a fantastic atmosphere, so long as you're not intimidated by it, and you get some very exciting fighting there. On the way there, I stopped to buy a paper and see what the commentator made of the prospects for the title fight. He forecast a walkover for the other fellow, Peter Craig, bound to win, he'd punch Bernie out of the ring. I slipped the paper into my pocket and got back in the van. Bernie says to me: 'You don't want to read it, do you?'

'Read what?'

'The fight prediction.'

'No, it's not that.'

He turned and looked at me. 'Listen, George, I've got faith in you and I'm going to win it for you. And me. All right?'

'Okay.' I drove on.

We got to Shoreditch and the place was seething. Packed out, and a lot of betting going on — not allowed but it went on. Bernie's opponent, Craig, was the red-hot favourite, that was obvious, but I knew one thing about him in our favour: he was having trouble making the weight (welter), he'd been drying himself out to get the pounds off, which always saps a boxer's strength. That didn't make him less of a puncher in the long run, but I knew our main chance was not to let him go the long run. Give Bernie the chance to hand him the old two-round frenzy, with a ten-round stamina to back it up.

In the dressing-room I told Bernie not to let Craig get into his stride. Normally you take a round or two to feel the other guy out, but this occasion called for a head-on attack. I said: 'Bernie, go out and jump him.'

And that's what he did. As soon as the bell went, he steamed out of his corner like a man possessed, walloped Craig all round the ring and KO'd him first round. He was fantastic; it worked a dream. Southern area champion. At the same time Bunny met John Kramer again, for the area title, and gave a hard-hitting demonstration of how unjust the earlier decision between them had been. Armistice Day 1968, appropriately enough. And what a thrill for me, that issue of *Boxing News* showing a picture of me with my first three area (southern) title-holders: Bunny Sterling (middleweight), Ray Brittle (light-heavyweight) and Bernie Terrell (welter). I'd read *Boxing News* for years. It's our almanac; gives the boxers' ratings, fight programmes, comments, everything to do with the pro game. I felt I was on my way at last. My first three champions.

Bernie Terrell eventually lost to the then British champion, Ralph Charles. But he did more than was ever expected of him; fought hard, above himself; living proof that you mustn't let anyone else impose limitations on you: it's what's inside you that counts. And a trainer's job is to release that inner talent, if it's there. Another memory of Bernie, this time at a show up north. Waiting for the preceding bout to end, Bernie was jogging on the steps leading into the arena, keeping warm, when one of the seconds in the ring corner, an old guy, keeled over. People rushed up and Bernie, who as a fireman had trained in first-aid, said: 'George, cut my gloves off, I don't think they know what they're doing.'

'You can't do that, you're due on,' I said.

Well, the old guy had died and there was nothing anybody could have done for him, went spark out, but on the way home Bernie was very quiet and subdued. I knew what was up and I felt sorry for him.

'I feel a bit choked, George,' he said. 'I might have been able to save him if I could have got the gloves off.'

Sadly, probably not, but you always blame yourself.

As area champion Bunny Sterling was now up for a crack at the national title. He beat four other boxers nominated alongside him by the British Board as the best five middleweights in the UK to fight eliminators, and won the right to challenge Les McAteer, the British and Commonwealth champion, for the title. But we stepped aside to allow Mark Rowe a crack first. Bunny was an excellent mover, nimble footwork, but McAteer was very tall and rangy, an unpredictable fighter, and I thought Rowe was a better bet for us: he was a solid puncher but no great mover; he marched forward and kept marching until he was stopped. He relied on his strength from start to finish. I was certain that Bunny's scientific approach and his natural skills and athletic ability would tie him in knots. And Rowe was popular; he could sell thousands of tickets. A victory over him would really put us on the map. He duly took the title from McAteer.

The Albert Hall, 8 September 1970. Bunny Sterling, the outsider, immigrant, black, no massive puncher but a brilliant technical boxer who used the whole ring — almost nothing in his act to be flashy, just to please the public. Mark Rowe, the title-holder, a toe-to-toe fighter, big puncher, odds-on favourite, the crowd's darling. If the struggle to achieve this particular bout had been tough, winning it was going to make the approach work look like a picnic. Except for one thing — whatever the crowd thought, whatever the pundits said — Bunny was a born champion. He knew it, I knew it, if no one else knew or would admit it. And this isn't nostalgia; we knew it then, too.

That sort of trust and confidence between boxer and trainer comes through long hours of training, the talks in between, the shared runs and walks, the total focus on winning which eliminates everything else from your mind — worries, fears, uncertainties. Before the fight there were exercises, drills, constant repetition of moves, combination punches, defence, attack. Once in the ring, the boxer's on his own, relying on instinct, reaction, and every scrap of skill, talent and training he's acquired, concentrated on the opponent; to master his fight, to snuff out anything he throws, to exert such pressure on him, by absorbing his attack and rattling his defence, to drive him onto his back foot. Once he is retreating, his balance is upset. He has subconsciously accepted that now he has to stop himself being beaten where before his aim was to beat.

Bunny was very calm. He had such an outstanding technique, a natural flair developed into comprehensive skill, that not even a heavy puncher like Rowe intimidated him. He knew he could stay out of trouble, he knew he could get close enough to hand out trouble. The bell went, the fight was on. The crowd were roaring for Rowe as I watched Bunny step into that noise and clamour like a surgeon in an operating theatre. He cut Rowe to pieces. Rowe hardly laid a glove on him. The crowd hated it, the clinical precision: duck, feint, lead on, swerve, sway and then one, two, three; hold off; lead on again, feint and one, two, three again. The referee stopped the fight in the fourth round because Rowe was so badly cut and held Bunny's arm up: British and Commonwealth title-holder. Sterling: a good name for a British champion, the first immigrant ever to win the title. Two new kids on the block, Sterling and Francis, and we'd done it. The crowd booed the place down; they didn't like the decision one bit, a black upstart, not even British, hammering their own boy. That was horrible for Bunny, just as he was breaking through into recognition. But you can't educate dumb ignorance and the fact is Bunny gave a demonstration of boxing skills that most of the punters couldn't have recognised in a coaching session. It was fantastic. If my pride in that attainment seems over the top, it's only because we'd had to overcome such odds. Everything that could have gone wrong seemed to have gone wrong — bad decisions, months without fights. I'd put most of my savings into the training work and got virtually nothing back. We'd had to scrape for fights, persuade the Boxing Board of Control to allow Sterling a title fight and now he was champion. As he climbed out of the ring, Bunny spotted Mickey Duff. That crude joke about his colour still rankled. He walked up and said: 'Well, I've knocked your ticket-seller over. And I remember the whitewash.' Duff wasn't being nasty, he was being realistic; I knew that, but it wasn't Bunny's style and that victory began to change things. No more whitewash.

Bunny had a great boxing brain, something that can't be put into a boxer. During the fight with Rowe he several times heard Rowe's corner shouting instructions — something I had told him to do and he got in ahead. Say they shouted to Rowe to try an uppercut, even as he bent his legs to deliver Bunny was in with his punch. It made me smile. The real boxing fraternity recognised his superior skill, and the Boxing Writers Club voted him Best Young Boxer of 1970.

Victory should be sweet, but verdicts in the boxing-ring — as in the criminal court — are rarely that simple. We maybe didn't expect instant acclaim for the new title-holder, but the mob shouting abuse made us feel as if Bunny had thieved the trophy out of the locked cabinet — barefaced robbery of what he couldn't possibly be entitled to own. That reaction riled him; not to mention the comments in the press that of course he couldn't do 15 rounds, that his win had been a fluke, a chancy punch out of the blue. It was the usual padding round a plain truth: that a first-rate fighter had beaten a workhorse in a dominating victory. Even Harry Carpenter, who has become such a close supporter of Frank Bruno and me, said at the time, dismissively, that Bunny was 'a kid from the small halls'. I didn't like it, but it was true, of course. It had to be accepted, but not ignored. No point in banging your head against a brick wall for the sake of it. You have to tread a path between not getting apathetic about the hard fact and not letting the hard fact get to you. However, not only did Rowe's fans boo us — and that was to be expected in some ways, unpleasant though it was — Bunny had stopped their man, the unknown had robbed their guy of a title he hadn't held for very long, they were upset and reacted badly. But that was nothing compared to the hate mail I got. 'Nigger lover, go home to Jamaica with him.' That was a complete shock. Rowe had nothing to do with any of that.

I honestly thought, in my naïve way, that once we had won the British title, life would be sweet, but it wasn't. I had assumed that a title was the great goal, the proof that Bunny, and therefore I, had to be taken seriously now, and that we would get fights. The pedigree of any title depends on the boxers who contest it. You know the old response, when someone brags he won a race. Who came second? I underestimated the obstinacy of the fans, the promoters, the whole boxing hierarchy. The truth is they still worked on the principle that when Bunny arrived for a fight he brought only his bag. I was determined to prove them wrong, but I had to take him across to the other side of the world to do it. And two months later we flew out to Melbourne, Australia, to challenge for the Commonwealth title held by Kahu Mahanga, a Maori. A hard man. The first international trip, November 1970.

One day in Covent Garden, a while before this, I'd finished work for the morning and taken my shirt off to sit out in the sun — never miss an opportunity to sunbathe, wherever it is; I'd sunbathe in the snow up a mountain if the sun was shining. I sat there, soaking up the heat, staring up at the sky. One of the buyers I knew came over and said: 'What are you gawping at?' I told him I was watching the planes go over. 'You gone soft in the head?' he asked. 'No,' I said, 'one day I'm going to be in one of them. One day I'm going to be travelling the world.' He nodded and said: 'Good luck, mate.' Twenty years or so later, when I was an established manager and trainer, I met that same buyer, I can't remember where, may have been a boxing show. Anyway, he came up to me and said: 'George! Remember me? You was the dreamer, right? You got there. I'm always reading about you, seeing you on TV. You got there!'

The plane to Australia was the first part of the dream come true. Arriving in Melbourne reawakened the nightmare. The immigration people took one look at Bunny and turned the heat on. They asked him how much money he had: very little. They snarled back that they didn't want vagrants coming into their country looking for handouts. They asked him where he'd been born. Ah, not a true British citizen. And what's this, British champion? Who are you trying to fool, mate? You know we have strict rules about immigration into this country? We don't want to immigrate, we're here to win the Commonwealth boxing title. So what? You just land in Australia, you expect the same treatment as anyone, you have to fulfil the same conditions. And so it went on, pretty objectionable stuff. They didn't actually call him a nigger to his face but they might just as well have done. We kept our cool for as long as we could, but I soon got the impression that they were enjoying baiting us — Bunny in particular — they were having a lot of nasty fun at our expense. My patience gave out and I rounded on them: 'Right, that's it. We've answered all your questions. Any more problems, we're going back home on the next flight, no fight, no nothing. But I warn you, I'll tell your press the whole rotten story and let's see what they make of it. We've come to fight your bloke and he's going to look more than a bit stupid stepping into an empty ring to defend his Commonwealth championship against the British and Empire title-holder who's gone home because he couldn't get through immigration answering poxy questions about how much cash he's got in his back pocket and why he's got such a deep suntan.'

In the end they backed off, but it was an hour and a half of very ugly interrogation, innuendo and worse, insults, snide and offensive remarks. If Bunny needed any stirring to get his dander up, they did a good job. He won the fight on 14 November, over 15 rounds. He was Commonwealth champion. As ever he relied on skill; he relished boxing and he boxed superbly. A whacking punch never really interested him as much as covering the ring, which he always did more than his opponent and with an ease and fluency that was a joy to watch, establishing his superiority so there could never be any doubt as to who properly deserved the verdict.

If that classic, meticulous technique in the ring won him few friends — by and large fans prefer blood and guts — Bunny's personality made him very popular outside the ring. People loved him. In Australia he was the only black guy for miles, which made him something of a wonder, but he had such an attractive personality that the locals warmed to him at once; he even convinced a lot of the betting fraternity, who had been sceptical, that he wasn't only champion but he was going to stay champion. They put money on him and, of course, he repaid them decent winnings.

I can't be sure, but it may be that Bunny, being black, wasn't what the Aussies thought of as a British champion. They love a sportsman, and he was certainly that. They like a good, hard, technically superb fight, and he delivered it. And he was so different from the whingeing Poms they were used to and loved to hate, that they warmed to him more than even his great charm and easy manner called for anyway. Maybe, too, they knew instinctively that the Brits hadn't given him an easy time, so they felt drawn to him. Whatever the reason, he was definitely a hit and a hitter. While we were in Sydney, one of the small bridges collapsed. The local Aussies took a particular delight in telling me: 'The Brits built that!'

The Aussie reaction was very heartwarming. It gave me a terrific boost. Ninety-five per cent of my stable of boxers were black and the struggle to break through with them had ground me down a bit. In fact, the television commentator Reg Gutteridge came up to me at one point and said: 'Hey, George, you've taken over from Jack Burns.' The generous reception Bunny and I received in Australia and later on Canada was a tremendous encouragement.

Even the local flies found him irresistible. We went out running the first morning and a whole black swarm of them landed on him, not a single one on me. We're running along, with the sea booming onto the beach, the sun blazing out of a blue sky and Bunny covered in flies. He was cursing and blinding, trying to bat them off, spitting and waving his arms about.

'George, why are they all on me?'

'They must like your taste, son,' I said, laughing.

Next day, I smothered him in repellent, togged him out with a hat and a net till he looked like a beekeeper and off we set. They still avoided me and what bits of him they could still get, they got.

We went back to Australia, Sydney this time, to defend the Commonwealth title against Tony Mundine. I got a fight on the same card for another of my boxers, Willie Reilly. Willie had been with Eddie Thomas, came to me and won the southern area title, then beat Jim Watt for the British lightweight title. Ordered to defend his title, I searched for a fight but couldn't get one at anywhere near the right money, so I offered it out to purse: all the promoters sent bids in sealed envelopes to the BBBC and the match went to the highest. Yet, even then, the fee was so poor that I refused to allow the fight and the Board called us up to see them. I went in and said it was very unfair to expect us to box for such a measly purse. Of course we wanted to defend the title, no problem about that, but why should we have to do so at a loss? After expenses, sparring and the rest we'd be badly out of pocket. I asked them to put out the purse tenders again. They replied there was no guarantee of any improvement and advised me to take the fight for the highest bid on offer. If we didn't, the chances were that Willie would lose his title. We went outside to discuss it. Willie said: 'George, I'd rather be stripped of the title and quit boxing than fight for peanuts. It's a matter of principle. I'm not going to be kicked about. You don't either. Tell them.' We went back, stood our ground, and Willie had to relinquish his title.

The plane trip took an age. Instead of flying direct to Sydney, we seemed to stop at every airport *en route*, dropping passengers off and collecting others. Eventually we arrived at eight in the evening, got a taxi to our hotel in Coogee Bay, next to Bondi Beach, and checked in. The hotel people were still cleaning our rooms, we were sick of being cooped up in a plane, the beach was only just across the road so I said: 'Let's go for a swim and wash the travel off.'

Bunny shook his head: 'Sharks, man, no thank you very much. I'll come and watch.'

We ran onto the beach; the sun was going down, the light failing, and the sea was pretty rough. Willie took one look at the waves and said: 'I'm not going in there, and you're crazy if you do,' but I was mad to get into the water. 'Don't worry about the waves — you'll be all right, just dive under.' And in I went, Willie following reluctantly.

I swam out some way, turned round to see how Willie was getting on and he was standing waist deep, gesticulating wildly, shouting out: 'Behind you! Behind you!' I turned round to see an enormous wave heading for me, high as a house. I just had time to dive under it before the whole weight of it broke on top of me and I was being churned round and round, upside-down, my arms and legs flailing in all directions like clothes in a washing-machine, my head twisted back and forth and nearly yanked off my neck, and a tremendous roar of surf pounding at my ears. It was appalling, I thought I was a goner for sure. I didn't know where the surface was and there was no way I could get to it under my own steam anyway. Eventually the wave spewed me out into the open again, like a beaten rag, gasping and retching. The daylight had virtually gone and for a moment or two I couldn't even see which way the shore lay. I struggled to regain my balance and felt an almighty undertow plucking at me and now I could see it was dragging me straight out to the open sea.

I struck out as strongly as I could across the current to the left, desperately kicking and thrashing, the water slapping like fists into my face, the noise of the ocean all round me and the roaring surge of the water. Suddenly, there was another mammoth wave bearing down on me. I didn't know whether to turn into it or go with it. There was little I could do but hope I could ride it out somehow.

It broke and I was in the washing-machine again, only this time it swept me right up onto the beach and pulped me up and down on the sand like a terrier shaking a rat. I tried to scramble onto my feet, but there was no way I could resist the force of that sea. All I could do was go with it. At last, to my incredible relief, the wave died and left me sprawled on the beach, vomiting up salt water, brine and snot coming in gouts out of my nose, my lungs heaving, my stomach twisting from the nausea, my legs and arms raw from the sand scraped . . . but alive.

I was a long way from where I'd gone into the water. Some people found me, bundled me in a blanket and delivered me back to the hotel. The medics bandaged me up and I crept off to bed.

Next day I thought the only way to get over the experience was to go for a run; so I hobbled out, stiff as a concrete suit, the scrapes, bruises and grazes on my skin stinging like ulcers, and tottered down onto the beach to supervise Bunny and Willie's exercises. A big, strapping lifeguard came up, looked me over and said: 'Are you the crazy Pom who tried to commit suicide last night?'

How could I argue?

'Now listen: you're bloody lucky to be alive, mate. That wave is what we call the Dumper. Not only does it land on you like a ton of bricks, as I am sure you can testify, but it has a mind of its own. It belts in like an express, divides, heads for the beach and swings back round again to join up and back out to sea in a big rush taking anyone and anything back out with it. See? And, you see those red flags? Any time they're flying, you stay out of the sea, okay?'

That business put Bunny off swimming for life. And I kept clear of that sea unless it was more or less flat calm. Even when we went running along the clifftops, the waves were so massive they were smashing up nearly at our feet. Then Willie got sunburn and blistered, which halted his training schedule for some time.

That apart, Australia was great. Bunny drew with Mundine, which meant he kept the title. Willie won his fight, too, and I got him another for a fortnight later, so we stayed on. In fact, he took such a liking to Australia that he settled there, quit boxing and took up football; he was always a tidy soccer player and being a Scot he got to know a few of the Scots soccer players out there and they persuaded him he'd have a fair living in Australia. I came home with Bunny to what seemed like another major disaster.

Before we left I had talked to the five other porters in Howgego's and cleared my leave with them. We agreed that they would keep my weekly retainer, split among them, plus the extra porterage that normally I would earn, so they'd be a lot better off financially, even at the cost of a heavier workload. They said that would be fine.

I got home from Australia at the weekend and went into work on the Monday, two weeks later than expected. I called in to say hello to the governor, the top salesman, and he said: 'I'm glad you're back, George, the others have got a new man coming in today to replace you.'

'Oh,' I said. He raised his eyebrows as if to say 'Just in time'. He mentioned this other bloke's name — I knew him, from another firm. I wasn't best pleased. All right, I'd overstayed a bit, but this was going behind my back. It wasn't as if they'd been out of pocket from my absence, quite the opposite, and two weeks was hardly a wild liberty. At 5.45 a.m. I got ready for the off and at six o'clock this new geezer checked in at our firm to make a start. I went up and told him in no uncertain terms to get lost: this was my job. I intended to keep it and I wasn't about to let the likes of him stroll in and snap it up while my back was turned. I grabbed my barrow and got stuck into loading. The Greedy Bastard was back. Meanwhile, the others had arrived but there was no 'Hello, George, how you doing? How did it go?' Only stony silence. I'd been sent to Coventry. I ignored them, pressed on with the work till ten o'clock, the breakfast stop. Usually I went in to take over from the foreman while he had his break and the others went off to breakfast, but this time no one moved. We all stood around uneasily in a crowd. My view was that either we smoothed this business out or there would have to be a showdown. The others looked very shifty, not wanting to let on what was going on in their minds, but I wasn't having any of that. I put it to them straight; 'What's going on with you lot, eh?'

Hands in pockets, shuffling about, sideways looks, who was going to pipe up?

'We don't think it's fair you doing this boxing business and leaving us to cover.'

'Cover? You lazy gits. You're getting extra out of my pocket — retainer and porterage. What more do you want?'

'You're the Greedy Bastard. Not everyone wants to tear round all day like a blue-arsed fly.'

'I thought we were mates. Some of you wouldn't even have a job here if it hadn't have been for me.'

Well, it went from bad to worse. I got more and more het up, they were that sour and surly where before we'd made a tight-knit team. And I didn't know what they were nagging on about me getting extra money from outside the market. There were plenty of porters who knocked off in the afternoon and went off to do other jobs, driving a taxi, scene-shifting, lots of things, for the rest of the day. Anyway, I could feel myself getting angrier and angrier, the frustration of arguing the toss, going round in circles and in the end I lost my rag — my impulsive nature, again. I gave one of them a shove and said: 'Well, if you're so keen on giving my job to some jerk as miserable as you lot of miserable sods you can stick it up your arse.'

I walked out. If I'd stood my ground, there was nothing they could have done. Only the governor, George Butler, hell of a guy, could sack me and I was his best porter, we got on a treat and he wanted me on the firm, no question. He'd given me the job after the trial and I always worked like a train for him; I wouldn't dream of letting him down. The fact is, those other guys made me sick. I had no desire to work alongside a bunch of creeps who had, supposedly, been mates. I was angry, hurt and dumbstruck — they were behaving like kids, spoilt kids: sneering, selfish, spoilt nambies.

I went straight up to the governor's office and told him I was leaving. He was disappointed, asked me to reconsider — which I wouldn't — was very sympathetic, tried to persuade me it would all blow over, but I'd made up my mind, and that was that. He shook my hand, wished me the best of luck in the boxing and I went home. It was a queer journey that. I was giving up something I'd worked at to achieve for many years. I had been going to Covent Garden since I was no more than a kid on the back of the cart. Most importantly, I was ditching a steady and not unsubstantial wage for complete uncertainty. I began to wonder what on earth I had done and what I was going to do. All at once I was terrified. When I got home and told Joan, I realised exactly what I'd done. She went mad, livid. 'You've done *what?*'

Leaving St Pancras had been throwing money down the drain. Leaving Covent Garden meant we had no money to throw. Her comments are better left unrecorded; except that when she'd got over the shock, she stuck by me, as ever. As soon as the kids had grown up and gone to school, she worked as much as she could to boost the money. And now, for me, it was back to doing whatever had to be done to survive. I put all my energies into boxing: building up the stable, going to shows and scouting for promising amateurs. I worked in corners for other boxers as a second (another name for a cornerman, and there might be up to three cornermen). Obviously, as manager-trainer I was always cornerman for my own guys, but another fighter might employ you if you got a solid reputation as a second. And I worked as a specialist cut man. In fact, in USA there are men who do nothing else. The idea is to staunch the flow of blood from a cut by squeezing the cut tight shut with a gauze pad soaked in '1 in a 1,000', the dilution strength of adrenalin — the only chemical substance allowed for the job in this country by the BBBC. If the cut is deep you can use a swab stick, close the cut over it and slide the stick away. Just before the bell, you smear Vaseline over the cut to keep it shut as long as possible. I was full-time professional with a vengeance.

It brought an awful lot of hard, unforgiving work, an awful lot of heartbreak before we began to get on top. In hindsight, leaving the market was the best thing I ever did; at the time it felt like the stupidest. But the thing that protects you against doubt — and doubt floods into you like natural adrenalin when you've chucked what seemed to be a secure job, a safe existence for uncertainty and no money — is the thought of yourself, sitting slouched in a chair, 70 years old, thinking: 'If only I had tried, if only I'd taken a chance.' Opportunity doesn't always look like opportunity. Only you can tell whether a dream is just idle fancy or a real passion. There's a big difference between 'I wish I were' and 'I'm going to be'. And however few things there are you can be sure of, you can be sure of one thing: regret is the most destructive, most poisonous, most negative feeling to saddle yourself with. If you have any desire at all buried inside you, don't give it away, give it a go.

Covent Garden gave me an education no money could buy. It was a tough job, a hard forum to work in and not infrequently dangerous. We had porters killed. One man I know was diving between two lorries with his barrow when, suddenly, the lorry in front backed into him and he was killed instantly, crushed. Everybody had a whip round, gave the money to his family — it was the same if anybody was killed or injured. Our attitude was matter of fact: life had to go on because life did go on; you couldn't change that. And here's a thing: a large percentage of the salesmen were Jewish and if any of their guys died, the others went into a panic, almost. 'You hear about Hymie? My God. Heart attack. Died. Forty-five years old, only. Same age as me. Who's safe? Gevalt.' And when you asked where so-and-so was, he'd be having a check-up in Harley Street, frightened out of his life. I'm not taking the mick, far from it, just the difference between them and us. The whole Jewish community took the day off for the funeral, paying respects to the dead man's family. That's the way they were.

The market was no place for hangers-on. You plied your muscle and you made bucks — a bit borderline now and then. At Christmas, for instance, everyone took a scrape or two of cream off the top, but that was for a fair reason: the nurses from UCH always had a special fund to give the patients on their wards a treat, stuck in hospital instead of being at home with their family. So the whole of Covent Garden rallied to the cause — even governors who were so tight they wouldn't give you the drip off the end of their nose in the normal run, dug into their pockets. And blokes who wouldn't dream of a fiddle twanged the strings at Christmas — praying for wet weather in the country so the wooden apple boxes got saturated and weighed that much more, so a few Cox's could disappear to help swell the nurses' collection and the box-weight of apples would still be even on the scales.

It was the finish of a lot of fun, too: like the night in the flower-power days when the hippies used to hang out in a bar under Munroe's warehouse, smoking dope, and I couldn't find my barrow; in fact there wasn't a barrow to be seen. Then I spotted a big crowd in King Street and went over to see what was up. Someone had pushed a whole load of barrows together to make a sort of stage, and suddenly there was a great cheer and applause as out of the club came a girl, stark naked and woozy with pot. She clambered up on the barrows and did a dance. It was a hell of a show — stopped the traffic for ages. The police tried to push through and break up the party but they couldn't, the circle was so tight. Live acts are quite commonplace in the piazza these days, but we had them, too.

I met theatre stars — Rex Harrison, Rudolf Nureyev come to mind — and I'm proud to have been a porter. My son, Danny, followed me. And through the contacts with Drury Lane theatre (scene-shifting, which I organised gangs of porters to do) he eventually became a dresser, then a personal minder after he quit the market. He it was, incidentally, who told me to pack in fighting. I must have been about 40, got into an argument with a guy I usually got on well with, and we went for a straightener. Danny said: 'Dad, what do you think you're doing? You like the bloke. What do you need to fight for?' The old street-fighter instincts died hard, but they did go and I'm glad of it, even if it took me a long time to cut loose.

'Cloth-cap man' was, still is, a stigma, a brand of someone inferior and I think it's misguided. I've seen more honour in so-called rough diamonds than in the supposedly upper-crust business world. Ironically, though I lived in a cloth-cap world, I never wore that standard working uniform of cap, muffler, waistcoat with deep pockets for the porterage tickets, canvas apron with leather straps, corduroy trousers with knee-ties and clodhopper boots. Not out of snobbery, it's just I wanted to wear bright clothes, and lighter clothes were more comfortable if you sweated a lot, which I did, hauling heavy loads at sprinter's pace. I wasn't the only one; a lot of the younger porters ditched the old-style duds. It was part of the '60s, I guess. In the summer, T-shirts started to come in, and I even turned up for work in shorts, which was unheard of. One of the older guys took one look and his eyes popped out of his head. 'The governor's not going to like that,' he said. Which is what a moaning minnie will always say out of envy that you've shown a bit of enterprise. In fact, the governor couldn't have cared less: so long as I did the work — and there was never any danger of me slacking — he didn't mind what I wore. It was just a new generation, changing the fashions of the old guard. Sometimes we carried the loads on our shoulders rather than our heads and that caused muttering and bitching. What did it matter? We did the job and we did it fast.

In later years, when I got publicity as a top manager-trainer, they would often refer to me as an ex-porter of Covent Garden. The way it came out I could never tell whether that was a compliment or a put-down. Myself, I regard my years in the market as very important and I wouldn't have had it any different. I still dream occasionally of being a porter, losing my job and being desperate to get it back. The whole place has changed now, obviously, but only on the surface, somehow. Other ex-porters I meet say the same. The spirit of the old Covent Garden remains alive and strong, and I get fired up just walking round, seeing the natty shops where the old firms once stood, and strolling along those cobbled streets where I hauled the loaded barrow with GB on the side.

On the other hand, that's my feeling and thought. I just don't see the special relevance of that period of my life to my career in boxing: George Francis used to carry trays of mushrooms around on his head and now he trains boxers. You might as well say what colour socks I wore. People pry for useless detail as if it gives them an insight into how you do your job, which no one can really know. A teacher once said to me: 'You'll never achieve anything: you're going nowhere.' Fortunately I ignored that; unfortunately, I also ignored almost everything else any teacher said to me. But then, who is to say what we achieve? It's having goals and going for them that counts: one goal achieved, on to the next one. As Jim O'Keefe used to say: 'Keep your spirit unbroken.'

You might be born in clover or in a stinking backstreet with disease rife; as the Duke of Bedford's motto over the big archway in Covent Garden says: Che sara sara . . . It's the luck of the draw how you start out. How you finish is what matters.

Chapter Six

Two World Champions: Conteh and Boza-Edwards

Bunny was booked to fight in Edmonton, Alberta — our next major trip — for a title defence against the challenger, Johan Louw, on 22 March 1971. From the moment we arrived Bunny was treated like a real champion, a top-flight sportsman, in contrast to the shabby neglect of earlier days in England. It gave us both a terrific boost in confidence. Victories are important and applause, even grudging applause, welcome; but immediate recognition of the quality and class you've always believed in and seen in action — despite the indifference of everyone else — is something special. Bunny was the title-holder and they gave him the respect that he so richly deserved. But they believed in their man, too: they wanted to see him beat someone worth beating.

Edmonton was shoulder-deep in snow, and when I asked where the running track was they looked at me as if I was crazy. I told them we had to run, so where was the track. Under six feet of snow is where the track is, Mack! There was nothing for it: every morning we turned out when the snowploughs started up to clear the roads and ran behind them, crunching through the snow in the pitch-dark. And the air was freezing. I don't know how many degrees below zero, but so cold your breath felt as if it turned to ice in you mouth. We had to run with a scarf tied round our faces and breathe in through mouth and nose alternately. Eventually word got round and the local ice-hockey team gave us permission to train round the perimeter of their rink. That wasn't exactly an Australian beach either; it was perishing cold, like training in a giant refrigerator.

Bunny retained his title and our next fight came a month later, a straight match versus Dynamite Bill Douglas (father of Buster, who became world heavyweight champion) in the Albert Hall. Another victory was followed by two more trips to Australia. One time, before we flew down under, the *Daily Mirror* got hold of the story that Bunny wanted to study law and they had the idea of togging him up in a lawyer's wig and gown as a publicity stunt. The Law Society kicked up a fuss — judges and barristers could wear fancy dress but no one else, apparently — so the idea was dropped. The Australian newspapers heard about it and they couldn't care two hoots about stuffy rules. So when Bunny stepped off the plane in Melbourne, he was wearing his legal eagle's kit. Next day the sports pages carried the headline: 'Here Come De Judge'.

After Australia, Jamaica, and for Bunny a sort of homecoming.

Our reception in Jamaica was the best of all. They treated Bunny as their man. Nothing was too much trouble for the skinny Jamaican-born kid who had become Commonwealth champion. It was fantastic. They gave us a white car to use with Bunny's name on the side, they treated him like a king. The first morning we went out for a run, going at a fair pace, the sun already quite high, I watched everyone else ambling along as if they had all the time in the world and I thought they must all be drugged, they seemed that dozy. But as the heat began to hit me I realised we weren't in London; this was sunshine of a very different sort to what we were used to. Where London's morning crowd is a mob of crazy people in a desperate rush, late to work, pelting along the pavements, the Jamaicans were taking their time, nice and slow, easy and relaxed. It was a style I got to like for our time off, even if I never relaxed the pressure in training. Palm trees, blue skies, hot sun and fragrant breezes.

One curious event in Jamaica. The old Craven A factory in Mornington Crescent — where my mother and a lot of the family girls worked — had moved some years earlier to new premises out in the country somewhere, Basildon, I think, and the firm's mascots — two ten-feet tall gigantic black cats — which sat outside the front entrance had gone. I used to scramble up and sit on one of those cats to wait for my mother to come out after work. And we found one of them in Jamaica. As Bunny was being sponsored by Craven A they invited us on a tour of the factory in Kingston, and there was the black cat. I hope it was the same cat. It brought us luck anyway, not that Bunny needed that. He won a good fight and now that the sun was literally shining on our hard work, after years of struggle against the odds, we decided to stay on and enjoy it for a while. After all, there was Covent Garden to return to.

One of Bunny's finest fights was the defence of his European title against Tom Bogs, the Dane, in Copenhagen. Bunny had already had a victory in Germany — invariably hard for the foreigner, boxing away from home in front of a partisan crowd — and in Bogs he met a real local hero. Bogs had beaten Chris Finnegan and many other British fighters and he was even more famous than the Danish Prime Minister. The whole of Denmark was behind Bogs, and the promoter had even booked the top floor of the hotel where we were staying for his victory party after the fight.

First problem for us: they produced a Danish referee. I objected and we got a German guy, a very fair ref who saw the actual fight, rather than his version of it, which a local man might have been badly tempted to see.

Bunny licked Bogs on points. That was a fantastic feat as Bogs had seen off most of the other opposition around at the time. I thought the first fight was a great example of Bunny's technical skill and courage, his coolness under pressure, his memorable stature as a boxer. In the hotel later, the manager called us and asked if we'd like to come to what was to have been Bogs' celebration do, with Bunny as star guest. We obliged. What with all the shouting and excitement, I was parched and someone gave me a big glass of orange juice to quench my thirst. I thought it tasted rather bitter but swigged the lot anyway and suddenly I felt very dizzy and keeled over. I came to clutching at my waist — I had a money belt on with Bunny's purse in it. 'Bunny,' I said, 'help, I've been drugged, I've got all your money.'

'You're okay,' Bunny said. 'Someone's just playing a joke on you . . . vodka.'

Next, Mark Rowe asked for a rematch.

I wasn't keen. It seemed a risk. Rowe was a big hitter and anything could go wrong; it seemed like tempting fate. But Bunny was still smarting after the spiteful reaction to that first victory which brought him the titles. He said to me: 'Nobody tells me I can't go 15 rounds, George, nobody. If they want 15 rounds, they can have them. Get me the return. I'll show them who's got stamina.'

If winning the title in the first place and defending it so handsomely took nerve, putting it on the line against the original holder showed real courage. A rematch is always tricky; the guy who lost the title has a lot to prove, and the new man has to be doubly hungry to keep what he was starving to win in the first place. But Bunny was a champion, a solid, sterling champion. Rowe jumped at the chance of regaining the title he (and the great British boxing public of the day) thought he should never have lost, and for 15 rounds he backed round the ring like a sparring partner, not knowing where the next punch was coming from because he was still wondering how the last combination had materialised. I kept telling Bunny to finish it off but he just shook his head and said: 'They want 15, they'll get 15.' Then he went back out to the deliberate, piecemeal demolition job. It was a boxing *tour de force*.

Bunny's last fight was at the Anglo-American Sporting Club in the London Hilton and it was a defence of his British title against Kevin

Finnegan — who was managed by the bookmaker Sam Burns. Bunny had won the first three-quarters of the fight comfortably then, all at once, his left elbow began to trouble him; I think he had bone-chips floating about in the joint. Mickey Duff spotted that he was holding off on his jabs. Because of Sam Burns' involvement in the fight, there were a lot of betting men at the dinner tables round the ring, and Mickey Duff started a chant: 'Fi-nne-gan! Fi-nne-gan!' The betting lobby took it up, then the crowd grew louder and louder over the last three rounds and it swayed the referee's decision. He gave the fight to Finnegan. I was disgusted, fuming, beside myself and I did something totally unacceptable: I gave vent to my feelings of anger and dismay in front of the boxers and the referee. I should have kept quiet; but the decision was so blatantly unjust I couldn't help myself, I let go in public.

It wasn't only my opinion either. Several punters crowded into the dressing-room afterwards in their dinner jackets to clamour for Bunny — saying they were outraged, they'd never seen so unfair a decision so patently for the wrong man. One of those guys was a man called John Smith, a businessman. He stood on the fringe of the throng for a bit, then reached into his pocket, took out a chequebook and wrote a cheque for £500. He handed it to Bunny and said: 'Bunny, you won that fight. Come and see me. We'll talk.'

Bunny more or less decided to quit boxing there and then. He went to work for Smith and became a businessman too. It was a sad way to end a brilliant career; but I sympathise. After all he'd put up with to get where he did, then to lose it on such a pathetic decision must have been the last straw.

Next morning I went in to collect the purse from Mickey Duff in a high old state. I hadn't slept a wink and I was very angry and uptight. I'm not saying the chanting had absolutely decided the fight, but it certainly hadn't helped us: I was convinced Bunny had won.

'Much obliged, thanks a lot,' I said.

Duff dug his finger in my chest and said: 'Why should you have all the champions? Come on, sit down, cool down, have a cup of tea or coffee, but cool down. Give me a chance to talk to you.'

He explained that as a promoter he had to wear different hats on different occasions. On this occasion he had to back Sam Burns. It was nothing personal, against me or Bunny, but Bunny didn't sell tickets. Finnegan and his management had brought in most of the audience sitting round the tables. Bunny had brought his bag. Boxing is business, it's not neutral. I still didn't feel persuaded.

'George, come round this side of the desk and tell me honestly, if you were sitting here, who would you want to win?'

I didn't like it but I could see the logic. It was one of many important lessons I learnt from a man I worked with for many years. And in every negotiation after that time I always asked myself: 'What other hat is this guy wearing?'

Of all the people I've trained, Bunny Sterling was special both as a boxer and as a man. I'm as fond of him today as I was when he first came into the gym as a kid. He fought in a different era, of course, and comparisons are misleading; but I do believe that if he was starting out boxing today, he'd be supreme. We pioneered together — both our pro careers started at roughly the same time — had a lot of fun together, tackled and cleared the first obstacles together. The one thing against Bunny was, ironically, what made him so exceptional: his mastery in the ring. The real fans knew how good he was, he'd make decent fighters look plain and ordinary, but the public never warmed to him. They didn't appreciate any one of his many finer points; they preferred an action-man slogger without the finesse.

As a trainer, the nicest thing you can have is a long-lasting association with a boxer, a strong friendship. Most of the time I never even had a contract with Bunny, but the reward with him was the closeness, the trust and the loyalty. It breaks your heart when someone sees one of your boxers doing well and they entice him away — especially when you build up the champion that no one else wanted to know. Then when he's made it, they're clustering round like vultures. In fact, after Bunny won the title we went back to the St Pancras club one evening to say hello to all his old clubmates, sign autographs, photos etc and some fellow sidled up and buttonholed Bunny: now he'd made it, how about going with a real pro manager, all that garbage. Bunny listened, called me over and said to the geezer: 'Now say to him what you've just said to me.' The bloke slunk away and that was that. Boxing isn't noted for loyalty but Bunny was as loyal as you can get. Whenever anyone asks me how is it going, about anything or anyone in boxing, I always reply: 'All right . . . so far.' With Bunny Sterling there was never any 'so far'. We never fell out; he was a worker, totally dependable and I missed him badly when he quit. Like losing someone who dies and you think you're suddenly going to see them in the street, alive again. Whenever we met the pace quickened and we'd hug each other — I've never hugged anyone else. In fact, one time we saw each other in the tube — he was going down the escalator, I was going up, and he leapt over to join me. A great guy.

When I became a professional trainer, a very experienced guy told me: 'Listen, one thing you must do is forget all that nice, pally stuff with the amateurs. It may work with them, but the pro game is strictly business. Don't fall in love with your boxers. They're here to do a job and so are you; sentiment doesn't come into it. Don't get close to them because, if you do, you'll get kicked in the teeth, depend on it. Be like a doctor, a lawyer, nothing else. Keep your distance or you've had it.'

I hated him at the time for saying it. I had always had a terrific relationship with the amateurs. Later, sadly, I saw how true it could be. There were bitter lessons to learn. The pro game is so different from the amateur.

An example of this came early in my career when I was training and managing a fighter who'd been an amateur with the Finchley club and, because he had a day job, I gave him the *nom de plume* Johnny Oliver. He had no rating as no one knew him. A promoter phoned and said he had a fight for my man Oliver, named the opponent, whom I knew. I also knew that Johnny would almost certainly give him a real hiding — the promoter had assumed my unknown couldn't be any cop. So I told him: 'I know this must sound crazy to you, but my guy will do this other bloke up.'

The promoter said: 'So what?'

'Well,' I went on, 'I know his manager, he's a friend of mine, I don't want to do his guy over, plus he's a ticket-seller. I don't want the other manager to think I'm pulling a stroke.'

The promoter wasn't having any of that: 'You're too squeamish. The fight's on as far as I'm concerned.'

He put the phone down, but I was bothered and called the other manager, Mancini, and reported the conversation. I told him I felt guilty about the match and I wanted to square things with him. I didn't want to stitch up his boxer with a fight he was bound to lose — nothing wrong with that, he'd do the same for me, I was sure. Well, Mancini phoned the promoter and asked for an explanation and a bit later the promoter phoned me, fuming. 'What do you think you're doing, phoning the other boxer's manager? I make a match and you talk to the opposition? It's none of your business. Putting boxers into the ring is your business and nothing more. You don't have feelings either, your feelings or anybody else's feelings. Feelings are irrelevant, they're a luxury you can't afford. This is strictly business and the sooner you realise it's business the better.'

My bloke did win, and handsomely, but it was a lesson learnt. I'd made a packet. In the pro game your own boxer is your prime responsibility: training him for wins, getting him opponents to beat; seconding him in the ring to make sure he does win. No one else counts, only your man.

Once, in the amateur days, at one of our shows in St Pancras, I saw that two of my novices were due to fight Mark Rowe (the same one) in a novice competition and I knew Rowe well. He was already a devastating body puncher, unusual among amateurs. So I pulled our two kids out of the competition. Our competition secretary went berserk: 'You can't do that. It's our show.' But I told him I wouldn't let them fight; they weren't ready for Rowe. And Rowe floored all his opponents and took the cup.

This seems as good a place as any to mention a guy who did help in the early days, one of the nicest guys I ever met in boxing, Bobby Diamond. He was in his sixties when I met him, a little fat guy with thick pebble glasses who was a walking encyclopaedia on the fight game. He knew the weights, ratings, records of any fighter worth consideration; he had more information on boxing in his head than the rest of us put together. He was an international agent doing a lot of work for Mickey Duff when I met him. I liked him at once, and he did his best for me and Bunny when we couldn't get fights at home. I suggested going abroad; anywhere as long as I could get Bunny in the ring to earn money. (Even when he did start to claim sizeable purses, my cut left me a long way behind what I'd pulled in as a porter. For the 1970 defence fight against Mahunga the purse was £2,500, of which I took £250 as manager, money I'd have taken about seven weeks to earn in the market, and how long did we work on that fight?)

Bobby told me: 'It's tough abroad. I can get you fights, but if you think it's hard getting a decision here, you try getting a decision against a foreign fighter in his own backyard.' But he was a hundred per cent committed and worth every penny of his ten per cent. Not only that, he impressed on me how vital it was to stay in a decent hotel, instead of accepting the crummy holes some promoters try to fob you off with. Stay somewhere pleasant before the fight and your morale will be better. Also, he told me: 'Check your contracts; take care of the boxer after the fight — if in doubt get them into hospital straightaway for tests.' He pointed out that not all promoters are lily-white and taught me to keep my eyes and ears open.

Once when Joan and I went on a package holiday to Italy — to get away from boxing, have some peace and quiet, absolutely free of the whole business — Bobby phoned our hotel. He could speak eight or nine languages, or maybe it just seemed that no matter where he was he could always communicate, he was that sort of guy. Anyway, he asked for me and the hotel manager said, 'Who?' and Bobby said, 'George Francis, you know, the man who trains the boxers, he's very well known.' Meaning that if Bobby knew you you must be well known. The manager ran down to the beach and called me to the phone; then puts the word out that I'm an internationally famous boxing trainer. Next morning I go out for a run and there's a line of blokes waiting for me to give them a training session. And the rest of the week we got VIP treatment. That was Bobby.

He had a sad, lonely end, to my great sorrow. He'd gone to the airport to meet one of Mickey Duff's boxers and gone missing. There were frantic phone calls backwards and forwards from the airport when the boxer arrived and no one to meet him. Eventually, they found Bobby slumped in a toilet; he'd collapsed, unconscious. Mickey heard he was in hospital, rushed him to a private clinic in Harley Street but he never recovered. I was away at the time, so never did get to see him. I came home to the sad news and felt his loss badly.

Once, after a fight in Paris, I brought the purse home all in French francs. They refused to pay me in any other currency. When I took it into the bank on Monday, the exchange came out way below the agreed purse. I contacted Bobby, he was livid and phoned the promoter in Paris, got some story that when the contract was agreed the exchange rate was different and they were sorry if we'd lost out, it wasn't their fault. That night Bobby took the French money off to a casino, did a special deal on the exchange, and managed to bump up the amount to something near the original figure. Bobby was never short of an idea, never content to let someone get the better of him.

As my stable of boxers grew, the gym at the Butcher's Arms got too cramped and we moved to a new gym that had been opened by the BBBC behind the Load of Hay pub (later renamed the Noble Art) on Haverstock Hill. The guy in charge, George Daley, was like a father to me. I owe him a lot. He'd been a terrific boxer, a brilliant technical fighter and for that alone I respected him enormously. I prize skill very highly. You don't see many superb technicians nowadays — the emphasis tends to be on showmanship — but George kept the old expertise alive. He'd excelled in the ring and he excelled as a trainer. You can always learn and I learnt masses from him.

I met John Conteh in 1972 after the annual race for boxers and trainers, organised by Danny Mancini from his sports shop. We raced between Lonsdale's in Golden Square to a pub he owned in Fulham, the Rifleman. I won it. There was a large crowd milling around at the end of the race. People congratulated me and I spotted Mickey Duff and his driver, Taffy Martin. I went over and he had John Conteh with him, an outstanding amateur with a lot of managers after him. Mickey introduced me. John said: 'You must be fit to beat all those other guys.' I told him I liked to keep in shape because I expected my boxers to do the same. He told me he'd seen me with Bunny Sterling and my other guys and thought, 'What a great stable of coloured boxers.' I told him: 'If ever you think of turning pro and you fancy joining me, get in touch.'

Some time later Taffy rang me and told me Conteh wanted to turn pro with me. He was 19, and things weren't so rosy. He'd just been beaten for the European amateur middleweight championship by a nobody. A boxer of his class should have walked the fight, but he fought badly and that cast a shadow over what had been an exceptional amateur career. Suddenly there was a question mark over his potential as a professional. Nevertheless, I signed him, then went to sound out Mickey Duff, who owned the rights to all boxing shows in the Albert Hall and Wembley Arena.

'You've got Conteh? You know he and his brother have been to see Jarvis Astaire [a licensed holder with the BBBC who worked closely with Mickey

Duff], came away with an unsigned contract, more or less promised.'

News to me. (Later I heard Conteh had approached several other people.)

'Sorry, George, in that case I couldn't touch him.'

You could say there was a bit of an argument; all very upsetting. I kept on at Mickey, said I had a signed contract; Mickey kept on at me, saying I had no business to interfere with what amounted to a prior agreement with Astaire. In the end Mickey said he couldn't use Conteh so I said: 'Fair enough' and went to see Jack Solomons instead. Solomons only ran clubs and shows, no large venues, but I needed fights for my new hope and I aimed to get him fights. Jack agreed to set up a couple of bouts and I accepted. Conteh won them hands down.

At this point, Mickey Duff came back. He'd changed his mind and wanted to take Conteh on. Of course that was a lot better for us, so I agreed. Solomons didn't like that. 'Hang on,' he said. 'We had a deal.'

'No, we didn't,' I said. 'You agreed you'd find him two fights, which you did and which he won. End of story.'

'You think I'm doing you favours? We had a deal,' he argued.

'No we didn't. Two fights and two fights only,' I replied.

Solomons took out a writ against me, a High Court injunction on the grounds that John Conteh would have brought him this amount of money and that amount of money; that as his trainer and manager I was breaking an agreed contract — albeit verbal — for three fights with Solomons as promoter. He even produced his partner as a witness to swear he happened to walk past the open door of Solomons' office at the precise moment I was saying to Jack: 'Yes, Jack, all right, I agree, I agree, you've got three fights with Conteh. Let's shake on it.'

'How very convenient,' the judge said in court.

Then Solomons reels off some figures, proving how much money he stood to rake in from the third fight based on previous takings.

So I pointed out that one of the two fights Conteh had already won had been on the under card, with three other bouts, at the Grosvenor Hotel, Park Lane, the World Sporting Club, where the principal guests for the evening had been Prince Philip and Muhammad Ali, therefore the punters certainly weren't coming to see John Conteh, however highly I rated his talents.

The judge said he was inclined to agree.

Solomons was claiming a substantial amount in compensation for my so-called breach of contract and, however sceptical the judge might appear to be, he decided that because it was two voices (Solomons and partner) against one, he couldn't give a definite ruling. He made no judgement and ordered me to pay the costs. The only relief was that he set them at County Court not High Court rates. It saved me something, but I was furious. Solomons' partner slipped off after the hearing, but I nobbled Solomons and said; 'Listen, Jack, I'm small, you're the big fish, what kind of game do you think you're playing?'

'I'm not after you, I'm after Mickey Duff.'

'So you can cheat me to get back at someone else? It's bloody stupid. Who pays the money, me or Mickey? And I tell you what, there's a Man Above and he repays, you mark it.' Then I walked off. I'm not a stupid man, and I didn't wish him ill beyond telling him what I thought of him. Ironically, he was taken ill shortly afterwards, suffered badly and died. So did the witness.

Looking back, I would say that John Conteh was the best all-round boxer/fighter I ever trained. He had in him what you can't teach, however hard you try: a solid punch, a big heart and an almost unquenchable thirst to learn, a dream to train. Tell him something and he'd do it, training, sparring, in the ring, he'd do it. He never took prisoners. If he got hit he'd come straight back with double the dose. He could not only box, he could unleash amazing energy and aggression. He could be as fierce as a wildcat in the ring. It is true that he had brittle hands which got very sore after ten rounds. It restricted his sparring but it never made any difference in a fight. As soon as the bell rang all hesitation went out the window, weak hands or not. Another boxer might have tried to nurse his fists early in the fight to last him through to the final bell, but not Conteh. He flew at it from the very start, no pain barrier was going to stop him winning. All that plus he was entertaining to watch: the crowd loved him. As soon as he became British champion people went crazy trying to get his autograph. He couldn't understand it. He was doing what he'd always done — win fights — he thought he was an unknown, but suddenly he was a hero. He didn't know what had hit him. The public simply took to him, and I can understand that. He had charisma, a personality that vibrated out of him — the sort of bloke who walks into a room and draws your eyes to him. Not that he manufactured that, it was natural for him — even when Ali gave him lessons in publicity.

We were in Paris for a fight one time and Ali happened to be there, too. He always took a shine to John, kept on saying to me and him: 'Come on, let's get a fight on, you and me, John, how about it?' Maybe he was not entirely serious, but it was his way of paying a compliment, I guess. I said the usual: 'He's too light.' But Ali just laughed and said: 'Come out and watch this.' We trooped out into the street by the Arc de Triomphe and Ali just strolled into the middle of the traffic, snarled up round the roundabout. He planted himself in the jam and pointed up into the sky. We stood and watched as first one driver then another got out of their cars, till there was a whole crowd round him begging for his autograph. Do you see who that is? That's Muhammad Ali for heaven's sake.

In the end the traffic got rolling again, and Ali ambled back to the pavement, rolled his eyes and gave us a broad grin.

John always trained hard, but he wasn't above taking a rise out of the trainer he christened the Sergeant-major. One Saturday the whole pack of us were doing our long run from the Pond across the Heath, over Hampstead Lane, down to the far side of the Heath extension and back. Just before the trees into Kenwood they all suddenly put on a terrific spurt of speed and left me. I turned on the pace and made off after them, came out of the woods on the other side expecting to see them but not a sign. I guessed they'd taken a side path round to the Pond and carried on. Still not a trace of them; and they weren't at the Pond when I got there. I came back out and was wandering around the fields when somebody who recognised me came up and asked if I was looking for my boxers. I replied: 'Too bloody right I am. Where the hell are they? You seen them?'

'Yes.'

'Where are they? You wait till I catch them.'

'They're up in the café.'

'They're where?'

I trekked back up to the Kenwood café, stormed in, fuming, and there was the whole row of them, sat at the tables, eating cakes and drinking tea. Conteh was in the centre, grinning. He stared at me, triumphantly, and said: 'I've always wanted to do that.' He'd instigated it; none of the others would have dared, but he faced me out. I was ready to sack the whole bunch of them, but in a while I saw the funny side and had a cup of tea myself. Naturally, when we finished, they all skedaddled out of the place before I could protest and left me to settle the bill.

John repaid it a hundredfold when, on 1 October 1974, at the Wembley Arena, he beat Jorge Ahumada of Argentina to become the first British holder of the world light-heavyweight title since Freddie Mills in 1950. It was a desperately hard fight. Ahumada was a very tough and determined opponent; he gave not an inch. Whatever Conteh threw at him he threw back again. Again and again John seemed to be faltering; again and again he came back. These were two guys who would go the whole way — even if it finished them off — and though I knew how obstinate and resourceful John was, I began to wonder if even he had enough power and stamina to beat this formidable champion. I could hardly tell which way the fight was swinging either, till the tenth round. I talked to John through the minute break between rounds; told him he was almost there, another bell would do it. His eyes had a remote, completely focused look in them. His concentration was total. He listened, nodded, his entire conscious mind taut with the effort to bring every scrap and shred of fight left in him to beat the man in the far corner. I don't know how his body had taken the battering, but as I rubbed his shoulders, I could feel the strength in the man, still surging, still on the boil. And when the bell went for the final round, the uncoiled spring snapped tight and he marched out and carried the attack right through Ahumada. The crowd was behind him, but I don't think he could hear them. Both boxers had had to dig so far into themselves they probably didn't know anyone else existed for those last three minutes and, at the end of them, the referee held up John Conteh's hand. He was champion of the world. I can't describe how I felt. A dream come true. Leave it at that. It meant even more as I, too, had been a light-heavy.

We were wined and dined at the Anglo-American Sports Club — where I'd often taken my guys — and one time I'd glanced up at the top table with the celebrity guests: Prince Philip, Sugar Ray Robinson, Ali, and thought: 'One day, one day I'll be up there.' And there were the two of us on that very same table looking down across the sea of punters, me in the monkey-suit I'd bought for the occasion. That was the only time I wore it. Next day I gave it to my brother Billy. I told him I'd had my moment of glory. Besides, I don't like functions; as a rule I avoid them — too much back-slapping and false friendship. People ignore you on the way up, yet they're all over you when you emerge in the limelight. You see through the times when you're ignored and adored; they both come to the same end — people trying to steal what you've slogged to get. Some guy came up to my brother the morning after one of my guys had a nice win and said: 'I see your brother got another champion last night, eh? We all know why — money gets money.' As if that victory fell into our lap, like a loose apple out of a box. He couldn't say: 'Well done, he deserves it.' He had to slag us off as if we never did a minute's work for the success.

Something happened to John during the fight with Ahumada that I can't properly explain and I doubt if anyone can, even John himself. It was an awfully hard fight and, all right, he won and it was a magnificent win, but there are things you go through subconsciously that you shy away from facing again. It was as if he'd plumbed greater depths in his spirit than he could possibly have imagined, a dark, dark tunnel and he couldn't see light at the end of it. He came out, and he came out on top; yet some voice in his ear whispered: 'Never again.' Because there is no question that fight changed him, disturbed his make-up. He was never really the old Conteh — skilful, unstoppable, strong. He had reached the pinnacle of his career by the most astonishing display of courage, pluck and sheer will not to surrender. The climb up there had been so exhausting, his reserves were so depleted, he somehow didn't have the wherewithal to stay up there. And no one should underestimate how doubly tough it is to stay champion after you've become one. Every one is out to topple you. You're on the perch, vulnerable from all sides. And the raw hunger to get what you never had is like a wolf in your guts — hard to match that when you've sat down and eaten the champion's feast, especially after such a torrid combat. When you're going for it, you apply every ounce of willpower and determination. When you've made it, you reflect for a bit and suddenly you realise just how backbreaking the whole struggle has been and that realisation can eat into you, you go soft, you don't need the victory so badly. It's a very unusual man who says, 'Okay, let's do it all again, I enjoyed all that pain and hard labour.' And, of course, it's extra difficult to keep your mind on early-morning runs in the pitch-dark, cold-water plunges and long hours with the medicine ball, the skipping-rope and sparring partners, when the razzmatazz that surrounds a world champion starts to ring in your head and dazzle your eyes. Money, acclaim, hangers-on, know-alls all diverting you.

John, at first the modest, industrious bloke from Liverpool who was on top of the world, couldn't work out what was happening. He simply could not believe that he was the centre of this ecstatic attention, that all these people were clamouring after him, fawning on him. He'd come from a large, close-knit family in Liverpool but in London he was on his own. Gradually, he softened and began to go along with the easier side of life. He believed the publicity they were shoving in his face day and night. He began to drink, though never in training, and he had some great fights at the time. But there was little I could do to turn back the clock. I had other boxers to consider and John was his own man. I could do no more than try to keep him in fighting shape.

Conteh defended the WBC title against Lonnie Bennett, the American, at Wembley in March 1975 — stopped him halfway into round five. After that fight he decided to challenge Willie Taylor in the USA for which he needed permission from the BBBC; they refused, so he took them to court. The judge gave him the verdict; he said the Board of Control couldn't take away a boxer's livelihood so the fight was on, but without me as manager. I didn't want him to fight abroad, but he insisted and went with other people. It was the only time John fought without me and the consequences were painful: he broke his hand. I had always looked after his hands as they were fragile. The bandaging is always important but in Conteh's case it was crucial. That break affected the rest of his career.

John beat Taylor over ten rounds, came back to England and we patched up our differences — he managed himself, with his brother and Bobby Nydo, while I trained him — in time for another defence of the title, against Alvaro 'Vaqui' Lopez in Copenhagen on 9 October 1976. Fifteen rounds and a win on points.

In March the next year he stopped Len Hutchins in three, and in May he was due to defend again. He had trained pretty hard and I certainly had enough confidence that once the match drew nearer the old fighting instinct would surface in him and he'd be as tigerish in retaining what he'd fought so hard to win. But when we were ready to go, and the fight was a few days away, he sat in my room and said: 'I'm not boxing. It's my title. I'm not boxing.' I couldn't believe my ears. I said: 'John, you've signed a contract. I think you'll beat him. You're crazy not to fight. Sure, it is your title but it's only borrowed and if you don't fight, the powers that be will strip you.' He wouldn't budge. I couldn't persuade him to fight and he was stripped of his title.

It's difficult, no, it's impossible to summarise what I felt. So much of a trainer's job is teaching, coaxing, persuading, bullying even, pushing for more work, more concentration, more skill, more everything. I always tell them when things get a bit tense: 'Listen, when I holler and cuss at you it's nothing personal, it's my job.' It's amazing, too, that more of the boxers I've trained haven't taken a swing at me, some of the insults I've stung them with. The whole time it must feel to him I'm saying, 'Do this, do that, do the other thing, that's no bloody good, start again', day after day. The guy must get heartily sick of it and, more than once, they have nearly given in to the temptation to let rip and punch me on the nose. But that is the test: I'm there to teach and motivate, the boxer is there to learn and respond. It's a two-way process, and that's only one aspect. Once you're outside the gym, you have to concentrate on helping your man relax, taking his mind off the business, talking him through the other side of the fight, the mental preparation, the consolidation of energies, physical and mental, all the time thinking: 'What next? Have I left anything out? Is his mind right?' Working to the peak, making sure we don't go over the peak. It's talk and thought and pressure one minute, easing off the next. But then there comes the point when the boxer decides something and there is nothing you can do. You're helpless. He's your boss, finally. He's the one who goes into the ring and when the fight is on it's more or less up to him what happens. You can watch in amazement as he wins, and in dismay as he throws away everything we've painstakingly rehearsed, month after month, and the fight slips out of his reach. And then, outside the ring, he goes his own way and there is nothing you can do. You're his trainer, you can try to dissuade him, but your authority has been turned over. As a trainer your job is on hold. As a man you could have ceased to exist. All you can do is to shut up.

John's decision was very painful for me and I hated it. He was, in my view, chucking away a brilliant career, for what?

He soon came to feel something similar. That experience jolted him, as hard a lesson as he'd had and the harder for being self-inflicted — or that's how I saw it. Anyway, a year later, he came to his senses and buckled down once more to try to regain the title in a match with Mate Parlov of Yugoslavia in Milan on 17 June 1978. He lost, from a bad decision and an unpopular one. Everyone thought he'd done more than enough to take the title back. A terrible disappointment that we needed all our tenacity and strength of mind to get over it.

As we got into the ring before the fight, I looked across at Parlov and I was shocked. All over and round his eyes were thick layers of what looked like some glue substance or, perhaps, new skin. I'd never seen the like — layers and layers of it. I went over to grab the referee, pointed to Parlov and said the fight would have to be called off unless the stuff was removed from his eyes. The fight was being televised all round the world and on prime time in America. Parlov's cornermen were dancing around, the organisers were telling the ref to get on with the business, the promoter was going crazy — he could see his money flying out the window. I went to our corner and told Conteh that Parlov's eyes were caked with glue and we should pull out, but he said: 'Let's get on with the fight.' I wasn't managing him, so the decision wasn't up to me, but the contest should never have been allowed. All through the fight Parlov's eyes were bleeding under that protective layer but the stuff held up and he got away with it. Nonetheless, the result was reckoned to be dodgy and on the strength of it we got a fight with Matthew Saad Muhammad in Atlantic City, in 1979, Muhammad's first defence of the WBA title that he'd taken from Marvin Johnson.

The fight is well known. John cut Muhammad's eyebrow and his seconds used a banned ointment to staunch the blood. At the rules meeting before the fight — attended by all the officials and representatives from both camps — it was agreed that only Adrenalin 1 in 1,000 was to be used. However, in one of the early rounds, I saw Muhammad's cut man putting what looked like Monzal on his man's cut — it dries dark and solid like cement. I immediately protested to the referee. He wouldn't listen, so I sprang into the ring. The referee told the cut man to lay off, but as soon as he turned his back, on went more Monzal and the bell went. Next break I was shouting round the ring, but got nowhere. And John kept blinking; he must have got some of the Monzal from his gloves into his eyes and it's hellish bad stuff. The television commentator, Ferdy Pacheko, mentioned this, too: 'Why is Conteh blinking so much?'

Muhammad should have been disqualified on the spot, and if the cut had been let alone the referee would have had no option but to stop the fight and award it to Conteh. But it didn't happen. John soldiered on, fought as hard as he had ever fought and lost by a whisker, after a thrilling 15-round contest. Another bitter disappointment: the home guy helped over the fence; the interloper pushed off the top. The one encouragement was the WBA ordered a rematch, scheduled for 1980.

The cut man was banned for life, but that doesn't end the story. In Atlantic City some time later, his people approached me and asked if I would petition for the ban to be lifted. Rightly or wrongly I did that and he was reinstated.

We had our second bite of the cherry on 29 March 1980. Conteh looked magnificent in training at the Bahamas camp in Surfer's Paradise. The old John, full of spirit and go. I really believed he was going to go into the ring and storm his way back to the title that had cost him so much to win and even more to lose.

But in the dressing-room before the fight, he was edgy, nervous, twitchy, all over the place. The usual routine was gone and I knew there was something horribly wrong. Instead of busting to go out and do the business, he seemed almost sullen, apathetic. I had never known him like this. I could hardly bear to admit it, but my heart felt cold. Whatever was going through his mind, I couldn't tell, but this wasn't the Conteh I knew.

In the ring he was like a shadow, only half a man. He never got into the fight at all. He went down five times. It was an awful way to go out. He'd taken Muhammad all the way in their first encounter, lost when everyone agreed he should have won, and now he simply couldn't find it in himself to try to do it all over again. And this time the defeat crushed him; all hell broke loose. He went on a monumental drinking binge.

Next morning, a couple of boxing reporters told me I had better get over to John's hotel. I asked what was wrong. They said he was the worse for wear.

Two security guards had cordoned off the floor his room was on. He'd been shouting and hollering most of the night and at one point he'd been rearing up and down the corridor half-dressed. A hell of a commotion. I explained who I was and they let me through. I knocked on John's door. More shouting. I told him to calm down, let me in. More shouting.

Eventually I did get in and was horrified. One of the fittest, clean-living blokes, totally out of it. It felt like ruin, the same guy who had trained like a demon and fought like a lion. I was bitterly angry, but much, much more overwhelmingly sorry for him. It was tragic — probably the saddest thing I saw in my boxing career — my finest boxer so wretched. I managed to calm him down in the end and I left him to sleep it off. I had some idea of what he must have been going through. I knew what he had endured to get into such a state. Everything he had achieved with stupendous effort and talent had gone, lost, and the loss was simply too ghastly to bear.

Next day, the papers were plastered with the headlines. It was horrible, a humiliating experience for any man, but for a proud, noble individual like John, doubly so.

There was little I could do; we were in different worlds now. Anything

I said to him would only make the suffering worse, because I'd be saying to him: 'What do you want to do, box or booze? Hit world champions or the bottle?' And that wasn't going to do him any good. He didn't need my anger and frustration bellowing at him. I didn't know quite what he needed, so we parted company. It hurt me more than I can tell to watch what happened to him, but I had a job to do, other pro boxers to push towards the ultimate goal. One failed and broken fighter couldn't stand in our way. You see a boxer going down the wrong road, you've seen it before, but just as with parents and their kids, advice can be counter-productive; tell them 'don't do it', and they rebel. Wise words can be a stumbling block. And it is an odd set-up: you work for someone and you're in a position where you have to tell them what to do. Where do the boundaries of their self-reliance end?

About a month later I got back to our house in Highgate from a run across Hampstead Heath to find John sitting in the kitchen with Joan. He had always been very close to Joan; she was his London mum. He was soaking wet from rain and sweat. He looked at me and I saw a flicker of the man who'd been the best in the world in his eyes. But there was an awful, yawning sadness there, too. He'd run all the way from his home in Bushey to north London and it was miles.

'George,' he said, 'I can't leave boxing under this cloud. Please get me a fight. I want to go out with some pride.'

I got him a fight, for 31 May, against James Dixon, through a Liverpool promoter, a guy called Atkinson; a fight in his home town. The crowd were very supportive: he was their man and they felt very warm towards him, no matter what had happened. It was a great boost to his morale. They cheered him to the roof, he won the fight and it restored him a bit. I was so glad; none deserved it more after the anguish and torment he'd been through, which was made worse because he had to endure it on his own.

A trainer gives his boxers total commitment, shares in everything, triumphs and defeats, setbacks and success, but, just as the boxer is on his own in the ring, the trainer, even in the corner doing everything he can to support, encourage, motivate, is on the sidelines. He can only ever share a bit of the euphoria of victory, when the adrenalin and jubilation hoists the boxer on to cloud nine. It can be an awful bump coming back to earth, but the trainer never goes up that high and consequently he never has the crash-landing either. As soon as one fight is over, whether it be for a world title or one of four on the under card, he has to be thinking of the next fight, and the next. Psychologically, he can't stop for a minute; no breathers, no relaxing, always looking for more . . . greedy bastard. That's the way it is. Defeat and victory are the same: milestones on a long road.

John Conteh had a brilliant success and he suffered a sad decline but, in the end, just as he dug so deep into his courage and will in the ring, so he pulled himself up out of the ring. He did that on his own and earned my lasting respect by it. I even forgave him the Rolls-Royce. Knock on the door and there's Conteh, grinning like a Cheshire cat, hopping about like a jack-in-the-box.

'Come out and see my new car, George,' he said.

'Oh, no. You haven't,' I said. 'You get the money, you can buy a Rolls-Royce; so what? It takes an exceptional all-round athlete to win Sporting Superstars [which Conteh did] and that's worth a mint more in my view.'

In boxing, as in any top-level sport, you have to be 100 per cent fit in body, but also in your mind. Anyone who steps into the professional ring is, or ought to be, at the peak of condition. If not, he's a fool. The champions, though, are those who are above the rest in mental preparation, in single-mindedness, a total dedication 24 hours a day. Like Daley Thompson, who used to train twice on Christmas Day because he knew none of his rivals would.

When you win a title you instantly become hugely popular. Everybody wants a bit of you — hangers-on, leeches, piss-artists, no-hopers, groupies — everyone who wants to be spotted hobnobbing with celebrities. People with no personality being parasites to stars with an excess of personality. Pasty faces basking in reflected glamour. All manner of creatures slither and crawl out from under the stones, and it can be nearly impossible to cling — yes, cling — onto any sense of proportion and self-respect; you can easily start to believe the bullshit and sycophancy they shower you with. I'm a loner, I got streetwise to that kind of froth and nonsense early. I can spot the conmen as soon as they show themselves, smarming in bearing gifts: invitations to clubs, champagne on the house, free lunch, introductions to girls. They're good talkers and they come in all shapes and forms of disguise. They work on the basis that one free meal buys your loyalty, lock, stock and barrel. That's when boxers on a roll of success are at their most vulnerable; when they probably need the sergeant-major barking in their ears most of all, only the sergeant-major can't be there because he hates that false world. Nor can he be there to nanny grown men round the clock.

Trainer? The job doesn't stop when the boxer climbs out of the ring. You have to be their mother, their father, their doctor, nurse, guru, companion, Dutch uncle, bodyguard — an entire contingent of helpers and guardians rolled into one — and still somehow keep yourself emotionally separate.

In May 1973, when I was training Conteh to fight Chris Finnegan, a southpaw, for the British, European and Commonwealth title (which he won), I needed southpaw sparring partners and advertised in *Boxing News*. Often you phone round other managers and ask for their men. Anyway, one afternoon the gym door opened and in walked a smallish guy. I asked him who he was. 'Chris Sanigar,' he said, in a strong Bristol burr, and told me he'd come in answer to the advert.

'What advert?'

'Sparring partners for John Conteh.'

'How much do you weigh?'

'Ten stone six.'

'What? Are you crazy?'

'I'll fight anybody.'

And by the look of him he would, too. But I wasn't having it.

'Listen, Conteh's 13 stone, you've got no chance. You'll get murdered.'

'Give us a go. I've come all the way from Bristol. I ain't messing.'

'Nor am I.'

But he wouldn't go away; he was obviously bursting to get into the ring. So I agreed, took Conteh on one side, cautioned him to take it easy, but when Sanigar got into the ring I was flabbergasted. He didn't let up. He was bent on giving Conteh a good hammering. When John hit him he wobbled a bit but he came straight back into the fray. I was so impressed with the man's heart I said to him as he climbed out of the ring: 'You want to turn pro?' and signed him on the spot.

Sanigar had real fighting guts but he made every fight a war: tore in regardless; soaked up any punishment so he could dole it out when the opponent snatched a breather. I couldn't curb him. I told him: 'Chris, you're in too many wars, it's not the way I do things. You'd better leave.' The fact is I didn't want him to get hurt. He didn't care, he'd punch his way through an oncoming double-decker bus for all he would register the bruises, but a trainer has to take care of his boxers, not only as fighters but as men who stand to get injured in what can be a hell of a rough house. Chris could put on a terrific wild show, the crowd loved him, he brought the house down with his antics, but at what risk to himself? Well, he begged me for one last fight and I got him a match with Sid Smith for the southern area light-welterweight title at the Elephant and Castle leisure centre. I had a word with the referee before the fight and asked him to stop it if Chris looked like getting hurt, and sooner rather than later.

The fight started and Chris did several rounds toe to toe with Smith, absorbed a lot of heavy whacks and I decided to pull him out. As soon as the bell went for the end of the round, I sprang up to tell him I was calling it a day but, before I did, I glanced over in the other corner. Smith was slumped over, dead beat: he'd shot his bolt — used up so much energy trying to floor Chris early on — he had had it. Chris was on his stool, taking long deep breaths, reeling but still raring to go — he was a bit like me in my days on the streets: the more you got clobbered the more you went back in — and I leaned down and said: 'Look over my shoulder, he's knackered. You can win this. Pile in.' I rubbed him down, sloshed the iced water into his trunks over his private parts (which you do to make the fighter jump, liven them up), the bell went and in tore Sanigar, knocked Smith out almost on the rebound. And there he was, parading round the ring holding up his champion's belt. What a turn-up.

Next day he came into the gym and I said: 'Okay, you fought a blinder, it was brilliant, but this is where we part company. Go on fighting if you want, but it won't be with me.' We shook hands and he did go on fighting — every fight a war, as ever. He's a promoter and manager now.

He wasn't the only guy mad to spar with Conteh. There was Paul Rodgers, lead singer with Bad Company, for whom my son, Billy, was working.

We were training at the Sobell Centre when Billy came in with Paul and told me Paul wanted to spar with John. I just laughed and they left. Later, Billy came into the gym on his own and said Paul had been very upset. I told him to leave it out: Conteh was a light-heavy, a pro, and he'd punch Paul out of the ring. The whole idea was ridiculous. Billy wouldn't give up, he said Rodgers was a tough nut and he wanted a go. One of my other boxers, a junior lightweight, overheard this and said: 'He's the same weight as me, I'll spar with him.' So Billy went off and brought back Rodgers. I told my guy to take it steady, just move him around, not do anything elaborate, three rounds would be enough. Paul did take a bit of stick, but he didn't disappear and over the next three months he came back quite regularly — he kept himself in decent shape, anyway — and the boxing gave him that bit of extra edge. In my honest opinion he could have become an excellent professional fighter. Reg Gutteridge, the boxing commentator, even saw him one day in the gym and said: 'Who's he? I haven't seen him before. Who's he with?'

'Bad Company.'

'Never heard of them. Where do they operate from?'

'It's a pop group. He's a singer.'

The junior lightweight who gave him the sparring was a young Ugandan, name of Cornelius Boza-Edwards.

Boza-Edwards was something very special — unique, I'd say. I'd seen him as an amateur, boxing for the Fitzroy Club, and considered going after him, but he was light — bantamweight, perhaps even lighter — and he'd never make any money in this country at that weight.

By this time I'd moved from the gym at the Noble Art; a new publican was coming in who wasn't keen on having boxers round the place and wanted to revert to the old name, the Load of Hay (again). I was on the hunt for somewhere else when Ray Childs (former UK welterweight champion) and Vic Andreti (former pro champion) decided to manage a new gym at the Wellington Arms at the bottom of North Hill in Highgate. (The pub has gone now, replaced by a garage.) I approached them, asked if they'd like to give space to my stable of about 12 boxers, and they leapt at the offer.

We moved in and one day Mickey Duff gave me a call, said he wanted to bring me a young boxer to look at. He arrived next day with a white businessman, Jack Edwards, who'd been booted out of Uruguay by Idi Amin, and his adopted son, Cornelius Boza — now Boza-Edwards — born in 1957, now 18 years old. I took to him; whatever doubts I'd had about his potential as a pro disappeared and we shook hands on the deal.

As a boxer, Boza-Edwards was pure class from the start. As a ticket-seller he was a non-starter. Not his fault, and I thought with Mickey Duff promoting us we'd get lots of fights. But after a few matches, as he began to show his real ability, the fights dried up. Duff tried hard enough, but Boza-Edwards being categorised as a foreigner there was little room for him on any bill, that already named say three established foreigners. He might be adopted British, but was still categorised as 'foreign'. So we looked for opponents abroad. We fought in Italy and the USA and gained such a reputation that Mickey Duff steered him towards a fight for the world lightweight title against the holder, Rafael 'Bazooka' Limón of Mexico in Stockton, California, on 8 March 1981.

Boza had fought as an amateur for Britain at international level, but the inequalities of the system still prevented him from contesting a British title, and now he was challenging for a world title. And his opponent wasn't called 'Bazooka' for nothing.

It was one of the dirtiest fights I've ever witnessed; 15 rounds of blood and snot. It was savage, cruel and if I needed any reminder of Boza's — Corny's — stature as a boxer, that fight provided it. He had to drag out everything I had taught him, technique, ring-craft, the lot — and more. He had to reach right down to the depths of his reserves, and even I had begun to think that he couldn't possibly draw up any more, any more sheer courage, any more strength. He seemed to have spent himself twice over, and yet he still came on. And the look in his eyes. Before the fight, there had been something so steely and compact about him, I had rarely encountered such a total grip of willpower, physical and mental concentration even in Boza, that it was as if he'd gone right beyond the guts and pain of the fight into the realising of his ambition: to win. He was set on victory. I knew it, too. In fact, before we went into the ring, I asked Mickey Duff if he had any spare money on him. He had said yes.

'Well,' I said, 'put it all on Corny, because he's going to win. It'll take a sledgehammer to stop him tonight.'

It nearly didn't come off.

Bazooka Limón did everything he could, legal and decidedly illegal, to retain his title. He struck Corny in the crotch seven times. I couldn't believe it. The referee did nothing. It nearly finished Corny off; doubled him over and he took bad punishment when he was in that vulnerable state. But he absorbed it all, just somehow shrugged it off. Stood up and came back.

Limón was a terrific fighter. The man could — and did — loop punches, roll his wrists and corkscrew the punches double-power. He could — and did — throw wicked uppercuts, vicious hooks. Every punch in the armoury, delivered with mean savagery. The crowd, 3,000 strong, were firmly on his side. So often the case, of course: they get behind the champion because he is the champion. And, of course, being champion can lift a guy's performance so he's boxing out of his skin. Boza was in that ring on his own, trading punches with a hard merchant, no question of that. But he was boxing out of his skin, too. He caught Limón with a tremendous left hook in the fifth round and Limón went down. It might have ended there and then. I stood in the corner looking at Boza, the ferocious determination in his face, and at Limón, groaning as if he didn't know what had hit him. But he was struggling up. He wasn't going to let it go. Boza was going to have to tear it away from him, inch by inch.

Boza had never been beyond ten rounds. He'd never needed to. And if the first ten were hard, I was thinking, how was he going to survive the rest of the onslaught as it stretched into the far distance of five more brutal, crucial, three-minute toe-to-toes? Slowly, though, Boza's boxing skill began to tell. His defence was superb. He was taking fewer punches — the good and the bad and the ugly. The crowd recognised his class — and the underhand tactics that Limón was working in a desperate attempt to stay ahead. And instead of 'Lim-ón! Lim-ón!' they began to shout 'Bo-za! Bo-za!' It was fantastic. The entire place calling for him. Boza boxing his heart out. A world title belt within reach.

Between rounds I worked frantically in that single minute, my time, my job to spur him on, rub him down, clear his mind, clean him up. There was no need to stimulate him. He was so deep in the business, nothing could have disturbed that amazing focus he had. He was so fired up you could feel the energy pumping out of him like heat from an oven. Yet he never once lost his cool. Inside him there must have been such a chill of calm — difficult to imagine with all that passion driving him into the toughest fight he'd ever dreamed of — but there's no other way he could have executed such a ruthless display of attacking boxing and survival defence.

His character shone through. He became a man. At the final bell he was so tired he could barely lift his arms up. But then the moment came when the referee raised his arm for him, and he was world champion. Limón was in a heap. Boza was on top of the world and if his body was too shattered to show much of the exultancy of that moment, his eyes did. I could see in them the same certainty as I'd seen in them before we went into the ring. It was amazing. He'd been so sure of victory, right at the bottom of his soul and then gone through punishment of a sort he'd never met — and should have won on disqualification — but he never let himself be worn down by the cheating, the rank unfairness of his opponent's foul play. He weathered it, he shook it off, he never let it get anywhere into his mind. It was as much that he won a torrid psychological battle as a physical war and I never admired him more. It would have been understandable if he'd caved in — many men would have done — but that is what boxing can do: it exposes the inner courage, the hidden, spiritual courage, as well as the raw surface courage, in a way not many other sports can. This is the glory as well as the misery of the ring, the four corners of truth.

Boza held the WBC title for just short of six months; beat Bobby Chacon of USA in the fourteenth at Las Vegas in May, and then was knocked out by Rolando Navarrete of the Philippines in Viareggio that August — not far from the hotel we'd stayed at with Arthur Vaughan all those years earlier. Boza had been tremendous in training, but when he stepped into the ring it all evaporated. He was like a feeble imitation of what he'd been. Even as I bandaged his hands he was limp, listless, no strength in him. We never did find out what was wrong, perhaps he had a virus. Perhaps he did too much training after all, left too much behind him in the gym. It can happen; a boxer overtrains and, as we say, 'leaves the fight in the gym'. I couldn't, and can't, really believe that was the case, but something must have undermined him and it was no great fighter who beat him.

Sadly, he never regained the title. It wasn't that he weakened as a boxer, he had tragic luck in his personal life. Before the title fight he married a white girl, Jackie, and he'd been terribly anxious about it . . . what would her parents think, their lovely daughter wanting to marry a black guy? I sympathised. After Conteh became champion, I had a lot of hate mail, calling me a nigger-lover, for training a black, even a very pale black, fighter. I told Boza I was sure they'd love him as warmly as she loved him, and so they did. I guess I was biased: I got closer and closer to him myself, till he was like a son. Well, they got married, had a baby girl and then Jackie developed a kidney complaint, grew very ill and died. It was awful. Her parents came round to my house with Boza, just sat and wept. I tried to comfort them, said anything you can say at such moments, it all sounds pretty futile. They couldn't believe it: such happiness all gone, her young life finished before she had hardly got going. Boza's own life seemed to have gone, too. I thought he'd never box again. How do you come back to anything like what you had been after such a heavy blow?

A few months later he did phone, but he didn't say much. I asked him how he was making out, he told me okay and then said: 'I think I'll come back to the gym.' It was characteristic of him. He'd faced a devastating loss, somehow come to terms with an appalling grief, and then set out to face whatever else life had in store for him. Our codeword just before leaving the dressing-room had always been 'Let's do the business'. And I am sure being a great believer in the Man Above helped. He always went to church two or three times a week. I used to wait for him outside. I always reckoned I was too big a sinner to go in with him.

He boxed a lot in USA and took to the States in a big way — in fact he's now training a fair-sized stable of boxers in Las Vegas — married a girl who worked in Caesars Palace and got to be very popular, a firm favourite with American TV fans. They voted two of his fights 'Best Fight of the Year'. I went over to train him; we had to switch from the British style of fighting, which is light-footed, dancing, moving, using the ring, to the American fighting style, planted on your feet, fist-to-fist slugging it out. Because all his fights were televised, schedules were often changed at the last moment. A fight might be billed for live transmission at ten o'clock but because the sports channel was also covering other events across the country, across time zones, it would have to cover crucial stages in, say, a golf tournament, and the boxing would be held up, often more than once in an evening. Boza hated those disruptions.

One occasion, at Madison Square Garden, we got ready to fight twice. It was nearly midnight and he still hadn't fought and he said: 'That's it, George, cut my bandages off.'

'Okay,' I said. I could see he wasn't prepared to fight now. I went and told Mickey Duff. He said: 'I know, I know. I've been going crazy out here, but they won't listen. I don't blame you.'

It meant no money, but we were sick of waiting and walked back through the downtown streets of New York to our hotel. On the way we stopped at a shop — nothing ever closes in Manhattan, it seems — and I bought Boza six toy cars to cheer him up. He was a mechanic by trade, collected toy motors. We slunk into the hotel, pretty disconsolate, and at one o'clock in the morning there came a knock at the door. It was Mickey Duff.

'Well, boys,' he says. 'Surprise, surprise,' and throws a wad of money on the table. 'There's your purse!' It turns out that the television programmers had had to cancel the fight card so Boza wouldn't have fought after all. The postponements meant paying for an extension to stay in Madison Square beyond midnight which they couldn't afford. They knew nothing about Boza and me walking out, of course, but coughed up anyway, they had no option.

Mickey Duff felt a great attachment to Boza-Edwards; his was the first corner he ever came in to. Generally he was more a gym man, a true pro who let you get on with your job as trainer, never interfered or queried decisions, saw it as his job to put confidence in you and back you. I didn't suggest he come into Boza's corner, I thought he'd be too emotional, but he did come and he's always gone into the corner ever since. Into the corner, but never the dressing-room. Not like some, who bother you incessantly. In Germany, for instance, the dressing-room is like rush hour, troops of people flocking in and out. I always post someone at the door and nobody comes in apart from the referee and the Inspector.

I was still at the Noble Art when a tall, well-dressed black guy came into the gym, announced himself in a very posh accent as John Coker and asked if I would coach him. He boxed for his college and was going to box in the Olympic Games for an African country. He looked the part, so I took him on. He sparred, trained, I sharpened up his technique and then he announced that he wasn't going to be able to fight at the Games because his hands were too large for the gloves. This seemed a pretty bizarre excuse, and it made me wonder why he didn't check out the glove sizes before he started. In any event he left off and I thought nothing more about it until I had a phone call from the Zambian Embassy: 'Would you be interested in training the Zambian boxing team for the Olympics?' I suppose Coker had some high-up connections in their government and had recommended me. He phoned me a bit later and explained that they were very poor, they had virtually no gear and there'd be no money in it, but would I do it anyway? I took the job on, fixed a day for their team to come to the gym and, at the time appointed, waited. And waited. No sign. An hour passed and I gave up, got changed to go home, shut up shop and went out into Haverstock Hill. On the wall opposite sat a line of six black guys in tracksuits. Could this possibly be the Zambian Olympic boxing team? The cab driver had dumped them in the middle of the road and driven off before they could ask him where the gym was.

No time like the present: we went back into the gym and got started. Charm Sichula, John Munduga, Chisanda Mutti, John Schuler and a boxer I realised immediately was something special — Lotte Mwale.

They trained with me for six weeks and went off to the games, but in the upshot never fought, because the African nations boycotted the games, due to the presence of the South African team.

I assumed that was that, until a while later I had a phone call from a German businessman with business interests and contacts in Zambia. A keen boxing man, he was looking to help establish professional boxing in Zambia by ploughing back some of his profits into sport there. Could he bring a Zambian government minister to see me?

They arrived at the house. I took their coats, offered them a cup of tea, very English-like; they perched on our settee and said they wanted me to take over Lotte and the others to train them in England, as professionals. The idea was to build up a core of pro boxers here as the eventual basis of a pro circuit in their own country. They explained the hardship of Zambian sportsmen. The had approached me because they had good reports of my stable of black boxers, so could I help them out by putting their guys in with mine? I didn't warm to the idea of training them for nothing, but on the other hand they would provide me with a constant pool of sparring partners on tap, so I agreed.

Chapter Seven

Out of Africa

The Zambian boxers arrived and took up residence in a house I got through a friend, round the corner from where I lived.

I had worked with a lot of black boxers, mostly from the West Indies, and Boza-Edwards — though he had spent a long time in England — but those Africans were quite a shock. I'd never met anyone like them; they were a different kettle of fish altogether. Unpredictable, scatty, chaotic, full of fun and yet prone to deep glooms, hopeless with money, almost impossible to keep tabs on. If they trained well they were terrific; if they took it into their mind to have an off-day, it was so far off you couldn't believe you were dealing with the same guys. But you couldn't help liking them. They were like children: devoted kids who needed constant mothering.

In professional terms, though, I was back to square one in many ways: they weren't rated and they didn't sell tickets. Even their names were unpronounceable when you saw them written up. Lotte was the star among them and I knew I had to get him known; maybe he'd make the breakthrough for the others. So I pulled a stroke I am not particularly proud of, but it did the trick.

Tony Sibson of Leicester was on the hunt for opposition from abroad. A tough, relatively unstylish boxer, he had a very popular local following, always sold out any hall he fought in. I got in touch with his promoter, Ron Gray, and offered him a fight with Lotte. The usual response — 'Who?' — except that Ron knew me and was interested. I explained that Lotte was from Zambia and Ron could save himself the expense of flying in a foreign boxer. He asked me Lotte's weight. 'Light-heavyweight? Sibson's a middle,' Ron said. Which, of course, I knew, but he was always off the scales, so I told Ron: 'Come on, we both know Sibson has trouble making the weight, let's weigh them in at 12 stone and I'll shed the pounds off Lotte.' Sibson would go in heavier and Lotte would have to lighten up. He hummed and hawed a bit, then asked me: 'There's no danger, is there?' Meaning for Sibson, naturally. 'None at all,' I replied, tongue in cheek, meaning there might not be for Lotte but as for Sibson . . . Gray agreed.

Incidentally, when the fight was billed, Mickey Duff phoned and asked me not to go ahead with the match. It was obvious he felt there was a strong chance that Lotte would beat Sibson and, to be fair, he realised that Sibson was a bright young prospect and he didn't want to see him set back in a match that he didn't pressingly need.

He wouldn't say much more, but I remembered his words after Bunny's loss to Finnegan: 'Why should you have all the champions?'

'Come on, Mickey,' I said. 'You won't get me a fight for him. I have to do the best for these Zambian boxers.' And that was that.

Next day, another phone call; this time from Ray Clark, secretary of the British Boxing Board of Control. 'I really don't think it's right for you to do this, matching uneven weights,' he said. And I'm beginning to wonder what's happened to all of them — was this a fight game or what? The phone rings again; Sibson's manager, a local bloke, not particularly well established, still nervous and wet behind the ears. He's been hearing the rumours flying and got cold feet: 'I keep hearing these tales about your boxer.' (No doubt: he's eight feet tall, with club fists, skin like a rhinoceros and he crushes his victims alive.) 'Are you sure this fight's all right?'

I reassured him: 'All right, no danger at all.' I'd never had so many phone calls.

Gray decided to check up on the opposition, though, and fixed to send his brother down to our gym to see Lotte in action. Before he arrived I filled Lotte up with water till he could hardly stagger, then put him on the scales so this not so private eye could take a gander. Lotte sent the dial round to 13 stone. I shook my head. I told the bloke we'd need to lose an arm and a leg to reduce Lotte to 12 stone. Then Lotte sparred a few rounds; I'd primed him not to do anything fancy, just defend himself, plod about looking like a journeyman — dull and ordinary — on no account give him any flash of his real class. This he did, and the fellow went away very perky.

We travelled up to Leicester. There was a lot riding on this fight. I had another boxer on the same bill — a lightweight called Robinson, who knocked his man out — and now it was Lotte's turn. The weigh-in had raised a few eyebrows — Lotte certainly didn't look as if he'd sweated blood and tears to peel off a mass of surplus.

We walked out from the dressing-room into the hall and a gale of noise. The whole place was packed, standing room only, and every single guy in the audience rooting for Sibson, chanting 'Sib-o, Sib-o, Sib-o, Sib-o' to the tune of 'Amazing Grace'. I patted Lotte on the back to keep him calm, though he had a fantastic temperament, like ice when he was focusing on the job. I told him: 'Go for him. Don't give him a second to breathe in, from the bell, flat out.' And he did. He flew in like a bat out of hell, knocked Sibson over and out in the first round. It was amazing. The whole place was completely stunned, hushed. Sibson keeled over right in front of me and I had to climb into the ring to pull out his gumshield, slap his cheeks and try to revive him, saying his name over and over again – not to any known tune – but he wouldn't stir. Lotte had whacked him cold. I was a bit worried, until he moaned and began to come to. The crowd simply couldn't believe what had happened. Then they started hollering against the injustice of it, their hero knocked over by a spoiler.

As I followed Lotte away from the ring, a small posse of guys cornered me and blocked my way, did a real hoods number on me, faces all twisted with loathing, coming on extremely heavy. One of them leaned over and whispered in my face: 'We're going to get you, you bastard.' These weren't fans – and Sibson had an army of them – only jumped-up hard boys who thought this kind of posing was impressive, bullies with loose fists and no style, poaching on Sibson's name and prowess. Drunk, of course, and very out of hand. I certainly didn't choose to tangle with them; who knew what they'd try on? I nipped round to the cashier's office, picked up the purse, ran along to the dressing-room and told Lotte not to bother to change, we were getting out sharpish. We slipped out, found our way to a side entrance to the hall and off into the car. I put my foot down and didn't ease up till we were halfway to London.

As I said, I'm not proud of what we did, but that fight put Lotte on the map. He was rated. Mickey Duff took notice, at last, and took him on with the others. I was very relieved. They were costing me a fortune to train, so I would get some percentage at last. Above all, Mickey Duff could work his magic on them. We could start moving.

I did manage to repay Sibson for that deception. After he was beaten by Hagler, in February 1983, before Hagler called himself Marvellous Marvin (after his tenth successive defence of the title in 1984), I called Sibson's people and arranged for him to come to join my guys in the gym where I was working, in Vineland, near Atlantic City. It was out of the way, very quiet and peaceful, a great spot. He came, found it terribly hard; actually wanted to run home after only a few days – didn't take to the sergeant-major regime at all – but I kept him at it and fixed him a fight with the undefeated Irishman, John Collins, in Atlantic City. Collins was odds-on favourite to win by a mile, but Sibson put him down in the second round. It was a great win for him – and some recompense for the débâcle against Lotte. Curiously, before I took on Sibson for that fight, a promoter, Cedric Cushner, had contacted me and asked me if I'd train Irish John. I told him to send him down but then he changed his mind, because of the Anglo-

Irish troubles. He got cold feet, didn't want to stir up any politics. After the fight, Sibson and I were in the hotel having supper, and Cushner came in, walked up, smiled ruefully and said: 'I should have let you train Irish John, I made a bad mistake there.'

Another Leicester boxer from my Vineland stable fought and won on that same card — Chris Pyatt. He later became European light-middleweight champion and recently won the world title. A memorable fight that turned out to be, for the vacant WBO crown, in May 1993 against Sumbu Kalanbay, which went the whole distance, ten unbelievably hard rounds. Pyatt needed every ounce of resilience and heart to win.

The first time we went to Zambia I was quite shocked. Because of the war the country was completely cut off at the time. The whole of that part of Africa was on the boil. The Zambian borders were shut; railways were constantly being blown up so virtually no supplies could come in from the coast, food was desperately scarce — little else to eat but maize. They were badly up against it.

The whole place was rundown. Needless to say, the boxing facilities were pretty basic — toilets without bowls, ramshackle gyms, fleabitten gloves to train with and only a few pairs to box in at shows — as one fighter left the ring he'd have to pull off his gloves, slick with sweat inside, for the next guy going in to wear. As for bandaging, they knew nothing about it, it was bare hands straight into the gloves — if you could find any gloves. Anything that wasn't nailed down disappeared. Ask who had such and such and it'd be: 'Wasn't me, he took it,' without batting an eyelid, like kids, just like me and the Prebend Street mob in Camden Town. I recognised it well ... 'Mummy says she's not in', all that. The one huge benefit for me was training in brilliant sunshine. That I relished. The poverty got me down at first. Not the Zambians: they seemed just to shrug their shoulders and laugh. The more I went there, the more I enjoyed it, the place and the people. They are so warm and friendly, so wholehearted and appreciative of everything you do for them. Not that they are averse to asking either. They must have thought I waltzed into shops back in England and helped myself off the shelves. They were always coming up and asking me if I'd give them my shoes, watch, T-shirt, anything. Waiters in the hotel, anyone, not the least bit bashful. One time before I left, six of them came up in their white waiter's coats and handed me pieces of paper — shopping lists, of all sizes for this and that item. Hilarious. I'd have liked to inform them I had spent most of my expenses just buying the ticket to Zambia. Call me amateurish if you like, but some things you do for love and some for money. The Zambians might have been poor, but their exuberance and enthusiasm were fantastic, a real example to people who've got more than enough and can't raise any sort of energy.

John Coker, who had reappeared on the scene back home, had warned me about this. 'They'll ask you for the shirt off your back and, knowing you, you'll want to give it to them.' So I'd gone into Lonsdale's sports shop and bought 100 T-shirts. Our driver drove us in a station-wagon from the hotel to the gym, Lotte in the front, me in the back, two motorbike outriders with sirens blaring, and hundreds of kids lining the street, shouting and yelling, chanting 'Lot-te! Lot-te!' The car slowed to a crawl and I opened the box of T-shirts and started chucking them out. But instead of taking one each, the kids in front were grabbing all they could get and then fighting off the others who'd got none. I'd made a silly, stupid mistake. A policeman rushed over and yelled at me: 'Stop that. Stop. They'll tear each other to bits.' We distributed the rest, one at a time, from behind the railing that surrounded the gym building.

A boxing show might not seem such a big deal, but Zambian fighters putting on a show in front of a home crowd of 40,000–50,000 in the capital city, Lusaka, was a boost to national morale. That was the first of many shows, and when Lotte took the Commonwealth title, the local crowd gave us a welcome to remember. They carried me all the way round the stadium. I felt a real hero. Lotte, of course, they treated like royalty. I'd had a lot of hate mail for training black boxers, and to be cheered to the sky by all those black people I found very moving. I even got taken to see their President, Kenneth Kaunda. He shook me by the hand and thanked me for doing so much for Zambian boxing and boxers. And whenever I landed at the airport, I was always ushered straight through customs to meet the press and give them interviews, then out to a tremendous welcome.

The Zambians held the boxing shows in a vast outdoor arena. The tickets were cheap, but after the national anthem was played to start proceedings, there'd always be a whole horde of kids clambering in over the wall to watch for free. The police and the military (who both got in without tickets anyway) wanted to leap up and turf them out; and the promoters, of course — they don't change the world over. I told them not to bother. We wouldn't get any more punters in than we'd already got — most of the population it looked like — so let them stay. (I was probably thinking of my days bunking into the zoo, the Lido and the cinema.) And there was a hill opposite the arena, too, Humanity Hill — nice name — and a sizeable crowd of people gathered on it for a long, long-distance view of the fighting. How much they could possibly see, I don't know; matchstick figures in the haze. And the promoter said: 'We'll have to erect a screen so they don't get a free grandstand view.'

When Lotte fought — Zambian Sportsman of the Year, Commonwealth champion, increasingly likely to have a crack at the world title — we walked from the dressing-room into the arena through a double gauntlet line of his supporters, all wearing tribal masks and war costume, leopard skins etc, beating their hide shields with spears, just like in the film Zulu, making a din like you've never heard. Chanting blood-curdling war cries, it made me shiver and tremble. And they danced round his opponents on the way to the ring, and in the ring Lotte did the dance round them again. It was spectacular and chilling. Frightening, and I was Lotte's trainer. As the Duke of Wellington said of his army: 'I don't know what they do to the enemy but they scare the life out of me.'

One time, Mickey Duff came out from the dressing-room with us, on to the open-air path leading to the arena, stared down the double line of these guys whacking their shields, chanting and stomping, and whispered in my ear: 'I'm glad we're with them not against them.' It was certainly the hottest home support I'd ever encountered. And Lotte never disappointed them either, — didn't lose a fight. Can you wonder?

For one of the shows in Zambia, I took out some English boxers, including a barrel-chested battler, Carl Cantwell. He had to fight in the afternoon. Mad dogs and Englishmen go out in the midday sun, but this was 115 degrees, stifling hot and humid. Cantwell strode out to the ring and as soon as the bell went he ploughed in like a latter day Marciano, battered his opponent into submission and got a knockdown in the second round. He didn't even wait for the referee to finish the count. He leapt through the ropes and was off. Next day, the papers described him as 'like Charles Bronson in Death Wish', spreading mayhem. The truth is, because of his fair skin he couldn't stand the heat or glare. Before the fight he'd warned me: 'These temperatures will kill me. I'm going to wade in there and get it over with as quick as I can.' Well, he did the job, most impressively, whatever the reason.

In November 1980, Lotte challenged the holder, Matthew Saad Muhammad, for the world light-heavyweight title in San Diego. Boza-Edwards was with us for a fight on his way towards his world challenge the following year. Lotte didn't respond particularly well to America; a serious case of homesickness, maybe, and then an accident which rattled him badly. He'd gone out to buy souvenirs when Muhammad's entourage, about 12 of them, sparring partners and minders, caught up with him on the sidewalk, surrounded him and gave him a grilling. Didn't touch him, just put the frighteners on him, scared him out of his life. He mentioned it but wouldn't talk about it, and the day before the fight — when we were out running — Lotte was lagging behind. I went back to give him an earful, wake his ideas up — I knew these moods and the only way was to jolt him back to life — but he went silent, shut his lips tight and wouldn't speak, wouldn't even look at me. I could tell by his eyes that he'd sunk into a pretty deep depression and there was no way I could jolly him out of it, even if he'd let me close enough to try. Nothing would shift him. His sparring partner did say he'd had a phone call from Zambia in the middle of the night with bad news, but we never found out what the news was.

The day of the fight, he wouldn't say a word, went into the ring and fought, if you can call it that, given his talent, like a zombie, like half the man he was. Went down in the third round and didn't get up.

It was a sad business. I have no doubt that if he'd fought on his home ground, with those supporters of his doing the old Zulu act on Muhammad, he'd have won the title. But you can never tell. Lotte was a complex character, not averse to telling you a white lie and then flash a big wide grin as if that was enough to make you forget and forgive everything. A brilliant, passionate fighter who, alas, didn't go quite as far as he might have done. Always suffered from shinsplints, which tended to flare up mysteriously when we got to Hampstead Lane, halfway out on the run. 'Sorry, George, I'll have to go back, it's my shins again.'

Boza-Edwards makes another entrance here, in company with Barry McGuigan. I never trained McGuigan, but I did go into his corner when, as British and European featherweight champion, he took the world bantamweight title from Eusebio Pedroza. He was in Belfast, training for an eliminator, and I not only happened to be there with Boza for a fight on the same bill, but we were staying in the same guest house in Bangor. We got acquainted and took to each other. He saw me bandaging Boza's hands one day and asked me to do his in the guest house that evening; which I did and it led to me doing his bandages for his next two fights, and the start of a good friendship. I already knew McGuigan as a boxer, naturally: a real firebrand, Celtic fury and punching that smacked the vim and wind out of his opponents — 24 knockouts in 27 pro victories; not a bad record. And as a boxer, so the man: a terrific guy, bags of heart, warm good humour and as friendly out of the ring as he was undoubtedly mean in it. However, a week before the fight, his opponent pulled out and the promoter rematched McGuigan with a southpaw. We heard the news as we were waiting up the driveway to the guest house. The promoter had sent someone over. Barry shook his head and said: 'No way. I'm not fighting any southpaw, I've done no training with any southpaw, I'll pull out myself.' At which point I saw our fight going out of the window, too, and I didn't want that. I grabbed his arm and said: 'Hold on, hold on. Boza's a southpaw; why don't you come in and spar with him, give it a go, at least, and if it doesn't work out by next week, then pull out. What do you say?' Of course I knew that one of his specialities was a left hook that could fly in under any slack defence and that was perfect against a southpaw. With a bit of persuasion he agreed; the sessions with Boza worked out well, he stayed in the fight, and won it, and he and I became very close, to the extent that when he fought Pedroza for the WBA crown in the open-air at Shepherd's Bush on

8 June 1985, he asked me if I'd do up his bandages for the fight — a specialist job that can win or lose a fight. Putting on the bandages is probably the most important aspect of the entire operation of preparing to go into the ring from the dressing-room. Bind them too tight and the hand can't move; too loose and they give no support. You mustn't tape over the knuckles, but you must get close enough to afford the knuckles some protection. If a man's knuckles get bruised on the hard corners of his opponent's shoulders, head, hips, he'll have dodgy hands and be at a disadvantage for the rest of the fight. The official inspector has to see the bandages and sign them to say they are approved. Get it wrong and you put your boxer's chances in jeopardy. Barry also requested that I go into his corner. I squared it with his trainer, of course, and was delighted — and honoured — to be part of McGuigan's back-up team.

McGuigan fought 15 bruising rounds against a man who'd been champion for seven years; an undisputed points decision from boxing of astounding force and channelled aggression. He served up Pedroza, as he seemed to all his opponents, a relentless beating, never stopping till either he put him down or wore him down. And I was proud to be associated with him.

John Mugabi, who won a bronze for Uganda as an amateur in the 1980 Olympics, was, pound for pound of body weight, the hardest puncher I have trained or managed. He was also the strangest and most unpredictable. I had my eye on him after the Games; mentioned him to Mickey Duff; I thought he was a great prospect. We contacted him and he was keen to turn pro so we brought him over to England and he joined my stable at the Wellington.

I'd never met a boxer like him. He changed from minute to minute: wild mood swings — all happy and likeable, full of fun, outgoing one moment and in a wicked state the next, blue depression, snarling, miserable, evil humour and impossible to get through to. It made life very difficult; it sometimes made training downright unbearable, an ugly battle of wills, which I hated. I believe my success as a manager and trainer is, and has always been, in gelling with boxers. Like a tree in the wind you have to bend; be rigid and you break, snap, you're useless to them. And if they go off the rails, you have to be able to haul them back, by coaxing, if you can, by pressure if need be. With Mugabi I found myself more and more having to bully and pester when he refused to co-operate, only for him then to turn round and be as sweet as pie, as if nothing had happened. It was exhausting. That said, he was a hell of a boxer.

His first fights were in Germany, all victories, all knockouts. Mickey Duff decided we should go out to the States — Mugabi was obviously world-title material, he'd best go where the world-class opposition was. He stayed in

Tampa, Florida, for two years, boxing and training with me when I went out. John became a local favourite, because he fought the way the Americans like, a real big hitter. But he was a headache to train. There were constant problems. Every fight he was booked for he'd try to pull out of at some stage, early or late, even the last minute. He'd lock himself in the hotel room, refuse to come out to train, ignore me shouting through the keyhole. Letting people down, me, the fans, the promoters, whoever, wasn't in his vocabulary. It got ridiculous, the same old 'No I won't . . . Yes you will' routine; and it always ended the same way, with him reluctantly opening the door, standing there glum and morose, like a kid who'd been spanked and me taking him out to the shops to buy him a nice present, buttering him up, telling him what a wonderful guy he was, what a great fighter, how important this fight was, much more important than any other fight we'd ever gone into etc. If it hadn't been such a grind it would have been comical.

He always fought in the end and he always won, but what a struggle just to get him into the ring. He had a vicious streak in him, too, and his sparring partners got the sharp edge of his temper, as if he was taking out all his anger and frustration — about what, who could tell? — on them and then me, for putting him through the ordeal in the first place. It's not regular practice to open up in the sparring ring, but if John was feeling irate for some unexplained reason of his own, he'd let go with all he'd got. I would wheel the sparring partners in and he'd wheel them out, very much the worse for wear. This reputation got round, as reputations will, and the locals loved it; they called him The Beast. One occasion, a packed house, he stopped his opponent in one round. One round, show over. I thought the crowd would go berserk, he'd robbed them of an hour's worth of steady mauling, but they adored it. The whole place erupted, chanting: 'Beast! Beast! Beast!' They loved him; but they didn't have to train him.

He didn't only box hard, he smoked, drank and over-ate hard, too. He was due to fight Hard Rock Green, one of Lou Duva's boxers, and he came in at the perfect weight when we put him on the scales in the afternoon before the weigh-in at six that evening, the eve of the fight (generally, weigh-ins happen the same day). I was chuffed, things were going according to plan, for once, and I went off to train Boza in the gym. We emerged at 3 p.m., walked back to the hotel and I saw John Mugabi coming out of a hamburger joint with smears of tomato ketchup on his chin. I nearly lost my rag, stormed over and said: 'Have you been eating that junk muck?'

No,' he says and tries to pull away but I grabbed him, marched him back to the hotel and stuck him on the bathroom scales. Seven pounds overweight. He must have drunk a gallon of Cola. Full to the gills with a load of artificial sugar.

I said to myself: 'Stay cool, George: desperate cases, desperate measures'. And marched him straight off to the gym. I wrapped him in towels and tracksuit and had him skipping out in the heat of the sun to sweat the extra out of him. It's a very dodgy thing to do, as not only does such a rapid fluctuation in weight drain a boxer's strength, but wholesale sweating like that can seriously dehydrate him. By five o'clock we'd skimmed off five and a half pounds, but he was still a pound and a half over. We couldn't go on like this, so I gave him a big ghetto blaster to carry and walked him along Tampa Bay, out and back for 50 minutes. On our return he was spot on weight. A close shave. I put the liquid back into him and eased him into some solid food.

I was worried, though. A man so undisciplined and erratic as Mugabi couldn't be trusted; if I didn't watch him like a lynx there was no telling what he'd eat or drink, even on the eve of a fight. What to do? Search his hotel room? Check the fridge? Chain him to the bed? Post guards on all the stairs and elevators? Halfway through the fight, I could see how weak the previous day's antics had made him; but he was nothing if not a fighter when the chips were down, and John Mugabi knew all about chips, believe me. Hard Rock Green was beginning to get to him, and the fight shaped up to be a real humdinger. Mugabi gritted his teeth, hung on and eventually stopped him.

The world title fight with the champion, Marvellous Marvin Hagler, on 10 March 1986, was Mugabi's first loss in 26 bouts, all of them knockouts, so it was no disgrace. However, it was the end of the line for me. I had had my fill of his behaviour, enough tantrums, sulks, hot moods, cold moods, indiscipline and unpredictability to last me several lifetimes. The pressure of his insecurity had got to me at last and we parted company. He did become champion in the end, but not with me.

Several years later, Mickey Duff rang me: would I take Mugabi over to France for a fight. I did; he won, but that was the finish. I always feared he'd end up the worse off and sadly he has ended up penniless — and a cataract growing over one eye which must spell the end of any boxing career he might have hoped for.

One thing which I do owe him, indirectly, I will describe here.

I was in Arizona, training Mugabi for the Hagler fight, and one Sunday we were out for a walk with Boza-Edwards into Nogales, a town on the border with Mexico. Off the road we saw a little church, nothing very unusual, a white adobe building with an open belfry, tiny windows, wide arched door at the front, you've seen them in hundreds of westerns. For some reason, though, and I believed at the time it was no more than curiosity, I said: 'Let's go and have look inside.' It may even have been so hot in the sun that I fancied a moment or two of cool in the shade of the interior. I don't know, there were any number of reasons why we did go in there except the one which really counts.

We went in, it was empty, nothing particularly special about it, except that it had a friendly feel, a pretty little church, colourful ornaments and decoration, statues of the Madonna and child, a clean, looked-after smell in the air. There was a man down by the altar sweeping up the tiles, he put the broom down, dusted off the altar table and started lighting candles. Nothing strange or unusual in that either, just the caretaker getting the place ready for a service, except he was wearing a boxing jacket. Of all the churches in all the world we walk into and the janitor is wearing a boxing jacket with a club name on the back. I was intrigued. We'd sat down to enjoy the cool for a while and the guy disappeared. As soon as he'd gone, the main doors opened, sunlight filtered into the shade and people started to drift in. Within quarter of an hour the place was packed. I suppose I'd gone into a sort of daydream, feeling lulled and relaxed. As I have said, I never felt lily-white enough to go into a church and suddenly I heard myself saying to John and Boza, 'Let's stay for the service'. We did, and I nearly fell out of the pew when the procession of choirboys came in, with the priest — the same guy who'd been wearing the boxing jacket. 'That's the man,' I said.

I found the whole service very touching: his preaching was so direct and simple, but warm and understanding, too. The singing was beautiful, everybody in the place seemed to be putting their heart and soul into it. Afterwards we trooped out with all the others into the sunlight and the priest shook hands with every single member of the congregation. When it came to my turn he said: 'We haven't met. You visiting here?' I told him we were but that I was puzzled to see a priest wearing a boxing jacket. He explained that he was coach at the local boxing club.

'Well,' I said, 'we've got something in common: this is John Mugabi, I'm training him for the title fight with Hagler in Las Vegas.'

He stepped back, stared at us wide-eyed and when it had sunk in he went crazy. 'Fantastic. In my tiny out-of-the-way church? I don't believe it.' So he introduced himself, Father Clark, an American. We chatted, got on really well, told him where we were staying and went back to the hotel. A few nights later, as we were having dinner, he turned up with six of his Mexican kids from the club. They sat down and Fr Clark said, 'I've been checking up on you. You're a trainer, right?'

That didn't take much checking up on.

'No,' he said, 'you're one of the best.'

What could I say?

'So how about you come over one night and coach my kids? I'd love you to do that and I just know they'd be so thrilled.' He'd brought six little persuaders with him and their faces lit up like mine used to when I was staring into the cake shops. How could I refuse?

'One thing,' he said, 'the club is across the border so you have to bring your passports, okay? I can't tell you how thrilled they'd be, how thrilled I'd be for heaven's sakes. Will you do it?'

Of course, I agreed. John Mugabi insisted on coming, too.

We followed his directions to a shanty town outside Nogales. The club hall was a rickety, broken-down, leaky, grubby old shed and the only equipment was a box half-full of worn-out gloves. I felt I was going back in time to the urchins' playground along the canal and in the totter's shed, but the enthusiasm of those kids was something else. They all lit up like Piccadilly Circus when they saw a real live champion contender and his trainer. They were the liveliest bunch of livewires you could imagine. All evening they were at it, hammer and tongs, energy bursting out of them, they lapped up everything we said and did. Father Clark couldn't stop smiling, he was so pleased, the professionals giving his kids so much attention. Before we left I suggested next time they come to us. 'Come to the hotel and have an evening's training there. Boza loves kids, he'll pitch in. He was a world champion, too.' It was fixed and we fought our way through a mob of excited Mexican kids who would have gone on training and sparring all week without stopping if we'd asked them to.

Fr Clark walked with us back to the customs post at the border, the American guards scrutinised our passports, checked mine and handed it back then took John's and said, 'We have to detain you, sir.'

I asked why. He ignored me and whined at John: 'We have to detain you, sir, your visa is out of date.'

'I've only just come across the border, what do you mean it's out of date? A few days? I have to get back to the hotel for dinner.'

'I can't help that, sir, if you'll come in and wait there.'

We left Fr Clark outside and followed the guard into the hut. It looked dodgy. I could see this getting out of hand. We knew the visa was out of date and we'd applied for a replacement. I told the guard, 'We've sent off for a new one. To Washington, somewhere, I don't know, but it must be on the way. It's only just out of date.' That cut no ice.

'It makes no difference. Out of date is out of date. Days, years, it's out of date. That's the law.'

'Oh, come on.'

'Your visa is out of date, sir, and we have to check it out.'

John started to get very hot under the collar.

'Hey, man, what is this? You crazy? We've only just been over the border to help some poor kids in a boxing club. I need something to eat. I'm a boxer, I've got to have food.'

'I can't help that.'

Don't you just love petty officials doing their duty, more than their job's worth, playing a power game, watching you roast over their rules?

'You know who this is?' I said. Maybe the guy was a boxing fan, though by the look of him the only enthusiasm he would work up would be for a rubber stamp refusing immigration. He looked blankly at me. 'John Mugabi,' he reads out from the passport.

'You know who he is?' I repeated. He sniffed. He knew all right but he wasn't going to let on. He turned the pages of the passport again, looked at the picture, at Mugabi, at the picture again.

'This is supposedly the passport of John Mugabi.'

'What do you mean supposedly?' says John, his temper flaring like a Texas oil-breather pipe. I leap in: 'He's fighting Hagler for the world title in a few weeks' time.'

The customs man was enjoying every moment of this; you could tell by the total lack of human emotion in his face. 'Makes no difference to me: this passport is not valid and I'm going to hold you till we get to the bottom of this. That's the law.'

At which point I thought John was going to vault over the counter and chin the whole lot of them in the office. I had to restrain him. I was pretty close to taking no prisoners myself. I could see we were going to get nowhere. I asked if they could bring in Fr Clark to explain. I thought maybe they'd believe a priest though, in the event, that only complicated matters.

Fr Clark joined the argument. Mugabi had gone into a black depression, brought on by hunger as much as anger at thick-headed officialdom. It turned out that the customs people had assumed that John's passport must be false, not believing that a world title contender would be traipsing across the border to spend two hours with a bunch of poor Mexican kids. And Fr Clark pitching in didn't help much because it also turned out that he was awaiting trial with 11 others on charges of helping illegal immigrants from the dictatorship in El Salvador to escape into the USA because they were sick and in a desperate situation. The customs guy had obviously seen Fr Clark coming and, immediately suspicious, decided we might well be trying to hop the frontier. Our priest only made matters worse. Nerves were fraying, tempers were getting hotter and hotter, the argument was getting nowhere, we were getting nowhere and John Mugabi was getting hungrier and hungrier.

Finally a big cheese customs officer arrived and asked what all the row was. Thank goodness he recognised John for the real, genuine article, the world title contender in person, can you credit that? He gave the other bacon bonces in the customs post the bum's rush and let us go, with plenty of apologies. He was probably angling for a free ticket to the fight. We crawled away nearly demented after two hours.

The training evening at the hotel a few nights later was a great success. Father Clark brought not only a small contingent of his boys but several nuns from a convent attached to his church. They supported the boxing club to help the poor kids of the parish.

Before they set off home again, Fr Clark and I had a talk. He asked me if I was Catholic and I told him I wasn't, I wasn't anything. So he asked me if I'd ever thought of being baptised. I told him I couldn't really think of such a thing, I was a sinner.

'But God has a special place in His heart and house for sinners. Why don't you consider being baptised? I would count it a pleasure and a privilege to instruct you. Think about it, won't you?'

I didn't need to think about it. Something told me to say yes and I agreed on the spot. And John Mugabi said he'd join too. For the rest of our six weeks in Arizona the two of us attended classes with Fr Clark or, if he happened to be out of town, with the nuns.

We were baptised one Sunday morning in that little church in Nogales. Boza stood as my godfather and one of the women who helped with the boxing club was godmother. Six of the kids we had trained were my special little squad of padrinos [sponsors]. It was a very moving occasion for me, answering the catechism and taking my first communion I felt as if I had found something I had been searching for — without knowing what — for a long, long time. At the conclusion of the mass, a line of 12 children who had fought in a boxing show the night before walked on — nine of them with trophies. All nine said they had won 'because of Mr Francis' and the whole congregation applauded; in a church, at a baptism. It made me so warm inside.

When Mugabi fought Hagler, I invited Fr Clark into our corner. Later, when another of my Ugandan fighters, John Mondooza, shared the same bill with a boxer managed by the Patronelli brothers, Hagler's managers, the Patronellis said: 'What about that Mickey Duff, he's always got something up his sleeve . . . whips up publicity for some so-called priest in Mugabi's corner when you can bet your life he was no more than a truck driver with a dog-collar on.'

(I did hear that the American President, Reagan, had wanted to make an example of Fr Clark and the others accused with him of aiding illegal immigration into the USA, but that only three were convicted and then of only very minor offences.)

About being converted, finding God, whatever you like to describe it as, people often say: 'Oh, born again, found God, you think you're saved', all that. As far as I'm concerned, that belief is there when you want it. Perhaps not in the times when, all things considered, you probably need it most, but when the realisation dawns. And, to paraphrase Voltaire, I believe that if God wasn't there He would have to be invented. That belief is part of something inside us, needing help, needing security, above all not feeling we are completely on our own. Some people point an accusing finger and say that religion causes terrible wars and hatreds that persist for centuries — Catholics and Protestants, Moslems and Christians, Jews — and I'm not

Einstein, I can't fathom it out except to say that the violence doesn't come from the religion, it comes from the people who practise the religion and they only use the religion as an excuse for murdering people, claiming it's in the name of God, their God. That's not the sort of God I believe in.

In your early life you're a bit befuddled, it's difficult to work things out. Time moves so quickly and there doesn't seem to be many spare moments for trying to work things out either. If calamities happen there doesn't seem to be any reason for them — I lost two sisters, a brother and my father, for all we didn't get on and for all I hated him in my childish way. But when anybody talks to you about God loving you, you say: 'How can there be a God with all those people in my family dying of disease?' It's only when you're older, when you've been through a bit yourself and seen that disease isn't some kind of vengeance, that it swoops here, there and everywhere on every sort of person, that you come to any understanding. I was nearly finished off several times — the tram, rheumatic fever, the gas oven — but I was still alive and kicking. I might have said about all those mishaps: 'Why me?' But again I might have said about me surviving: 'Why me?' There's no obvious logic in it. It's a question almost without an answer. All right, those early brushes with disease and illness made me a fitness fanatic. I never smoked or drank because I knew from bitter experience how vital health was — having had it taken away from me a few times and nearly popped off more than once. But here I was, training a man for a world title fight, strolling along a dusty road on the Mexican border and I see a tiny church and, for no clear motive, walk inside. Being baptised wasn't a pat answer, I didn't suddenly see a whole stack of reasons for a whole stack of unexplained mysteries in my life. But I did see a kind of pattern in much of what I had experienced during my life. For instance, the cross that someone planted up on Kite Hill, overlooking the Pond on Hampstead Heath every Easter. As I went for my morning run during Holy Week, long before I was baptised, I used to look up at that cross and run up to touch it, and say thank you for the day and for me being there to enjoy it. It might be slashing down rain — if it was Easter in England it more than likely was — but it was still a new day to be got hold of, worked out and enjoyed. And when I told Fr Clark he said: 'There you are — the feeling has always been there; it just needed the moment to make itself known to you.'

He gave me a booklet titled *Footsteps* and in it there's a story about someone having a rough time, imagining himself in a barren wilderness, a desert, empty and desolate and all he can see in the sand is one set of footprints, which means that he's on his own. He gets scared, angry and bitter and accuses God of abandoning him. 'God, why have you forsaken me?' And God answers: 'I haven't forsaken you. Those footprints are mine, from when I was carrying you in your time of troubles.'

After my baptism I have never felt alone and a whole lot of things fell into place. That was the nicest thing — those times of going to church the few days I did attend school, the singing and the stories. All I had felt then made sense suddenly. Material rewards don't mean that much to me. I should say I'm happiest sitting out in the sun meditating, thinking: 'Thank you for all this.' A little bit of heaven.

As a postscript to this I grew up believing that I wasn't baptised and then, in 1992, I was out running on the Heath and coming the other way was a guy I'd seen over the years and knew him as a runner. As we met, he swung round to run with me.

'Hold on, George,' he said, 'I've got a surprise for you.' Turned out he was a church warden at St Michael's church down in Camden Town.

'Oh, yes?' I said.

'You won't believe it, but I was looking through the parish register the other day and I found your christening entry, how about that?'

'You can't have,' I said. 'I was never baptised till a few years back in Mexico.'

Well, I was wrong, he had the record sure enough, he brought me in a copy:

GEORGE ALBERT FRANCIS
BORN 28 JUNE 1928
CHRISTENED 16 JULY 1928

Chapter Eight

Speaking Frankly . . .
Enter Bruno

I first met Frank Bruno when he came into the Wellington gym one afternoon in 1978 and stood in the doorway looking lost and overawed. This was where his idol, John Conteh, trained. Bruno was 17, raw and ambitious. Not recognising him, I asked what he wanted.

'I'd like to do some sparring, please, sir.' (He always called everyone 'sir'.)

A big lad, he seemed fit and when he told me his name it clicked — I'd seen him at a few amateur shows. Not a bad boxer. I told him to get changed and gloved-up and then stuck him in the ring — I forget who with. After three rounds he began to jump back out through the ropes.

'Where do you think you're going? I said.

He looked at me wide-eyed. 'I've done three rounds.'

'Get back in there. You came up here wanting to spar. You get out when I tell you.'

He climbed back in and carried on, another three rounds good and strong. His physique and pluck impressed me. He took his gloves off, got stuck into the punch-bags, the punchball, did some skipping and so on. I could tell he was overawed by the guys he was working out with — I had an outstanding stable of fighters then. At the end of the session I saw him loitering by the door, for all the world like an autograph hunter. I went up and said, 'What are you waiting for?'

'What do I get?'

'Experience,' I said.

He looked crestfallen. 'But I walked all the way up here from Kentish Town and I've got no money to get back to Wandsworth where I live, sir.'

'I'm not "sir", my name's George. Here's a fiver.' It was only a token, I admired his guts. He started coming up regularly — a long drag of a journey from south-west London — while he was training for the ABA championships.

I threw him in at the deep end; matched him with all shapes and sizes, all weights. He caught a few wallops but took it all in good part; he had a heart and he didn't give up, he came back and he came back. After a while I said: 'Listen, you've got a rotten slog trailing over here. Why don't you go and stay with Lotte a week or two in the house we got him in Hampstead, then you can join in the whole day's training?'

He jumped at the chance, moved in and began the early-morning sessions: 7 a.m., the long run, back to the Pond; exercises and cold-water plunge. His physique made him an unnatural runner, but he kept pace in spite of that. He was determined never to give in, give way, fall behind. One morning I decided to put him to the test, see what sort of guy he was, try his mettle, see if he had the stuff to make the grade.

It was mid-winter, bitterly cold and snowing. I took him on his own over into the woods this side of the Heath extension. The others had gone on. This was still unfamiliar territory for Frank but I said: 'Okay, away you go, back to the Pond. See you there.'

He stared round at the woods, snow drifting across the near darkness, and said: 'Which way do I go?'

'Up there,' I said, waving vaguely up the hill, 'follow your nose.'

He set off and I stood and watched him, then dodged off by another route. At one point I backtracked him to see how he was getting on. I caught sight of him floundering about, not knowing which of the criss-cross paths to take; then he spotted an old lady out walking her dog. He headed for her to ask her the way. She glanced round, saw this huge black man, hooded and swathed in tracksuit and scarf lumbering along the path, bearing down on her through the blizzard and morning twilight and made off smartly in the opposite direction.

Eventually he made it back to the Pond, staggered into the compound, puffing and blowing — he'd been plodding to and fro across the Heath for an hour and a half trying to find his way. He looked daggers at me but he didn't loose off. I put him through some exercises, told him to get stripped off and into the Pond for a plunge, then some skipping to warm him up again. He hated it, that was plain, but he didn't complain. He had determination in abundance, a lot of guts and I was so impressed. He was my sort of guy, strong and determined of his goals. Even today, when we're having a joke: he'll say, 'Which way?' and I reply: 'Follow your nose, son.' (Eddy Futch pulled a similar stroke on Riddick Bowe when he took him on.) And the fact is I knew how Frank must have felt, blundering about in the trees. I'd done the same in Germany once when I was staying in a little house on the edge of the Black Forest near Pforzheim, with John Mondooza, a gentle, Catholic guy — the opposite of his stablemate Mugabi

— training him for a fight on the same bill as Rene Weller, the outstanding German, later European champion. The two of us set off in the near dark one morning at six o'clock. The scenery was fantastic, real fairyland — miles and miles of giant Christmas trees draped in snow, the ground carpeted in white and as the sun came up in a clear blue sky the frost shone like diamonds. We got so carried away we kept on running, this path led to another, which led to another, and when we thought we should get back we didn't have a clue where we were or even where we had to get back to. I didn't know the name of the place we were staying and, even if I had known, there wasn't anyone around. We came to a road, saw some signs but in German which was no good to us. Eventually, after five hours' trailing around, we pitched up at a police station and stumbled in. Luckily the guy spoke a bit of English. I asked if he could help. He asked us where we were staying, I told him I didn't know, but it was somewhere not very far from Rene Weller's gym in Pforzheim, could he possibly take us there? Turned out to be 12 miles away.

Frank came to the Wellington on and off for about six months. He took the ABA heavyweight title, at 18 years old he was the youngest-ever champion. I would have liked to manage and train Frank at that time, but it wasn't to be. Mickey wanted Terry Lawless, a top manager, to take him on, with Mickey promoting. Terry Lawless was a decent fellow, I knew he'd do all right by Frank. He had the chance to prove it almost at once. When Frank had his professional medical, for the licence, the optician found he was short-sighted in one eye. Terry flew him out to see a world-renowned specialist in Bogotá and Frank had a very expensive operation to cure the defect.

Terry and Mickey did a fine job with Frank; got him a few fights (all victories) then sent him out to Germany on one of Wilf's shows. The morning after his fight he was sitting in the hotel lobby at 6 a.m. when I went out for my run, keen as mustard and ready to join me. That summed him up: greedy to work, always asking questions, thirsty to learn, keen to improve his skills and fitness.

In 1981 I was in Florida helping prepare Trevor Berbick, a Canadian holder of the Commonwealth heavyweight title, and his trainer knew I was very quick on the pads so he asked me to do some padwork with his man. Terry sent Frank out to get experience with as many top heavyweights as he could.

It was late winter and he'd never been to Florida before and turned up for the run next morning wearing the full British cold-climate outfit: woollen bobble hat, gloves, scarves on top of the tracksuit — the works — like an ad for a skiing holiday. I was clad in singlet and shorts. I shook my head: 'You won't need all that stuff on, you'll boil over and melt,' but he wouldn't listen, he had a very pukkah British approach — you had to wear the full sweat-out rig. And did he sweat. After three miles the perspiration was pouring off him and he divested himself of one layer, then another. By six miles he was about ready to perspire his last drop of liquid and expire on the spot; he was flagging, the jet-lag getting to him, and by the time we got back to the hotel Frank was just about on his hands and knees. We tipped what was left of him into his room and that afternoon, when he came into the gym for the training session, he was so weak he could barely lift his arms up. I gave him a smile: 'I told you.' He scarcely had the strength to nod.

Frank boxed about 50 to 60 rounds with Berbick and got very good experience. All the time I'm giving Trevor instructions do this, do that, try this, try that, and Frank is coming up to me after each round saying: 'What do I do? What should I try?' till I have to put him off and say: 'Listen, son, just get on with it. You're here to spar with him not the other way round.' I had to be thinking of the main man and Frank was, as yet, no more than one of the sparring partners. He was still in that arduous, sometimes very unforgiving, process switching to the pro game from the amateurs, but the measure of him is that he did get on with it, buckled down, got stuck in without a murmur. He was unstoppable, eager as a kid — and I mean that in the nicest way — you couldn't help liking him, an enthusiast to his bootlaces.

Trevor lost his first bid, against Larry Holmes, to become champion, but eventually beat Pinklon Thomas to take the WBC title in March 1986, two weeks after Hagler beat John Mugabi. Frank was in Las Vegas for that fight, preparing for his own crack at the WBA champion, Tim Witherspoon, scheduled for June at Wembley Stadium. Terry Lawless gave me a call and asked me if I'd take care of Bruno in his dressing-room for the fight. He had three other boxers on the same bill and he wanted Frank to have someone's undivided attention for the most important night of his life so far.

'You've always had a good relationship with Frank,' he said. 'I know he'd appreciate it.'

I agreed, naturally. I'd always liked Frank and was more than happy to sit with him in the quiet of the changing-room before he went out to face Witherspoon.

I watched from the corner. Frank boxed extremely well, he was ahead by a long way, he was teasing and provoking — guying — till Witherspoon landed an almighty haymaker in the eleventh round. That close and yet to lose. It was my first personal measure of Frank Bruno's considerable character: noble in defeat but even more hungry for the win. What a journey we launched on that night, the two of us.

It was after that fight my full professional association with him began.

I was wondering what to do next. I'd been abroad, on and off, for a long time, John Mugabi's defeat had probably brought him as far as I could take him, and Mickey Duff phoned to say that Terry Lawless was keen for me to come and train his stable at his gym in Canning Town, east London. I was dubious. The trainer who'd been down there for ages had just parted company with Lawless, I didn't know why. I didn't say yes straight off, but Mickey Duff was persistent; he set up a meeting with Terry and I agreed to go, providing I wouldn't be treading on anybody else's toes.

They had a large stable, about ten boxers, including Mark Kaylor, Jim McDonnell, Gary Mason (the three who'd fought on the same card at Wembley) and Horace Notice. The priority was to rebuild Frank's confidence after the Witherspoon defeat. He had relinquished the European title he'd won in 1985 and his sights were firmly fixed on a world crown. I felt that he had acquitted himself more than adequately in the Witherspoon fight. In fact, I always felt he had something special, that he would come again — he was only 24 — and eventually become world champion. I agreed to take over at Canning Town. There were some outstanding prospects there apart from Frank, though he was the only full-time pro. Where the other guys had to fit training round day jobs, Frank could devote his whole day, from the early-morning workout at the Pond to the afternoon sessions, to boxing. Another great asset he had was that he cleared his mind very quickly. It's a valuable part of his make-up, the ability to leave a defeat behind him and throw himself at the new job; not to get stuck in the past but to forge ahead to the next possibility. Nothing puts him off course, and he works as hard and with as much determination as any other boxer I have known or seen. The nice thing, too, is that we gelled from the start.

The first day at Terry Lawless' gym I was astounded to find not a single medicine ball in the place, so I got two in straightaway. I can understand why some people, Terry Lawless included, are suspicious of the medicine ball as, wrongly used, they can severely damage a boxer. The other thing I introduced was music. The boxers said: 'Terry'll go mad.' I asked them why. They told me he'd never had music, he was a quiet individual, he hated the booming ghetto blasters, not his cup of tea at all. Different people, different tastes: they're definitely my cup of tea for training. I replied that he wasn't going to have music now: he'd be in his office, we'd be in the gym, getting on with the work. They insisted that he wouldn't like it. 'Forget that,' I said, 'do you like it?' They said yes, so in came the sound system. Loud music with a strong beat for the exercises — punch-bag, skipping etc — and softer for the sparring, so I could call out any instructions when necessary.

I believe music is an excellent aid to rhythm, though you might think that in training it would interfere with concentration. However, you must remember that when the fight is on in the big ring, another sort of music takes over at full volume: the chanting of the crowd, catcalls, boos and abuse — unfortunately — as well as cheering and support, roaring and singing 'Bru-no! Bru-no! Bru-no!' The boxer has to concentrate in the middle of that uproar so, in a funny way, training to music helps him prepare for that. Moreover, a crowd can lift a boxer, spur him on, and he needs to be able to hear that, not just blank out all the noise and retreat into a cocoon of his own silence.

Apart from Frank the boxer I got on best with was Horace Notice, what I'd call a real Jamaican: happy-go-lucky, enthusiastic trainer, warm personality, a lovely guy, all heart and very strong with it. He won all his fights with me, became British heavyweight champion and then, one day, we were sparring with the pads (wide, flat-palmed padded gloves not unlike the discs that airport marshals use for guiding a plane into its parking space). The idea is that the trainer wears these and offers them as targets for his boxer to hit. By this method the trainer can imitate the fighting style of his man's opponent and school him for the eventual meeting in the ring. At the end of the round Horace blinked, screwed up his eyes. I asked him was anything wrong.

'I keep getting a black spot in my eye.'

I recognised the symptom and it wasn't pleasant — I had the same experience years earlier — it meant detached retina. Praying it wasn't, but fearing the worst, I phoned Terry Lawless immediately and told him. He came down, and we got Horace to Moorfields Eye Hospital without delay and they diagnosed a detached retina. It was a rotten blow. They performed an emergency operation and I got there as soon as I could and when Horace came out, I sat with him. I knew what he was going through. I'd been through it myself. He was still groggy from the anaesthetic, didn't even know what had happened to him. When he recovered sufficiently, I broke the news. He knew it was almost certainly curtains on his career. I felt so choked for him. A hell of a nice person, a fine boxer just coming into his own and what might have been a glorious career cut short. The British Boxing Board of Control always refuses a licence to a boxer who has suffered a detached retina. They are the strictest boxing authority in the world on that count, and justifiably so, I believe. In fact, our Board is, I reckon, the best in the world all round. Their rules are inflexible, but they need to be. In many other countries boxers are fighting who would never be allowed to fight in this country because they risk permanent injury.

I'll always be sorry for Horace: if ever a man deserved success and rewards, he did. He worked so hard and made such progress and it came to virtually nothing. Boxing can be so cruel to some and so over-generous to others.

With notable exceptions, the work at Lawless's stable was enjoyable, and we had success — a number of champions and a lot of attention. Most of that came courtesy of Frank, the undoubted star of the place. We always had the press in the gym, to see Frank, after some copy; he was a natural, a publicist's dream; bags of charm, a neat way with words and plenty of wit and jokery. People love him. He's modest, even unassuming with a gentle, bubbly sense of humour but no fool either; and he seems to draw people to him without making any effort or song and dance. Being the size he is helps, but it's more, much more than that. He doesn't put on airs and graces, never did — perhaps he's still like a little lost kid at boarding-school that he once was — and that gives him a soulful quality in amongst the laughs and repartee. It's not only the boxing fans who love him either. He's a nice, normal guy who has the way of making other people feel good about the human race, which is uncommon enough. It doesn't endear him to some other boxers. Whatever his attractiveness is, it riles other men who are envious of his public status and his boxing record. I could take other boxers who were eaten with resentment to one side and try to explain: 'Your turn will come. Don't resent it; learn by it.' Only to get the reply: 'I'm not one of the boys. I'm doing my own thing.'

'Doing my own thing' turned out to be mostly not training even a quarter as hard as Frank. But you can't plant a frank attitude to hard work and patience where there's no open spirit to receive it.

During 1987 Frank had fights with four leading heavyweights, including the man who had controversially deprived the popular favourite Henry Cooper of his British, European and Commonwealth titles, Joe Bugner. That was undoubtedly a showdown: Bugner trying to make a comeback by toppling Frank off his perch; Frank haunted (as he puts it) by the spectre of the man who had twice gone the distance with Muhammad Ali. A defensive fighter, a boring fighter, but still going strong, and still talking twice the fight he ever delivered.

Frank had beaten James Tillis in the fifth with Mike Tyson (who had to go the distance with Tillis) sitting at the ringside; Chuck Gardner, KO'd first round — a farcical non-event; and he gave Reggie Gross a solid, workmanlike hammering till the referee stopped the fight in the eighth, several rounds too late, according to most people. These victories were pushing Bruno towards a match with Tyson. The defeat of Bugner in the eighth, after a sound battering, put Frank number one in line for a crack at the world title.

Preparing for that fight was a terrible strain. Normally we train for about ten weeks before a fight but our training for the Tyson bout dragged on for ten months. Tyson withdrew three times, drove his car off the road, got into a brawl at a nightclub, had very public rows with various people close to him. And while all that was going on, postponements, new dates, stop and start, Frank was trying to stay at his peak. It was impossible. At one point he went down from his regular super-fit weight of 16½ stones to 15½. The pressure to maintain concentration and physical condition was almost unbearable.

Eventually the fight was on, but switched from London to America. We flew out to train at Fountainhills, Arizona. The USA was better for us; it supplied a much larger pool of sparring partners to draw on. I knew most of the pro managers out there, so the contacts were all in place and an excellent agent, Johnny Boss, helped no end. Frank had no lack of fresh opponents in training. And in the fight he very nearly pulled it off. He took a hard punch from Tyson in the first and a lot of people thought the contest was over — an 18-second knockout — but Frank stormed back with a level of aggression and hard hitting that nobody, bar me, had ever suspected him capable of, let alone witnessed. As I told Frank early on, more or less what Jim O'Keefe had told me, men like Tyson will pull any trick, any stunt to win, if they think they can get away with it. They'll scrap rough, brawl and butt, elbow and shove. Boxing is no polite board game; it's a tough, uncompromising, no surrender battle and the sooner 'Mr Nice Guy' transformed himself into 'Mr Mean' the better. I promised him not only the most arduous training schedules he had ever imagined in his worst dreams, but a crash course in professional gamesmanship with the sort of ploys, just on the borderline of the rules, perfected by great fighters like Ali. Frank not only needed to harden up his style, he needed to wise up on the pro business. All the old pro tricks: unbalancing your opponent by a nudge of the shoulder, pushing down his neck to crowd him. And in the Tyson fight he showed how much he had come on from the routine dismissal of no-hopers like Gardner. One trick he shied away from was the oldest trick in the world: he wouldn't hang on to his guy when he'd been hit. That's what even the best boxers do, especially on the ref's blindside, hold and stay out of trouble till you're ready for more. It's an escape route, not a surrender. I had wanted him to be nasty and spiteful in the ring — it doesn't come naturally to him and that is no discredit; why should it be? I wanted to introduce him to the American style, bobbing and weaving and making full use of all his considerable gifts. Well, that was to come, but not yet. He certainly got a severe introduction to the American style that night.

Whacked by Tyson he reacted as if he'd been stung out of his younger uncertainty about his own powers and prowess. He came back on the volley, punching and clocked Tyson with some of the hardest punches Tyson later admitted he'd ever been caught with. The man was in serious trouble; but he wasn't champion for nothing. He weathered the storm, grabbed breathers and then he slammed Frank with a real piledriver and the fight was over.

There have always been queues of people saying that Frank is not a natural fighter. Charming bloke, mellow character, wouldn't say boo to a pantomime goose, but they seem unwilling to examine the evidence, as if his own soft talking, his gentlemanly manners have fooled them into forgetting that he has been a first-rank contender for a world title for some years. He has fought extremely hard men and worried them badly, come within an ace of beating them. He shook Tyson to his boots, when every heavyweight in the world trembled at the thought of the street-fighting kid turned savage boxer from New York City, the guy who walks into the ring in shorts, gloves and boots, no socks, no fancy gown, for all the world as if he's stepping out onto the sidewalk to settle who rules the block. Frank has not only boxed his heart out in every fight he has gone into; he has often boxed his opponents off their feet.

That night after the Tyson fight I went up to Frank's suite to say goodnight. He was there with his wife, Laura, and he told me he was going to give boxing a rest. I said, 'That's up to you — I'm sure you'll make your own mind up. You fought a hell of a fight tonight.' When we arrived home the crowds at Heathrow were massive, cheering and waving — you'd never have believed he lost.

The difference between fighting and boxing is temper. I've done both; I know. My street fighting was all rage, not necessarily with the guys I was belting and being belted by either. It was rage with myself, my unhappiness at home, with poverty. Then in the market, tempers flared, you whacked each other and the argument was settled. There were very rarely any hard feelings. Boxing is different. If you get riled up and mad, if you let your deeper emotions spill out, you lose control and I would say that control of yourself is central to boxing. Control and discipline are what makes it the sport it is. Technical skill, fitness, toughness — both mental and physical — are essential, but command of a very basic human instinct — aggression — is vital, especially because boxing is rooted in aggression. Men have always fought and they always will. In mean times in mean places, if you couldn't use your fists you couldn't walk the street. Mining villages in south Wales, slum areas in London, the ghettoes of New York and Chicago, and every seaside port you can name, fighting was a way of life.

The lower West Side of New York City was always known as Hell's Kitchen, not from the gang warfare that went on, but from the rough and ready methods employed by the local Irish priests to keep their tougher parishioners in order and meek in the eyes of the Lord, so help them. I don't know if he was Irish, but a priest called Fr Bernard Vaughan was friendly with an early world heavyweight champion, Tommy Burns, who held the title between 1906 and 1908. He wrote him a letter in which he said: 'Boxing is an education — you learn self-control, to give and to take, to punish and be punished, smiling all the time.'

I don't know about the smiling — they were different times and the only boxer I know of today who talks about smiling is Naseem Hamed. In the heavyweight division there's little room for joking, whatever the psychological games being played. But the old priest was right in spirit at least. Boxing was always called the noble art, from the days when John 'Gentleman' Jackson taught the aristocracy how to box, in the early nineteenth century. Lord Byron was one of his fighters and when someone chided him about spending so much time with a common boxer, a pugilist as he was called, Byron said Jackson's manners were 'infinitely superior to those of the Fellows [bigwigs] of the College in Cambridge whom I meet at the High Table'.

Boxing became a fixed part of the public school curriculum. It was standard training for army recruits and officer selection. Boxing really started in Germany in the nineteenth century, because the German army copied the British, and British soldiers were reckoned to get their fighting spirit from the ring. And for these reasons boxing was taught and developed:

Self-reliance
Mental discipline
Physical strength
Alertness and quickness of thought
Physical dexterity
Steadiness of nerves
Courage

Just as aggression is a wholly natural human instinct, so is fear. They go together. You're aggressive because you're afraid. Both can be useful if they're controlled. Fear can reduce you to jelly if you don't face it, if you don't take it on, if you don't understand it. But fear can bring the best out of you, too, and the whole point about boxing is that you have to face your own fear and overcome it, consistently, as a matter of course. The basic appeal of boxing to spectators is that they can observe two men matched in strength and fitness testing each other's will to win and capacity to beat the call of fear. Fear is telling you to get out, to escape the pain, to duck the challenge. No one forced you to go into the ring, after all. And you square up to the fear and say no. That fear never leaves you; it always comes back; it's with you morning, noon and night; it dogs you all the way to the fight. You conquer it, it goes, it returns. You conquer it again. And as you conquer it, you learn how to control the aggression that lies behind it so you can have ice-cold aggression.

All sport involves physical and mental pain and success depends on breaking through the pain barrier. What makes boxing unique is that the pain is inflicted by your opponent; it's as close to the old-style duel as there is and it is the ultimate test of physical manliness. Some people may say who needs manliness in this day and age? Some people may disagree with the whole concept and there's no way I can convince them, except to say that whatever brutality there may be in boxing, it is incidental, it isn't the main aim. As the referee always says at the start of a contest: 'May the best man win.' By skill, by guile, by superior physical condition, above all by sheer heart and strength of will.

It's a common saying that the one thing you can't afford to do is to take any of your own problems into the ring, and it's true — any revenge, any resentment, any personal anger isn't only useless to you, it's positively harmful. Emotional luggage only weighs you down, spoils your judgement, gets in the way. Naturally, you can't step into the ring thinking your opponent is a sweet bloke, the loveliest guy on earth and wouldn't it be a rotten shame for you to hurt him, or whack him so hard he doesn't know what hit him. You're in there to do the business and so is he. But the business is temporary domination of another athlete, not a public vendetta, or blood on the canvas, or lots of hate. Naturally, too, you have to psych yourself up to fight, to hit and be hit. Even that process of steeling your nerves against a bruising encounter with another fighter is part, I believe, of the value of the sport. Perhaps of any sport, but boxing more than others, because boxing is one to one. There is nowhere to hide in the ring, no team-mates to carry you through a bad patch. The boxer has the loneliest responsibility of any athlete and that is what gives it its appeal with true fans, not any bloodlust. On the street hot temper overrides fear, in the ring hot temper is a catastrophe; it has to be replaced by discipline and that is what is impressive: the deliberate and controlled mastery of the basic instinct to run away from threat or to go completely berserk.

In boxing that threat starts long before the actual meeting in the ring. Some boxers talk a good fight. Ali was the genius at it, so classy in the ring he could assume total superiority outside it and turn it into a joke at the same time. Other boxers rely on generating such menace, their intention is to force their opponent to go into the ring already beaten in their mind. That's the style of Mike Tyson, born in the slums, who's never shaken off that almost animal savagery which grew out of the rage at being kicked around as a kid. The sort of intimidation he boils up is formidable. The black kid in New York, having to fight his way home, eventually fights his way out of the ghetto by putting the gloves on, but every fight he has he carries all that into the ring. It makes him a nasty boxer to deal with, but it's just as obvious to me that all that intimidation pouring out of him is a cover for a monumental fear. Unquestionably, though, he can turn that fear onto his opponents; everything about him, his body language, his eyes, even his outfit — black shorts, black boots, no socks — is calculated to overawe and frighten.

When Frank Bruno fought him in 1987, he got the eyeball treatment all right. There was such venom and naked hostility in Tyson's face, such contempt and arrogance. I don't think Frank had ever seen anything like it. An object lesson in just how mean the fight game can be, or how some fighters can make it. Frank showed extraordinary nerve that night, too much, in fact. I had only just taken over his training and told him at the outset that Tyson wasn't ever going to take prisoners. In those days Frank was by nature reluctant to go down on one knee when he got hurt, to take a short count and give himself a breather; or else grab his opponent and lean on him, rock and roll until he'd recovered from the shock and was ready to get going. That reluctance was partly physical — it is true that he has tended to be a bit immobile and inclined not to rely on his feet, which speedier movers have taken smart advantage of. But as I have said, he was too proud to go into a clinch. He's basically an out-and-out sportsman, with a decent attitude, more honourable, at times, than is good for him. What he never lacked, though, from the beginning, is heart; heart and nerve.

He demonstrated both in abundance in that fight against Tyson. It bore him through a pretty torrid first round, when many lesser men might have succumbed. And when he caught Tyson with a massive punch, it was more because he didn't have the killer instinct — the quick viciousness of a born fighter — that made him hold off, than any fault of skill. The fact is that nobody had put Tyson on the deck and Frank could hardly take in what he'd done. A split-second hesitation in the ring and you can throw away your gains. Frank stood back when he should have moved in for the finisher and Tyson snarled his way out of trouble and, sadly, we know how it ended.

Nonetheless, the fight did reveal qualities in Bruno which many commentators, pundits and punters alike have stubbornly denied him, even in the face of convincing evidence to the contrary: he is a man of enormous heart and, more importantly, of utter and total dedication to learning, to improving, to eradicating every weakness in his boxing. To lose against Tyson was hard, but Frank was still in an early stage of transforming himself into a champion, even if I knew from the start that he was champion material. To climb back after any defeat is tough. To climb back after being defeated by someone as dominant as Tyson — the man who terrorised the heavyweight division — was doubly tough. Not only do you have to convince yourself that it's worth carrying on, worth the grind of training and learning, you also have to convince yourself that you really are prepared to go through another cruel examination of your will and courage, voluntarily.

I was out running a short while after we got back from that fight and pulled an Achilles tendon which laid me up for about six months. When I did get back to the Canning Town gym several guys had left — Dent, MacDonald and Hughes had gone to Barry Hearns; Horace Notice had had to retire; and Terry Lawless had brought in a new man to work alongside Frank Black, who had been there for years. I told Lawless there wasn't enough work for three trainers so I'd go my own merry way.

I went out to South Africa to visit my daughter, Mary, and her family, and took a long break from boxing. While we were out there I even thought of emigrating. I was in my element; popping into gyms when I felt the urge, running and horse riding over open country in brilliant sunshine. I got on well with the locals and I could see there was a heap of raw, boxing talent around, just begging to be moulded and schooled. Several offers of managerial jobs came my way. There was, too, a huge potential market for boxing and sports centred on Sun City, the Las Vegas of South Africa. I could have made a decent living, I know. However, I detested the apartheid politics. I'd worked with black fighters all my life and to see the way the blacks were treated, despised, downtrodden, made me sick and I wouldn't stay. The old all-white policy stank. We can only hope and pray that the new democracy has a chance to survive the terrible hatreds that it seems to have stirred up.

After I got home from South Africa I saw Frank a few times. We went running up at the Pond, did some training; he was just ticking over, keeping in trim. Then he gave me a call and said he was going to resume boxing and would I train him? I agreed, but then came an almighty shock. At the medical examination, which he had to undergo before his licence could be renewed, the retina of one eye was found to be damaged. The British Board wouldn't hear of allowing him to box unless he passed stringent tests on the eye. One of the top eye specialists in the country, Professor Macleod, carried out the operation with lasers and, though he pronounced the eye sound, the Board insisted that one of their consultants examine Frank and give him the all clear. In fact, Frank suggested that he would be happier if several consultants nominated by the Board examined him: that way there could be no possible grounds for doubt about his fitness to box.

That meeting went on for two hours — stewards, doctors, consultant specialists called in to give evidence and deliver opinion. I had been called to attend but wasn't asked to go before the Board. In the end the Board's physician, Dr Whiteson, cleared Frank, on one proviso: from now on, every time he fought he would have to undergo an eye examination to check the continuing wholeness of the repaired retina.

Now that Frank was managing himself, he decided to move our training to a small gym in Plaistow, property of Triamond Construction, which Johnny Kramer, ex-boxer now a trainer, put me on to. I bumped into

Johnny one day, told him I was looking for somewhere halfway between Frank's place in Hornchurch and me in north London. A friend of his runs Triamond and we made the approach and the deal.

A string of fights through Mickey Duff brought Frank a match with Lennox Lewis. Frank beat them all, fought hard and aggressively and won no praise. The same old story. We match him with a guy who's just won a hard fight and people say to me: 'Hey, that's a tough fight you've got yourself.' Then Frank marches in, blasts the guy out in the first round and suddenly a tough opponent is a load of rubbish. Still, if Frank hadn't earned respect yet, he was going to earn it in Cardiff in October 1993.

The Sunday before the fight, Frank and I wandered unannounced into St David's church for mass. Inevitably, he was recognised quite soon, but I want to record my feelings about the service. There was a fairly large congregation, the sunlight was streaming in through the stained-glass windows, and the choir, all dressed up in their red cassocks with dazzling white collars and cuffs. Their singing was something glorious. I was so moved I could feel the tears pricking at my eyes. I had to wipe them away before anyone saw me blubbing.

Before any fight there's a lot of hype — not something I ever had any time for — but that's the business and other camps seem to think it's part of the deal to try and rattle their opponent with a lot of wild talk — and this match was no different. But it was worse. The needle that came Frank's way was barely short of disgraceful. Lewis said a lot of things about Frank which wounded him. Unnecessary jibes. Unworthy contempt. All pretty rude and out of order. On top of that, Lewis's trainer joined in the mouthing off: uncouth ranting, insults. I never take much notice of that kind of barracking and I tell Frank to ignore it. But trading abuse is not to be expected from trainers. The boxers are getting wound up, so they let off steam, it shows how nervous they are; and for some boxers that kind of fandango is normal. But I don't respect trainers who are mouthy: their job is to keep the temperature down, not heat it up. The nettle and stick that Lewis's camp handed out took the fight onto a personal level. It went far beyond pre-fight hype and posturing, it was on the level of Riddick Bowe calling Lewis a 'faggot'. It's grubby and I don't go along with it: boxing doesn't need that kind of stupid name-calling. All credit to Frank that he didn't let it get to his boxing. I told him: 'Leave it out. Don't take it inwards. Rise above it.' And though some of the things they said were meant to be very damaging to his pride and sensitivity and you could see he'd been stung, he did rise above it. He boxed a clean, ruthless, well-disciplined, hard professional fight. But when he did lose, the poison that had been injected into the rivalry made the loss even more bitter.

Frank boxed his level best against Lewis; in fact he outboxed him. He pushed him all round the ring. He hit him, he hurt him, he gave him no room, he showed him no gaps. We had worked hard for that fight. We knew Lewis was a solid puncher, we knew he had a good jab and right cross so we countered him. We rehearsed right cross and jab, jab and right cross till we were sick of it, and then we worked on it more. I don't doubt that Frank was doing it in his sleep: right jab, no cross, no jab. Right? It paid off. Frank matched Lewis in everything; the crosses came and went, the jabs got lost and it really seemed as though it was on and the title was coming our way. But, and I blame myself for it, of course I do, I didn't prepare Frank well enough for the left hook and it was that which clocked him. Up till then people at the ringside were aghast, they were witnessing an astonishing fight; Frank handing out a lesson to a boxer some commentators had called the best of the best. Beating the champion of the world all round the ring.

Frank was ploughing in like a man possessed. He knew he had this fight for the taking. There was no let-up. He was driving punches into Lewis and Lewis was having to pull out everything he'd got in his armoury. There's no question, he's a hard fighter, a hard man, a hard opponent in every sense. But, against all predictions, Frank was handing him a boxing lesson, driving him on his heels. And Lewis was on the ropes. The crowd was roaring for Frank. I felt my throat tighten. Could this be it? But sometimes a man is at his most dangerous when he's in the corner. He's taking punishment, he's retreating to get a rest, he knows his opponent has got his dander up, thinking this is the end in sight, and he's tired, maybe he's going to make an error so he's waiting for the chance. It's Ali in the ring with Foreman. Foreman's coming forward. Everybody thinks the great Ali is done. He's got his back to the corner, Foreman is hammering him this way, that way, every way, and then, suddenly, Ali springs out. It's as if he's lulled the other guy into a false optimism, lured him into a fatal slip of concentration, to make him drop his guard and . . . bang.

Who can know? Was Frank on the point of finishing Lewis? Was he going in to do the business? We can't say; only what they say in the trade: he zigged when he should have zagged.

My hands flexed into fists with the tension. 'Come on, Frank,' I was saying to myself, willing him on, as if it could be me inside him. It couldn't, but the closeness between us is something very remarkable, very special. 'Come on, Frank, you've got him. One punch. One punch.' Suddenly it was one punch: Lewis threw a vicious left hook, caught Frank plum, Frank reeled back, didn't go down — didn't look like going down — but he was badly dazed. He should have sunk to one knee, taken a count, to give himself breathing space. He could have rolled and weaved to narrow Lewis's target. He should have held. But he had too much pride. His arms dropped, he was wide open and Lewis sprang at him. Now Frank was on the ropes. I couldn't believe it. I didn't want to believe it. 'Hold him. Hold him. Hold him.' But he wouldn't. It wasn't in him to do what he thought was demeaning. He'd take what was coming, and it cost him the fight. Lewis piled into him without mercy — why should he hold off? He'd as near lost his title and now he'd been given a last-ditch chance. He hit Frank ten, 15 times. Still Frank didn't go down but he was badly hurt. Still he wouldn't hold or lean or move in to get some rest, anyhow, somehow, just ride out the storm till the bell. And now Lewis was holding his head with one hand and punching with the other. It couldn't go on. It was over. I threw in the towel — which is something I've done only half a dozen times in my career and hated it every time — none of us ever wants to do it, but I couldn't let Frank take any more punishment, I couldn't expose him to any more risk. I owed my man that. I have a big responsibility with Frank. He's a much-loved person. We trust each other. The referee moved in and stopped the fight.

Ironically, there'd been non-stop rain in Cardiff for some days and because the contest was taking place in an outdoor stadium, the organisers had introduced a special ruling that if it started raining after round six they would stop the fight and the man ahead would be declared the winner. Frank was well in front, but (there's always a but) after the fateful bell for the start of round seven, I kept glancing up at the skies and thinking: 'Come on, come on. You've been pelting down for two days, please send some more.'

It was a bitter lesson. It might have been worse; it might have been simply the most disappointing, most desperate defeat he had ever suffered. but he came back. He turned that loss into a final learning process that would take him to the WBC heavyweight championship of the world. It was an awful way to learn. As for me, how did I feel? Exactly like the way they say it: I wanted to dig a deep hole and disappear into it. After any loss there is a question I have to take on the chin: 'Who trained him?' I'm a pro, I should, even at such moments, be able to put the defeats behind me. That's my job: always to think ahead to the next time. Reputation doesn't win fights, it's what you do in the ring next time that wins or loses the fight. But there is no getting away from it: of the three, only three, defeats Frank has suffered when I have been training him, that one against Lewis was the most painful. Coming away from the stadium there were still people calling out to Frank, they were still behind him, urging him to come back, to keep going.

A boxer can only be as good as his opponent allows him to be, and Bruno made Lewis look distinctly run of the mill. It certainly wasn't his boxing that let him down, he got whacked and never gave himself the chance to recover. Afterwards, at the press conference, one of the scribes who have tended to gather like self-satisfied vultures round their latest meal of dead meat — Frank's inability to box — stood up and said: 'Well, we've got egg on our faces now, all right.' And if a journalist admits that in public . . .

You never know when you're at rock bottom until you start coming up again. For a brief time after occasions like that wet, dark, unhappy night in Cardiff, the prospect of having it all to climb again and then some more, and then some more still, was outside my understanding. Whatever the stakes are, high or low, whatever the reward for achievement, the climb from failure is the same: a hard route from the sense of failure and lost confidence back to self-belief and the elimination of every shred of negative thinking.

Take a marathon run, with the top athletes doing the fast time and the fun-runners slogging on after four and five hours. They both hit the wall somewhere. The trained athlete pushes himself or herself to greater and greater demands. The amateur makes far fewer demands on an untrained physique and psyche but the final test is the same for both: do you give up or do you go on?

Some people might say: 'Ah, well, it's different for the top guys, they're earning huge pay packets, they don't need ever to work again. What's the odds? Retire at the nearly top and sit on the money.' And I say that's to miss the whole point. Of course the money counts; I know all about the pressure of not having money. Poverty can stunt you, can crush natural talent. Unless you can burn through the dreadful grind of having no money with sheer physical and mental energy, you're sunk. But nothing, nothing, in the entire world can pay you off if you have a dream unfulfilled. I don't mean the sort of casual dream everyone has now and then, the sort of 'if only' attitude which gets nobody anywhere. If only is admitting defeat before you even start. It's saying: 'If only I had such and such I'd be home and dry but I haven't so what's the point in even trying?' No, I mean the dream that drives you on against all the odds. The dream you know is central to your life. The dream that has no price. You want to be heavyweight champion of the world like Frank; you want to train such a champion, like me, and nothing, no money ever accumulated in one place can buy that off. Only winning the title can do that, and we had just lost.

It was rock bottom. It felt like a huge nothing. It was a very lonely sense of disappointment. But the old spirit came back within hours. And the principle that's guided me all the way through, from the rough days on the streets of Camden Town, through the trials at the Old Bailey, through the hungry years of my early career as a pro trainer/manager: stand and deliver.

That loss turned out to be the breakthrough; my worst, most dismal and harrowing experience in the ring yet, but the greatest spur we could have wished for.

It might seem odd to finish this chapter on a defeat; a low point. But that has, somehow, turned out to be the pattern of my life so far. There's always a 'so far'. Who can tell? But I always dreamed of training a heavyweight world champion. I felt it as a destiny and that is one, only one, of the many things which clicked between Frank and me. He had a similar sense of destiny. He never gave up. I never gave up. Now we have the reward for it: the destiny came through. He's on record as saying that if he had never won the title he'd have got over it and resisted any bitterness. It's as much a mark of inner strength to overcome your worst disappointment as it is to keep striving after success. But, and it's for this reason that I saved the worst till last, success wouldn't have come through without that determination to continue come what may. I've said it before, there are some things which happen in your life which you choose, and some things which you don't choose but which can lead you into unfamiliar areas where you may excel, or you may come a complete cropper. And without Frank Warren's intervention, who can tell what the future would have been after the Lewis fight? When Frank Warren first came into the boxing game, I didn't think he'd last. But he proved to have as much staying power as his namesake and, dare I say it, his namesake's trainer. He's had setbacks but he's dusted himself down and got going again. It's a quality I greatly admire, and now he's one of the best boxing promoters in Europe. He took Frank Bruno on when almost all the experts were saying that Frank was finished and that he wouldn't get another crack at the title, and that he didn't deserve another crack at the title.

Well, Frank proved that he not only deserved another crack at the title, but that it would have been a crying injustice had he not been given the chance. For making that chance possible, for extending that great opportunity to a boxer who has only now been given the full credit in talent and moral power that I always had total belief in, we owe a lot to Frank Warren. And to Bruno himself. No one can reach down into your boots for you. Only you can do that, if you have the character to do it. As for me — the third Frank — well, as I always say when I drive past the cemetery: 'I'm still here.'

Chapter Nine

Fitness and Conditioning – the George Francis Method for Boxers and Boxing

CONDITIONING

People have always said that my boxers are in fantastic condition. Training is one thing, conditioning is another. It's not a bit of use knowing what to do and how to do it, if you're going to fall over dead on your feet before the end of the fight. In my book it's the greatest crime to allow a boxer to enter the ring in bad condition. It's hard enough in there if you're in peak form, without exposing yourself to unnecessary injury because you've let yourself go soft or slow. Certainly in the early days I told my boxers I wanted them in top form all the time, so that if they went to a show where they weren't billed and there was a chance of a substitution to replace someone who'd dropped out at the last minute, they could step in and have no problems. It was so tough getting them fights I had to make sure they were always trained and ready. I used to go into weigh-ins and pray that the doctor wouldn't pass a guy fit; or that some boxer billed to fight on the card would fail to show up. That happened with Lennie Gibbs, for instance, at the Albert Hall. I had one boxer on the card, but I gave Lennie a ticket and told him to bring his gear just in case. A boxer didn't show up, so I nipped over to Mickey Duff and told him I'd got someone to replace him. He asked me who it was and where he was. I told him, 'In the audience.' Mickey said, 'Fine. Get him changed as soon as you like.' They put out a tannoy call, Lennie scrambled into his gear and won the fight.

The only time I saw a boxer I had trained go into the ring out of condition was in 1976: Bunny Johnson, a Jamaican heavyweight from Birmingham. Technically excellent and a sharp fighter, he came to me in late 1973, from Al Phillips, with a match already made against Richard Dunn — an eliminator for the British heavyweight title. This might have seemed a silly move: Dunn was a lot bulkier and had beaten Johnson two years earlier. But I wasn't worried. I could see Bunny's potential: he was a far better boxer than Dunn, much faster, well able to put his whole weight into a punch. He knocked Dunn out in the tenth. The British Board ruled that because I hadn't made the deal, I wasn't due any money — even though I trained Johnson for the whole seven weeks before the fight. Nor did I argue. Again it was that amateur attitude, trying to be fair, leaning over backwards, most unbusinesslike.

In January 1975 he took the British and Commonwealth heavyweight title from Danny McAlinden and was on target for a possible match with Muhammad Ali . . . if he beat Dunn again. The winner of that fight had been promised a match with Ali, my hero, the greatest thing on two legs. We'd agreed to it — Dunn held no fears for us — and though Bunny Johnson had no chance against Ali, it would have been a substantial pay day. (Incidentally, I later worked quite a lot with Ali, provided him with sparring partners, got to know him quite well, had boxers on the same bill, a wonderful guy and it breaks my heart to see what Parkinson's disease has done to him.)

We went into training, Johnson commuting backwards and forwards from his home in Birmingham. Then he opened a nightclub in Brum and phoned me one day to say he was tied up, sick of flogging up and down the M1 and how about letting him train up there? I was against it; I hated the idea. I didn't want him going into so important a fight without making sure he was as fit and ready as I could make him. But he put such pressure on me, I had to give in and agree. I got him to promise to train as hard as I could train him (impossible), and put down the phone.

The Saturday before the fight, Johnson arrived in London and came to my house and we set off for our regular run across the Heath extension, approximately seven miles. He was all right on the way there, but coming back he was tuckered out; he was puffing like a steam engine, mouth hanging open, gasping for air, he was so knackered he had to keep stopping for breathers. He was in terrible shape. He knew it and he wouldn't look me in the eye. It was as much as I could do not to bawl him out. My immediate instinct was to pull him out of the fight and I told him so. He went berserk. He was going to fight, I couldn't stop him, who did I think he was, I'd agreed he could train his way and he'd licked Dunn before, he'd lick him again. He was very het up and, in the end, there was little I could do. I didn't like it, but I had agreed to let him do his training out of my gym. I wanted him to pull out but he wouldn't pull out. I was working for him and his decision was final. 'I'll be all right,' he said. Famous last words. He lost the fight and Dunn got to fight Ali. That hurt badly.

Before the Ali v Dunn fight, Mickey Duff approached Ali and asked him he would. Ali put Dunn on the canvas in the fifth and when Mickey scrambled into the ring to get the gloves, Ali said: 'Take a look at these.' He'd written on the palm of the right-hand glove: 'KO Dunn in five.'

To round off the story with Johnson — we parted company soon after that disaster — he switched to being a light-heavyweight. Being quite a small man, on the border of heavyweight, that posed no great problem for him and he became and retired as British light-heavyweight champion.

Everybody has their own methods regarding conditioning and the seeds of mine were sown when I was young and witnessed the Royal Marines gym in Deal. I thought the Marines were the toughest in the entire services, so they inspired me. They used the old Indian clubs a lot — something you don't see much now — which through the various repetitive exercises those light weights build up pliant muscles, co-ordination, rhythm, speed, endurance; flexibility was the key. Big heavy weights build up thick solid muscle, but they don't improve speed or elasticity and, in the end, power without quickness of movement is no real advantage.

The Marines also used the medicine ball in a variety of exercises, all of which I adopted and adapted for my training programme. The attraction of the medicine ball is that it's a moving weight; a weight that you can catch and throw, hold and pass, again it encourages strength along with movement.

Another Marine exercise was the fireman's lift — one man heaves his partner across his shoulders, right arm clasped round one leg, the left hand holding the load steady by his free arm. Run a hundred yards, swap places and the carrier is carried back. We did that up and down the slope in front of Kenwood House on Hampstead Heath. Everybody lines up at the bottom of the hill to pair off, in matching weights so far as possible. (If ever there was an odd number, guess who made up the evens.) The first man carries his partner up at full speed, the two of them amble back down to recover. Then the second man does the carrying. We always made it a race, to gee everyone up, develop team spirit and to help the weaker guys, to push them to get better till they could keep with the others. That spirit of rivalry was essential to my work — and making it a race added a bit of fun and distraction. Training can get very dull if you allow it to, mindlessly monotonous; variety is the spice and I rang the changes constantly to keep everyone alert, on the hop and interested and, above all, competitive. I even adapted kids' games, the sort of team races we did at the camp when I was a kid: 'overbacks', where the boxers run in a single file then, at the command, the man at the head of the line crouches down for the rest to vault over him till he's at the back of the line and so on. Always keeping everyone on the hop. For instance, in the runs we did, I never used the same route twice in succession, so nobody knew exactly which way we were going. And on days when the stable divided in two for the run, I took the first group out, tied a ribbon on a particular tree at the far end of the extension which the second group would have to retrieve as proof they'd covered the full distance.

Those runs got to be known — and still are — as 'George's Run' or the 'Boxers' Run' and although I don't run them any more, because of my knee, I walk them with hand weights. That's how the heath has been so important in my life and my work: in the middle of a vast, polluted, overcrowded city, sprawl 791 acres of heathland, meadow, woods, parks, lakes and ponds. You can train in what amounts to countryside; enjoy various aspects of nature; breathe fresher air. The contrast couldn't be greater or more welcome of being outdoors than pounding hard-stone pavements in city streets or even working out in the completely enclosed world of the gym.

Five days a week we did the Boxers' Run: from the Pond, via the White House (Kenwood) to Jack Straw's Castle, back through the Vale of Heath or East Heath. Twice a week we took half-hundredweight sacks of sand out to the extension and sprinted up and down the sandy hill through the woods with the sack on the shoulders.

After the run, in the Pond enclosure, we did group exercises on two areas of the body:

1. Top

Standing up with the arms swinging to build up the shoulders, trunk-swivels, arms stretched out to the side and hands rotating, chin rocking to build up neck muscles, star jumps, crouch jumps, knee-lift running on the spot.

2. Bottom

Lying on the floor mostly to build up abdominal strength. There's an old saying in boxing: 'If you kill the body, the head dies.' It's true. The stomach is what holds the boxer together: upper body to put weight behind the punches, legs to dance round the ring. If the junction in the middle is weak, both bits will be useless. Any flutters there and you're finished. I've seen guys lift their knees up till they're bent double when they've been hit in the midriff; and that's where the medicine ball comes in: bouncing on the abdominal wall. I first saw the medicine ball used by the Marines, then a clip of film showing Sugar Ray Robinson using it, and it's been a standard piece of equipment with me ever since, though I have two weights of ball. One heavier for the bigger men. I use it not so much to build up the strength of the abdominal wall — though, naturally, it helps — the strength comes from other specific exercises: feet together, holding the ball and raising and lowering it, up, down, up, down. The bouncing ball is to train the solar-plexus muscles to ward off punches, to clench tight instantly. I drop the ball from two or three feet, the boxer takes it on his stomach then passes it back to me. What you want is abdomens which will contract solidly the second they're even grazed; that heavy ball dropping onto the midriff is no macho trick, it's more subtle, it trains your reflexes. At the weigh-in I always look at two things in the opponent: scar tissue round the eyes and any sign of slackness in the stomach muscles. If I can detect any sagging there, I tell my man to have a go at some body blows.

More exercises with the ball:

1. One man with the ball, the others run by in a line, take a pass from him and pass back, all at speed. The keeper, therefore, gives and receives up to 20 passes. Change keeper and proceed.

2. Keeper in the middle of a ring, giving and taking passes round the ring.

3. Keeper in the middle again, but two balls on the go. This makes it more testing as you need to have very sharp reflexes and to keep your wits about you, otherwise you pass one of the balls, the second one is on the way and lands on your ear if you're not ready.

These exercises increase alertness, speed, instinct and reflex; and speed of reflex is essential in boxing. The rhythm of swinging the heavy ball plays a large part in developing poise and balance, both vital to the athlete. In my training methods I owe no small debt to the work I did as a porter in the market where I hauled huge weights against the clock; speed and drive were crucial, not to mention balancing the barrow so it didn't tip over — all components of boxing conditioning, which put together make for one of the most important ingredients in any athlete: toughness. But he or she must have stamina, too, and where toughness comes from exercises, stamina, in my view, can come only from running, miles of running, to build up staying power.

Every man is different and, as I've stressed, a trainer cannot afford to be rigid, he must adapt to each individual's pace, weight, style of work, while at the same time inspiring him to strive and strive towards a limit in himself he never knew existed, so that he can find the extra punch when he needs it, the precious second wind. In the old days, fights lasted 15 rounds; a solid hour of boxing, a tidy old battering sometimes, but 15 rounds or 12 you still have to reach down into your reserves, where the long hours of running have deposited the precious stamina.

Some boxers have a natural greed to push themselves and increase their endurance, others have to be educated how. And training is never all belt and bully; you'd wind up with a bunch of muscle-bound morons if you behaved like that. You must make your boxers train because they want to, they want to for you, their trainer, and, if you achieve that, your boxers will go into the ring at their peak. Reach that peak too early, and you leave the fight behind in the gym. Over-training is as harmful a mistake as not training enough.

After our sessions in the Pond enclosure came the unique George Francis secret ingredient of success — courtesy of the old reservoirs converted into the Highgate Men's Pond — a cold-water plunge. Ask the regulars who swim all year round — it's magic.

I'd always take amateurs to the Pond and a lot of guys who met up there took an interest, bought tickets to come to shows. So, when I started taking Lennie Gibbs and Bunny Sterling in to train, the Pond men more or less adopted them, a sort of fan following. My boxers were virtually the only black kids frequenting the Pond and, as I got more and more boxers to train, there were up to 14, even 20 at one stage, going into the compound. We didn't crowd the other swimmers, we went in first thing and in mid-winter there were generally more boxers than swimmers around.

So after the exercises everybody stripped off, ran down the jetty and in snow, sleet, rain or wind, it made no difference, in they had to go. They never liked it much. Freezing water? No thanks. And one time one of the Africans, who dreaded it, took off, ran flat-out down the jetty, along the springboard and flung himself into the Pond. Two mistakes: he didn't know how deep it is and he couldn't swim. One of the regulars hauled him out, coughing and spluttering and shivering from head to toe, and brought him back into the open-air enclosure.

'You nearly lost one of your boxers there, George.'

He hadn't told me he couldn't swim; I assumed he'd just climb down the steps, stick his head under and then come out, like the rest of the guys.

One guy who told me later in no uncertain terms he hated the freezing dips in the Highgate Pond is the boxer I've been associated with one way or another since the mid 1970s — Frank Bruno. He's never complained about anything else, never told me to back off or sworn at me, or questioned my methods; even when I've bullied and chivvied him, he's never lost his cool and taken a swing at me, and I'm very glad he hasn't. He's always stuck to his task, listening to what I'm telling him, and he may not be the most talented boxer I've worked with but he is the most patient student I've had by a mile, and with what deserved results; but the one thing he never saw eye to eye with me on was the daily ritual of baptism in the Pond. I told him there are 80-year-old guys swimming in there every day — it keeps them going. He just looked at me and said: 'They're welcome to it, know what I mean?'

Training Camp

For the last few fights, Frank and I have set up camp at the Springs Hydro, run by Steven Purdue outside a village near Ashby de la Zouch in the Leicestershire countryside. Although it is situated off Gallows Lane, luckily I'm not superstitious. It's perfect for us: remote and unpopulated — except by cows and hedgerow animals. When Frank and I go for our evening walk, there isn't a crowd of fans pestering us. He never gets tired or impatient with that and it's to his credit; it drives me crazy, but he says they're his public and he owes them a bit of notice whenever they're there, in return for all the fantastic support they give him.

So, how does the week in our camp go? Whether in a Leicestershire village in damp 'olde' England or in the dry heat of the Arizona desert, the pattern is pretty much the same.

I always scout out the local terrain to find suitable routes for our early-morning runs. Hard pavements or pathways are out if they can be avoided — the metalled surface has no give and jars and shakes the vulnerable knee- and hip-joints. I go for grass verges if there are no fields. I don't like going out in the dark, unless it's unavoidable, so, according to the time of year, we set off some time after 6 a.m. for an average five or six miles over as many hills as the land can offer. At every hill I call for a flat-out sprint to the top and a slower, half-pace lope down the far side to recover, shadow-boxing as you go. That sustained burst of speed and rest reproduces the rise and fall of explosive energy followed by controlled recovery in the ring: unleashing 15 shots at a time and then pull back to regroup before the next onslaught.

After each sprint I observe the reaction, to see how hard he's blowing and for how long he goes on blowing. An ignoramus will look at a man who's sprinted flat out and say, 'He can't be very fit, he's panting.' but that's the point of a sprint, to expand the lungs to their full extent and draw a capacity volume of air in and out. The lungs are pear-shaped and most people don't normally breathe from anywhere near the bottom of their lungs to draw the whole volume of wind available. But an athlete must, in order to work at maximum efficiency, pumping as much oxygen into his bloodstream as he can. In the corner after a round, I always tell the boxer to breathe deep, big steady gulps of air from the bottom of his lungs to circulate the breath. And, would you believe it, I've heard a TV commentator say of one of my guys: 'He's breathing very heavily, he must be exhausted.' That's as much as some so-called experts know.

If, after the sprint, the guy blows and goes on blowing, he may be unfit or overworked. A trainer has to be on the alert, to recognise the signs and judge whether to pile the work on or slacken it off for a bit. Maybe you go down the hill shadow-boxing and then sprint back up the hill a second time without pause. I frequently use Kite Hill on Hampstead Heath in that way: sprint halfway up, shadow-box, then sprint to the top — two hills for the price of one — and always ringing the changes, never the monotony of the same routine but variety and the unexpected. If a boxer knows what's coming, he can tend to get lazy, like a horse in a riding-school going over the same jumps day after day. I tell them: 'Get used to everything I throw at you. And from whatever direction I throw it. Your opponent isn't an automaton any more than you are. He'll try to surprise you, you have to try and catch him napping.' I may get them to wear weighted anklets or boots, even lead-lined jackets in the early days, and carry hand-weights, so when the weight does come off they bounce about like ping-pong balls.

Sometimes I may cancel the run if they've been having it too hard and they turn up for the afternoon sparring session a touch lethargic. A break gives their tissues and cardiothoracic reserves time to build up and make them that bit livelier. Training when you're below par is counter-productive: it breaks down strength and mental sharpness instead of building them up.

For the record, my best runners have been:

1. Chris Pyatt.
2. Jimmy McDonnell.
3. Frank Bruno (for a large man).

Boza-Edwards, John Conteh and Bunny Sterling were also good runners. Usually after the run, though not always, six to ten minutes' skipping, followed by the time-honoured callisthenic exercises described in 'Top and 'Bottom' on page 206 and . . . the medicine ball.

As they wind down from this, the first training period of the day, we may run through some different moves, with me on the pads, say, or talk for a while about the opponent, the tactics we'll use and the tactics he favours. Perhaps we might discuss what we might try in the afternoon sparring and then take a shower. The boxer's day is filled with showers. Change, work, shower, change, work, shower . . .

Relaxed, cooled down, nice and settled, it's time for a fair intake of liquid – the bulk of which will be water – plus a supplementary concoction I make up, full of salts and minerals. I do favour fruit juices, but you can't drink gallons of them to replace the fluid loss. And breakfast: a bowl of fruit – diced in small portions to ease chewing and digestion – yoghurt and cereal or muesli, and in winter, porridge. While in America we eat the breakfast favourite – pancakes. Some guys like grilled kidneys, say, to follow a grilled fish – trout, kipper, any type of oily fish – and, note, grilled. The frying-pan is out. Though I don't tell a boxer exactly what he can or cannot eat, and tastes vary so much, I do follow certain unwavering guidelines. I always eat every meal with my boxers. In fact, before a big fight I'm with them practically every waking hour. The one thing I do make a rule about is never to talk about the fight over food. Mealtimes are for relaxation, general chatter, anything but talking shop.

Breakfast eaten and digested, we go for a couple of miles walk, whatever the weather, but this is leisure – the run is work. This loosens the muscles and gets the boy moving in an easier rhythm than the high-octane exercises do, and it's important to get steady draughts of fresh air. Following the walk, a rest period – to read, listen to music, lie down . . . whatever –

it's the boxer's time. While they rest I busy myself with the laundry bags, checking the gym equipment and training gear, bandages, headguards, gloves, gumshields, to ensure that everything is ready in tip-top condition for the afternoon sparring session.

Lunch, between 12.30 and 1 p.m., where the emphasis is on light, nutritious food: consommé for the lighter boxers, thicker soup for the heavies, grilled fish or white meat. When I first started boxing, people told me: 'Eat lots of steak.' Oarsmen, weightlifters eat it for the same reason: to build up muscle. So I used to take my cotchel from Covent Garden down to Smithfield and swap any fruit for thick steaks. But I soon turned against red meat as it's so much harder and slower to digest and the sort of muscle it does build isn't necessarily quick or lively muscle; it doesn't encourage the 'twitch' muscles which aid reflex and speed of reaction.

Unfortunately, there are very few nutrition experts who have advised on diets for boxers. Other sports have whole panels of dietary brains working on the best foods for this and that aspect of physical development. In boxing, however, it's been largely hit and miss, each trainer learning for himself — if he can be bothered, and he ought to be. In my case, I read about footballers being forbidden to eat a large meal on the day of the match and followed suit. You can't fight on a full stomach, of course, but it was the arguments for and against red meat, for instance, which interested and inspired me. In the days with the amateurs, my boys always had abdominal walls like iron and the number of flabby guts I saw on other boxers made me wince. And, following the weigh-in, I'd see those soft bellies getting filled with sandwiches and drink immediately before going into the ring.

Regarding vegetables: I favour greens for their iron content, the fresher the better and the darker the better — broccoli, spinach, spring cabbage, spring greens. Starch from turnips, jacket potatoes — preferably fresh out of the ground with the minerals still packed in them. And always fruit: bananas to replace potassium lost when the muscle gets tired and begins to break down. Apples — did you know that they have arsenic in the pips? — to build up resistance to all sorts of ailments, plums, pears, always straight off the tree and juicy if at all possible. Grapes off the vine. Grapes are, as anyone who knows me will testify, my absolute favourite; they contain everything the body needs for nutrition. If a boxer comes back into training a bit overweight, I put him on a grapes and spring-water diet (three or four pounds of grapes and at least a gallon or more of water per day) to clear him out and evacuate all the toxins from his body. Not a crash diet to shed weight, only a cleansing process which you can monitor — the stools come out small and white, which is the sign that the poisons have been voided. The toxins are flushed out, the bloated feeling goes and we can start afresh.

Why mar the goodness which you are taking in with fruit and vegetables by eating cakes, sweets, biscuits, chocolates? Most soft drinks, for example, are loaded with added caffeine and sugar; all they deliver is a quick high with nil nutritional value. I encourage drinking ginseng products and, in hot countries, specialised drinks like Gatorade.

A half-hour ramble through the lanes helps digestion and then it's back to the room to rest and prepare for the afternoon sparring session at 2.30 p.m. (That time will adjust forward if the fight is scheduled for later than 9 p.m., the usual witching hour.) Before the gym, a massage. The masseur(se) is a very important member of the team: he or she has first care of a fighter's muscles, stretching and working them to reduce any stiffness in them and to assist in the general relaxation. In training it is as essential to supervise and organise what a boxer isn't doing as well as what he is doing. No boxer can work flat out all the time and he'd be a muscle-bound wreck if he did. The periods of leisure not only help to recoup physical energy, they also recreate the mental freshness that is vital to producing 100 per cent on the night. The emphasis is always on looseness. Tight mind, tight body and you fight like a tin soldier.

In the gym, I bandage and tape my boxer's hands. It's a process repeated every single day in training till that last vital time in the dressing-room before the fight. And, clearly, it acts as a sort of psychological reinforcement of all we have done in training in those moments of last-minute concentration till we find out if the training has been successful. The one difference is that for sparring I always pad the knuckles for protection.

Before a boxer steps into the ring he does 20 to 30 minutes' stretch exercises, to loosen up and warm up. I use that time to talk to the sparring partners who have come in for the session and I tell them what I want from them. They may well have been primed by watching videos of our opponent, so they can imitate his style and any quirks. This way they can give my guy the feel of what it's going to be like in the fight: getting backed into a corner, say, or putting him under a lot of pressure from the bell. And, of course, tell my man what I'm looking for from him, reminding him of all the points we've covered. That's the trainer's job, to think of everything and to remind constantly. Finally, everything depends on the boxer and his instincts. But the object of drills — in the gym as in the army — is to attune a man in body and mind to the possibility of any danger so that when it comes, and from whatever direction, he doesn't panic, he adjusts, reacts, dodges, uses his initiative, all under tremendous pressure. The ring can be a daunting, exposed, lonely place; only those who have been there can say how tough it is. The more training back-up you've got the better placed you are to survive it and come out on top.

The main meal of the day, a more substantial version of lunch, is served around 6.30 or 7 p.m. Eat any later and there is no time to digest properly before going to sleep. Towards the end of training, the last five days or so, we switch to pasta — carbohydrate loading — for a reservoir of energy, but that's really the only dietary trick, if you can call it that, beyond fresh stuff and food which doesn't cling undigested in the stomach or intestines too long.

After dinner we always go for a long walk, at least three miles. We talk about anything and everything. No hangers-on — they are like grit in the machine, they spoil concentration, irritate, prevent the smooth running of mind and, therefore, body. I don't believe in hangers-on at any stage. As far as possible a fighter's mind has to be left undisturbed by extraneous influence. Like the creeping poachers who blow in a champion's ear. The twilight round the boxing ring is full of such half-people. The real business is a one-to-one relationship: the boxer and his trainer.

I occasionally lay on a video of the opponent, to talk through his style and methods and pinpoint errors to capitalise on, or a tape of my man to correct errors and weak spots and encourage strengths; but generally after the walk, I leave my boxers on their own, to be private, unless they specifically ask for company.

This is the pattern through the week and I keep a diary of the work we've done and brief comments as to how I feel we were progressing. It's little more than a sort of shorthand really: 'Opponent strong left. Frank's getting stronger . . . Still a tendency to get backed up . . . Watch for the cross . . . Drop, breathe, gather your strength . . . Don't do all the work . . .'

And after the fight I always make a present of it to my man as a memento. It's of no value or interest to anyone else: a private code which half the time even I can't work out afterwards.

On Friday evening we analyse the week, go through my assessment of the sparring work and itemise a complete breakdown of the training to date — pluses and minuses. The diary and analysis serve a double purpose: as a record of the training, to keep my guy posted on his progress — to judge whether we are overdoing things, something to be guarded against at all times, especially with a boxer who is a glutton for work — and also a way of keeping our objectives sharply defined, part of the vital process of keeping the mental faculties honed as well as the body.

On Saturday, if you've worked very hard through the week, the morning run may be reduced, even replaced by a long walk, to stretch the legs and retain the stamina without flogging either to death. On the other hand, if there's work to make up, I lengthen the run to as much as eight miles. The afternoon is free time and in the evening we go for a walk. On Sunday we go for a walk and have a light breakfast.

Most of the boxers I have handled have been churchgoers. In the early days, notably with Boza, I took them to church at ten o'clock and waited outside for them. Nowadays I go with them. It's a special time: to contemplate, to clear the mind of rubbish, to feel that great companionship of the church congregation, as well as the opportunity to hear the singing and familiar prayers of the service, to think in private and to enjoy fellowship.

Sunday is the day for walks, particularly when we're lucky enough to be in the countryside. A day for the boxer to recuperate and settle after the week's efforts; when he can take his leisure; perhaps go for a swim, which is an excellent way of relaxing the muscles with little chance of pulling them and without putting any strain on the joints.

Some camps swear by games: chess, draughts, cards. For me it's a reading day, a chance to catch up on the papers I have earlier had to leave aside, to keep abreast of current events, the political scene. What shocks me most about the state of the world today is how viciously and inhumanly we go on behaving towards each other: in what used to be Yugoslavia, in Northern Ireland. The enemy from across the border is one thing: but to inflict these atrocities on their own people grieves me. The truth is that hatred breeds hatred and it builds and strengthens hatred, too.

Fan mail arrives almost every day, so one of my Sunday jobs is to sift through it and send off signed photos and so on. I rarely leave the camp; I have to be on call whenever the boxer needs anything, even if only to talk.

The day of the fight, all the preliminary work done — and done as thoroughly as it can be — the most important job I have is to keep tension to a minimum, to preserve some kind of normality and to regulate the build-up to the moment when the boxer steps into the ring and is, to all intents and purposes, on his own.

We arrive at the fight venue and occupy the dressing-room an hour and a half before the fight. I lay out the clothes — boots, shorts etc — and hang up the dressing-gown, sort the towels, make sure everything is how we want it, where we want it. Staying cool, calm and collected, my aim is to refine the boxer's concentration; to remove all other thoughts from his mind than the fight. In those times before the moment of truth, thoughts can crowd in and set up a fight of their own in a guy's head. A world title is at stake, he's going to face a ferocious barrage of punching before he emerges victorious and never think about losing — this is a time to exclude all doubt, all negative influences, all thoughts which conspire against winning. Positive thinking, direct focus on winning, on repeating all the lessons of training, on fighting the fight we have prepared, not the kind the opponent wants. You can overtrain and leave the fight in the gym; you can also lose the strenuous mental battle and leave the fight behind in the dressing-room.

I give my man a rubdown, like shaking out cloth to get rid of the creases, smooth him down and frisk his muscles to warm them, help them relax and not seize up with tension and nerves. We might ease any tautness by doing a bit of shadow-boxing with the pads. There's a massage table for him to lie on if he chooses to doze and settle himself.

We have passages of stony silence in there, little exchanges of conversation, a bit of music if that's what he likes. It's a mixture of his own routines and me keeping a surreptitious eye on the clock so as to know how to make the gradual transition from mental, emotional and physical readiness to the decision time. One thing I always lock out — superstition. If a boxer ever tells me he hopes he gets the red corner as opposed to the blue, I say: 'You have to stop thinking like that. If you don't like the blue corner and you get it, mentally you're already losing.'

All boxers have their own routines. For example, when I was training Frankie Lucas, we had a reporter following us around for an article and having seen Frankie go off to the toilet about six times, he asked me: 'Has he got the runs?' Next time Frankie popped out, I beckoned the journalist over: 'Come and take a look.' Frankie was on his knees, in private, praying. And he turned in the best fight of his life: ten hard, solid rounds, the best I'd ever seen him.

I'm a strict disciplinarian about the dressing-room. It's my policy to keep everyone out: no intrusions, bar the official visits. I even keep the pile of 'good luck' cards unopened till after the fight — it's enough to know they're there. If necessary, I park someone at the door to stop the would-be traffic of handshakers, snoopers and interferers. The sort of guys who pop their head round the door and say: 'Frank, would you sign my programme?' Then, as the boxer signs, it's: 'You want to watch this bloke, he's got a lethal left hook.' Then, 'Good luck, I'm with you.' You push him out into the corridor and he creeps round to the other fighter's dressing-room, same routine. Well-meaning, perhaps, but a pain in the neck when you're trying to screw all your concentration onto one thing: the fight.

I bandage my man's hands; we're getting close to the business now. Binding the hands with tape is at once calming and the final gathering of energy, to contain it in those two hands on which he will have to rely so heavily.

The referee arrives and talks over the rules and what he will and will not allow. This is to mark the boxer's card, almost as routine as the safety procedures on an aircraft at take-off.

Now comes the moment to step out into the corridor leading to the arena. The noise has started; you can see the glare of the lights ahead, making the corridor lamps dim. The boxer walks on, I keep my hand on his shoulder. It's the two of us for these last few minutes. His concentration is total, mine is total. The crowds don't exist. You don't see anyone else; you pay no one else any heed at all. People say to me: 'You never smile as you go into the ring.' But that's because I am completely immersed in the fighter, our vision is the same as that tunnel leading into the ring — 'on the way to the forum' as we say. In training things can go wrong, minor scrapes and abrasions, a cut eye, flu, setbacks, both minor and major, and there is time to take them in your stride, overcome them as you go, but now the fight is on, everything has to be right; nothing can be left to chance and no outside influence or individual must be allowed to come between you and the ring. We walk with that one unswerving purpose: it's our fight.

From now on my place is in the corner, my time the single fleeting minute between each round. From the corner I watch two men, watch my man and the opponent like a hawk. If I spot something in my opponent — the way he is letting his left hand swing at his side after landing a punch, instead of bringing it straight back to guard his chin, and my guy hasn't spotted it, I'll tell him. It's an opportunity to exploit a chink in the armour: 'Feint him on that, then he'll leave you an opening.' Your man's not always going to be able to see everything from his close-up perspective. As soon as the bell goes you have to fly up into the corner like a rocket, often with a styptic to close the cut just opening over an eye and barely visible to anyone who hasn't spent years keeping an eye out for the early signs of broken flesh round the eyebrow. If his flesh is puffed up from a punch I apply the ice swell, a piece of metal that I keep in the ice bucket or bag. And here's something you may not know: if my guy is swelling round his nose, I tell him not to blow his nose. It's better to swallow the blood than snort it out, otherwise the swelling can puff up worse and impair his vision. It's not very pleasant for him, but I just wipe the blood away from his nose and he has to put up with the discomfort. Then you make time to give him a gargle to cleanse and lubricate his mouth, a rub of his shoulders, all to get him bright-eyed and bushy-tailed. And a few words of advice about the opponent, what to work on, what to avoid. You can take that too far. There's an old joke about the cornerman telling his boxer, 'You're doing fine, he hasn't laid a hand on you.' And the boxer replying: 'Well, it must be the referee, then, because someone in that ring is knocking the hell out of me.'

Once the fight is on that minute in the corner is all a trainer has, and if there is a secret to the job it is to concentrate on that minute whichever way the fight is going, to let nothing distract you. If you are telling your man to show ice-cold aggression you, in the corner, have to be showing ice-cold calm and an intensity of commitment on the fringe of the fight to match his in the thick of it.

A cornerman can change a fight. Sometimes a fight can be won from the corner. And a cut man is worth every bit of his ten per cent if he can keep his man going after a bad cut, not only by fixing the cut but instilling the precious confidence that the fighter can keep going.

Two fights come to mind when talking about how the cornerman can help a boxer win a fight. The first was when Micky Hughes fought Gary Jacobs. I knew Micky quite well from training him in Terry Lawless's gym. He'd since gone over toe Barry Hearn but wanted me to come into his corner. Jacobs was a clever all-round boxer, in my opinion a much faster and more skilful fighter than Hughes — who was trained by one of the top American trainers, Teddy Atlas, one of Tyson's first trainers. I thought the best hope we had was to let Jacobs do all the work early on and then try to jump him. And that's how it worked out.

Hughes was losing round after round and Jacobs was so far ahead on points he was getting cocky almost to the point of arrogance. Hughes was slumping so I told him it was time for the second part of the plan, throw caution to the winds: 'Listen, he's knackered, just go in and fly at him, give him your left hook, the full works.' Which he did; went in like a tornado and knocked Jacobs over. It was a terrific result against all predictions, and Micky paid me a nice compliment, said he owed me the victory in a TV interview afterwards. I went over to commiserate with Teddy Atlas; he'd come a long way to see his man beaten.

The second was the Clinton McKenzie versus Des Morrison bout: Morrison, the taller man and a fine boxer. Clinton got severely cut in the early rounds — two cuts over the eye, one under, and he grew more and more dispirited. He was so much the worse for wear I had an idea he was simply going to surrender, so I bullied him. I had to, I shook him out of it, I yelled at him: 'Stop feeling sorry for yourself, get in there and take it to him.' He won the fight. Afterwards he paid me a great tribute which I am proud to say he isn't alone in saying: 'George is magic in the corner.' His words, not mine.

The fact is, if you've been with a guy all through training you go through every punch in the fight with him, and you have to keep your nerve, stay calm and steady even if things look black; his confidence may take a battering but yours mustn't. You have to believe in him and he must know that, he must feel that in the corner, feel it bubbling out of you, every pore. Inspiration, I suppose you could call it. And, sadly, if the towel has to be thrown in it's your job, your responsibility, to throw it in. You owe your man that regard for his safety. However badly it hurts to admit defeat, it's unthinkably worse to have to live with the consequences of carrying on beyond what you believe is admissible punishment. It is the referee's decision to stop any fight, although in some countries if a corner throws in the towel that ends it. In Britain a referee is empowered to ignore the towel; a boxer may look finished but then get a jolt of a punch and wake up from the shot of adrenalin it releases — adrenalin being the body's natural resistance to pain or shock.

In that McKenzie fight I did such a good job patching up his eyes that the Board of Control doctor confiscated my Adrenalin 1 in 1,000 to analyse it and, when he stitched up the cuts, he admitted he couldn't believe how well they'd held up in the fight. 'That comes with experience, doc,' I said.

A note about Clinton McKenzie. I signed him after the Olympics and was pleased to take him on: he had a lovely style and I'd followed his amateur career. I went down to see him and his family at their house in Croydon to sign the contracts. It was a long trudge for him, all the way to Highgate, but he did it, and I thought he would go all the way. He had enormous talent, not a devastating puncher but very skilled, a splendid athlete and very entertaining. He was ABA light-welterweight champion in 1976 and picked for the games of that year, he became British pro champion in 1978 and won the European crown three years later.

After a while, the long journey from south London began to get Clinton down; understandably, and he asked me if his father-in-law could take over his training but I'd still be his manager. I wasn't happy about it, but he persisted and I agreed. As his trainer I was employed by him; I had no choice in the end. He was preparing for a defence of his European title in London and one Sunday morning, just before the fight, he came over to my gym so I could have a look at him. He got into the ring and started throwing low punches. I was furious, I bawled him out: 'What do you think you're doing?' He told me his trainer had told him to go for the other guy's body, stop him early on and that's what he'd been working on. I told him straight that if he went in punching low he risked disqualification. It's not so dodgy if the guy comes in standing tall, but if he's crouched over the chances of landing a foul punch are very high. And the following Tuesday he was disqualified and Robert Gambini went home with his title.

I remained McKenzie's manager, but he started listening to other people, the usual stunt: you lose by being an idiot, you blame the guy who warned you off being an idiot. He wanted to box on other shows than the ones I picked out as best for him. In the end we got into a dispute about who told who to do what. Unluckily, word flew round, some unfounded rumours were stirred up and one weekend *the Times* printed an article featuring most of the gossip. I was so angry, I took Clinton before the BBBC, who decide and govern disputes, and they settled in my favour.

Needless to say, the relationship with Clinton was never quite the same and I suggested he find a new manager. I was in his corner when Terry Marsh took his British title, at Shoreditch in September 1984, but then we parted company completely. I always liked him and we stayed friends, but it was a sad conclusion. That's boxing. I still believe he could have made it to the top.

Chapter Ten

Boxers and Boxing

There are many different sorts of people who make it as boxers. There's the journeyman: strong, tough, go the distance, not a big winner but a useful man to pit your up-and-coming fighter against, to give him the experience of ten hard rounds, which he may or may not win.

The warrior: he will listen to you talking to him all day, day after day, and then charge in and do his own thing which is to aim straight at the opposition and keep going, no surrender, making up in courage and determination what he lacks in skill. You can sit in your corner and encourage or advise him, knowing that, win or lose, you'll always get a good fight out of him. Match two warriors and there'll be a rough and tumble, very popular, and even over two or three fights, it will never be sure which of them will win — it can be very hit and miss — but marvellous business for the promoter.

The technician: so skilled he makes other fighters look ordinary — great for the real fans but no entertainment value for the general punter.

A trainer can do many things for a boxer, but certain qualities a champion must possess before he even starts. Muhammad Ali, for instance. Ali was my great idol because he was a brilliant cumulative puncher with the skills of an exceptional technician, the flair of a showman and the naked audacity and courage of a warrior; one of the most accomplished boxers ever to grace the ring. He had the three things that a great boxer has to be born with:

1. A good punch or the ability to deliver telling combination punches.
2. A good heart.
3. A good chin or the skill to protect a weak chin.

These three qualities are the makings of a possible world champion.

Without the first he can't win; without the second he can't keep going when both boxers have more or less spent themselves or pull himself back from the brink of defeat and go on to turn the fight his way; without the third, he's going to get caught and that is very often the finish. No boxer can afford to be weak on the whiskers. Ali (and Bunny Sterling) was so technically clever he could let his guard drop, show his chin and entice his opponent to take a swing, knowing that his own reflexes were so fast that, as his opponent moved forward to take a swing, he could unleash and land his own punch first. As they say: 'You're only as good as your defence.' And where a slower, less skilled boxer has to keep his guard up permanently — and the referee always warns boxers: 'You must protect yourself at all times' — or else get hit. The superior fighter can play cat and mouse and not get hit. But once you are hit, properly hit, your time may well be ticking away. Some can hold a shot better than others, but a big sock on the chin does its job. Cooper caught Ali; Bruno caught Tyson . . . they went down. And those weren't lucky punches. Lucky punch? There's no such thing. You can go into a ring and from the first minute you're up there to throw punches and avoid punches. It's not luck, it's hard work in training. To go into the ring and rely on luck is a fool's game.

Losing? Sometimes it may even be a matter of how a guy felt when he got out of the bed that morning. We may call it a bad day at the office and, like pro sportsmen in any game, we always look for an excuse: a bad decision or the ref was against us, missed a whole stack of points etc. In the boxing game you're only as good as your last fight.

And finally, what makes a man box? I've heard people call it barbaric, mad, that it ought to be outlawed. One time at Caesars Palace, in Luton, at a dinner show, I overheard one waitress saying to another: 'They must be bloody crazy doing that to each other.' I suppose I had never really thought about it from the outsider's point of view. I had always been on the other side of the fence. My guy was due to go in the next bout and I felt a bit insulted. I was, and always am, so wrapped up in my fighter that I can't believe anyone else, whoever they are, isn't the least bit interested. But I thought about what the waitress had said and realise that boxing must seem pretty daft to someone who isn't keen on it. On the other hand, any sport involves risk. I've visited Stoke Mandeville Hospital a few times and seen the horrific injuries suffered by rugby players, for example. And if boxing were banned, it would only be driven underground and we'd be back to prize-fighting, no holds barred, a bloodthirsty, unrestrained, murderous pitching together of the sort of fighters who will stop short of nothing.

Boxers have died. No one who has read any boxer's account of when their opponent has died and the nightmare that such a tragedy entails can fail to be moved and to ask the question: 'Is any sport worth this?' For a man to know that another man died — even as an indirect result of the work of his fists — is a cruel burden to bear. But you have to consider another question: 'Is the aim of boxing to cause damage?' Emphatically no.

Of course, every professional boxer is paid to hurt his opponent. The point though is that this isn't unique to boxing. Every sport involving physical contact makes physical intimidation part of its tactics, from rugby to cricket (where the body-blow is dealt out by a ball travelling at upwards of 90 m.p.h.). Some boxers are thugs but rubbishing the whole sport on the basis that it has some dodgy practitioners is stupid. For the most part, however, boxers are quite the opposite of thugs; respect for their opponent and a desire to be respected in turn, is central to the code of the sport. Alan Minter tells how he visited the family of Angelo Jacopucci, who died from a brain injury 12 hours after Minter had wrested the European middleweight title from him, because he wanted to pay his respects to a man for whom he had the highest esteem. Okay, some cynics would say that was just a morbid attack of guilt; let them say it. Minter had boxed a fine champion and he wanted the dead man's family to know that he had lost to a decent man, not a murderous idiot.

I cannot argue away the misery of deaths in boxing; no one can, but nor can they in any sport. Life is so protected nowadays that the very idea of risking death in a so-called leisure activity, even a highly paid one, has become a subject of public outcry: Alison Hargreaves was killed climbing a mountain and she's called 'irresponsible' because she has two kids. The drive to test the human frame and the human spirit is still there, though, however safe 'normal' life has become. I would always support risk as against the cosy option, whether it be in how you try to further your ambitions and dreams, or in the perfecting of a talent. If the talent is for sport and the sport is for boxing, a true test of courage if ever there was one, then take the risk. Nobody succeeds in any endeavour without risking something: life, limb or fortune.

The perfecting of talent is a serious business and if you have a talent, not to perfect it seems to me a sad and bad waste. And while from the outside and from ignorance boxing seems to be fist-swinging violence and nothing more, it is a very precise sporting science. Most champions have won by sheer drive and willpower, true, but never without skill, the skill in stringing together combinations, like the relentless Ali stinging with punch after punch. That's something the anti-boxing lobby ignores. They bang on about boxers trying to batter each other senseless; they simply take no account of the care that a matchmaker generally takes to ensure a good, decent contest in the ring: checking with agents that the boxers are in shape, well-trained, and so on. Unfortunately, it can happen that a boxer arrives from overseas and isn't in the condition he ought to be, having been bouncing nothing heavier than beer bottles on his gut. That isn't the promoter's fault if he acted in good faith. The fans aren't fools, they know when a boxer is over-heavy. The home fighter goes out and does the job and then gets stick from the press for pasting a flabby, unfit opponent.

GEORGE FRANCIS

Another aspect anti-boxing people overlook is the skill, the athleticism, the courage. Even a great champion like Floyd Paterson, for example, couldn't take a heavy punch on his chin, so he perfected the peek-a-boo style of fighting to protect his vulnerable jaw: feinting, ducking, swerving, always carrying the fight to the other man. Ali described his own quickness in the ring as 'floating like a butterfly'. In the end it comes down to will; as the great man said: at the end of a hard, hard fight, when both men are nearly falling over with fatigue, when science has gone out of the window, it's who wants it more. That seems to me a noble test of a man's spirit and inner strength and the finest testimony to boxing.

I've been privileged to work with some tremendous guys, many of them champions, men like Frank Bruno, John Conteh, Barry McGuigan, Bunny Sterling, Boza-Edwards, top league men. But in some ways the happiest days were those I spent training the amateurs, helping the kids who thought that they were useless at everything to take a pride in themselves and in their achievements in the boxing ring. Not all of them were little bruisers either. Some of them were so quiet and soft-mannered you'd have thought they wouldn't have the first clue about boxing. Nor did the tearaways inevitably turn out to be the best boxers in the club. But every kid I trained learned the value of effort, of trying, of struggling against difficulty. They all developed a taste to improve, to take knocks and to come back more determined. Before joining the club many of them had been aimlessly kicking about, patrolling the street corners, killing time. In the club they found purpose. Black kids, white kids, all together — racism was never an issue with us. I came to boxing as a tearaway myself and I know the extraordinary change it can bring about in any boy, not only the wasters. Nothing gave me greater pleasure than when parents or teachers said of a kid they couldn't handle, who had no other ambition than to be a complete pain in the neck to anyone in authority: 'He's changed out of all recognition. What did you do?' All I did was teach him to box, made him physically fit, mentally alert and teach him a code of sporting conduct.

There is a natural aggression in boys: it would be foolish to deny it. The best approach, I firmly believe, is to channel it. In cowards that aggression comes out as bullying. I told you how I used to protect my weaker chums when they got picked on by the bullies. It's the only language a bully understands: till he's whipped, he's going to feel free to torment the small fry. Expose him by turning him into the victim and his image is shattered, he's finished and perhaps he'll learn some respect for himself. A kid in the paper recently said exactly that: he confessed he'd been a bully, until he ran into heavier opposition and realised why he'd been throwing his weight around. He learned to carry his weight instead. For years I trained kids packed full of natural aggression. Kids such as I had been, street fighters,

222

brawlers, out of control, mean, dirty below-the-belt fighters. And I trained them as I had been trained, redirected their aggression into something sportsmanlike, something disciplined, something, I believe, essentially decent. The better the boxer a kid became, the higher went his self-esteem and for all the stuff about ruling the roost out on the street, being the best scrapper on the block, that's as rough and short-lived a life as the life of the old gunslingers. With no rules to observe, it's always going to be the guy who is prepared to fight dirtiest who will come out top of the heap . . . for a short while. Of course, not all young boys launch out on a career of street fighting; I'm only saying that a lot who might have done got into boxing instead and used their skill and courage to much better effect.

Sport has an increasingly important role to play in our society, not just as a professional sport either, which is getting so money-obsessed. Sport should still, as it used to, occupy an essential, even obligatory, part of our education system. Many of the kids in schools are badly confused and baffled by their prospects: a lifetime of unemployment stares many of them in the face. They feel beaten before they've even started. I would encourage any method, any method at all, of helping them to get off the ropes and into a lust for life.

A boxer has to be completely in charge of his own will, his own drive. It is a very lonely sport where the commitment of one individual is pitched against that of another. Self-reliance is vital and that comes from hours of training, hours shadow-boxing your own image in the gym mirrors, that image which your opponent will see, while the trainer calls for more speed, more footwork, sharper reflexes, closer defence. Curiously, that complete dependence on the trainer during training is one of the hardest aspects of the boxing game. When it comes to the time to hang up the gloves, go back to ordinary life, the boxer usually hates having to depend on other people for anything. When the fight in the ring is on, there is no turning back: all the concentration is focused. The climb down out of the ring into civvy street is a long one and where can that ferocious concentration go? How can a boxer relive that fierce packing of will, energy, drive that came in the days before a fight, those times of total preoccupation when everything and everybody can grate on your nerves (which is why they so often go away into purdah), when they are fighting the opponent in their dreams? I admit that I've whacked Joan while we were in bed asleep more than once. Difficult to apologise for that, I can tell you.

In my experience, boxers don't generally cause trouble; they know what it is to take a punch on the nose and they learn to forget it, more often than not. Besides, they need to keep all their force for the real thing: the confrontation, the match in the four corners of truth.